INTRODUCTION

TO

MISSIONS

Dr. Lee Ann B. Marino, Ph.D., D.Min., D.D.,

Introduction to Missions

Dr. Lee Ann B. Marino, Ph.D., D.Min., D.D.

Published by:

Apostolic University Press

(An imprint of The Righteous Pen Publications Group)
www.righteouspenpublications.com

Book classification: Books > Religion & Spirituality > Christian Books & Bibles > Ministry & Evangelism > Missions & Missionary Work

All images as appear in text are public domain.

ISBN: 1-940197-48-1
13-Digit: 978-1-940197-48-7

Printed in the United States of America.

DON'T FEAR,
I AM WITH YOU.
FROM THE EAST I'LL BRING YOUR CHILDREN;
FROM THE WEST I'LL GATHER YOU.
I'LL SAY TO THE NORTH, "GIVE THEM BACK!"
AND TO THE SOUTH, "DON'T DETAIN THEM."
BRING MY SONS FROM FAR AWAY,
AND MY DAUGHTERS FROM THE END OF THE EARTH,
EVERYONE WHO IS CALLED BY MY NAME
AND WHOM I CREATED FOR MY GLORY,
WHOM I HAVE FORMED AND MADE.

BRING OUT THE BLIND PEOPLE WHO HAVE EYES,
THE DEAF ONES WHO HAVE EARS.
ALL THE NATIONS ARE GATHERED TOGETHER;
THE PEOPLES ARE ASSEMBLED.
WHICH OF THEM ANNOUNCED THIS?
WHO PREDICTED TO US THE PAST EVENTS?
LET THEM BRING THEIR WITNESSES AS A DEFENSE;
LET THEM HEAR AND SAY, "IT'S TRUE!"
YOU ARE MY WITNESSES, SAYS THE LORD,
MY SERVANT, WHOM I CHOSE,
SO THAT YOU WOULD KNOW AND BELIEVE ME
AND UNDERSTAND THAT I AM THE ONE.
BEFORE ME NO GOD WAS FORMED;
AFTER ME THERE HAS BEEN NO OTHER.
I, I AM THE LORD,
AND THERE IS NO SAVIOR BESIDES ME.
I ANNOUNCED, I SAVED, I PROCLAIMED,
NOT SOME STRANGER AMONG YOU.
YOU ARE MY WITNESSES, SAYS THE LORD,
AND I AM GOD.
FROM THE DAWN OF TIME, I AM THE ONE.
NO ONE CAN ESCAPE MY POWER.
I ACT, AND WHO CAN UNDO IT?

(ISAIAH 43:5-13)

TABLE OF CONTENTS

INTRODUCTION

Stand fast, stand firm, stand sure, stand true.
– Harrison Gray Otis[1]

WANDERLUST. Exploration. Gospel proclamation. Unspeakable faith. Helping others. Excitement. Renewal of faith. History is full of reasons why missionaries have ventured out from the comforts of their own lives into the unknown world of missions and missions' activity. If you are feeling the call to missions, you are not alone, but you, most likely, are uncertain of where to start.

Missions start within missionaries. They start as God purposes us to go and we take that literally, rather than seeing it as a call to evangelize and work within our neighborhoods and our friends. They start as we examine ourselves and develop the depth and love of faith and of seeing others flourish under the move of the Spirit. Missions start with good missionaries, with missionaries who dedicate themselves to the work and take the time to learn how to do a mission from start to finish in a way that will be productive, powerful, and purposeful.

In this text, you will learn about these foundations that make great missionaries. Text includes assignments and summaries at the end of each chapter, to help center missionaries for their upcoming task of true faith and test of life at hand. Missionary work is not necessarily an easy thing, but being prepared and ready for the work to take hold in your life and transform your perspectives on virtually everything: church, life, interactions of the faith, and what faith means to you will enhance your missionary perspective and enhance your walk as you fall in love with the things of faith once more.

Going forth for the Gospel can prove to be an ultimate life adventure as you watch God move on your behalf and intervene in the lives of those you reach for Him, time and time again. It's a blessing and an encouragement to see God's powerful hand, at work, as He brings spiritual sustenance to His people, no matter where they may be.

Missionary Amy Carmichael with children in India

CHAPTER ONE:
MISSIONS AND MISSIONS ACTIVITY

―――――――――――― ~~~~ ――――――――――――

When Christ calls a man, He bids him come and die.
(Dietrich Bonhoeffer[1])

IN its strictest definition, a mission is when one individual or a group of individuals go forth to accomplish a specific purpose. A mission involves a specific goal, specific purpose, and hopefully, a specific result. In the case of church missions, the specific goal of missions is the spread of the Gospel, the specific purpose is to reach people with the Gospel, and the anticipated result is the establishment of solid churches, wherever that mission has taken place.

But where do we start with missions and with understanding the work of missions activity? It seems so daunting to board a plane or get in a car and travel from one place to another. Where do we start with our educational endeavors? What if we feel called to go to a country that we do not even know much about? What happens if we do not even speak the language?

Being called to the missions field is a wonderful and amazing thing, but stepping out into the missions field is often something else, entirely. Preparing for missions involves stepping back, understanding the purpose and focus of missions, and seeking the face of God. While we step back and focus, we learn more about the work God has called us to do and what missions looks like, sounds like, and does in our world, today.

What are missions?

If you're in any way a student of Christian history, you probably have read about the great missionaries of the 1700s, 1800s, and early 1900s. It almost sounds exotic to read about the different missions experiences, especially given they were often the first endeavors that westerners made into continents such as Asia and Africa. The experiences we hear of these missionaries today are often second or third-hand accounts, and we don't hear about the pitfalls and difficulties of those encounters. We also seldom hear about missionaries of the early centuries of Christianity and the intense persecution and martyrdom they experienced.

From the earliest of times, missions have been a part of the church. Down through the ages, despite differences in culture, changes among churches and denominations, Biblical understanding, and yes, even the different understanding of missions, missions have always been there, expanding the church into distant lands. For this reason, we can understand missions to be at the very heart of the church and its expansion. Without missions, the church cannot, in and of itself, survive.

Missions are the specific sending work by which an individual or individuals are called by God and sent into different nations, regions, areas, or lands for the purpose of proclaiming the Gospel and establishing foundational roots for the spread of the church. Missions may be quick, short-term, or long-term in their duration and may or may not be successful in the bigger picture of church evangelism. An individual who goes on a mission or is involved in missions is known as a missionary.

The missionary

An individual who sets their sights on missions and missions activities is known as a missionary. The term "missionary" is not found anywhere in the Scriptures. The term itself appears to have come to existence somewhere in the seventeenth century. Prior to this time, missionaries were not noted with a formal identity, save whatever their credentials might have been through their existing denominations. None of this means that the identity of a missionary is unbiblical; in fact, examples of missions and missionaries exist in both the Old and New Testaments. What it does mean is that the

Bible does not outline special qualifications for missionaries (save qualifications listed for Ephesians 4:11 ministers and the appointments). If we properly understand the work and role of missions, however, it is certainly required of several offices within the five-fold, and this means that the qualifications to be a ministry overlap within the qualifications of the specific ministry office. To be a missionary, one must have the willingness to be sent, to travel, to experience cultural adaptation, to build and expand the church, and to have the ability to work in difficult, uncomfortable, and exasperating conditions as relate to missions work.

Assisting in missions

Oftentimes individuals assist a primary minister or missions team with missions. This is reasonable, as mission work takes great help and assistance. It is a beautiful thing to be a part of the spread of the good news, and it is an amazing experience for a Christian believer to see the growth and expansion of God's church. I personally recommend that the average believer assists in a missions experience at least once in their lifetime.

As with all things, an individual assisting in missions should receive the proper training and instruction, so they are informed as to what they are able to do and what they will be doing on the trip. When it comes to missions, everyone should receive proper training and equipping so they will understand where they are going, what it will mean, and what they will do during the mission.

It should also be noted that even believers who do not travel with missionaries should assist in missions through financial support, prayer, and interest in missions work. This is part of understanding the church as a missions-based organization, recognizing the role that missions plays within the heart of the church and the spread of evangelism. It may be hard to overcome attitudes that do not support missions given modern theologies, but it should be taught to each and every member of a church or ministry organization that if a leader or church member (or even a member of a sister church) engages in missions activity, every single member of that church should do something to help and assist in that endeavor, even if they do not go on the trip themselves.

Missiology

Missiology is the study of missions, missionary function, and the impact of missions in Christianity. Its main purpose is not just to review or document the history of missions (although that is certainly part of Missiology), but to look at the way in which missions can be relevant in our day and age. It covers a broad spectrum of theologically and culturally relevant topics and seeks to examine the way that missions can be most effective.

If you are participating in this course or in one that focuses on ministry overseas, odds are good you are encountering or have encountered Missiology. Even though the exact nature of its study and what classifies as proper Missiology often varies from one scholar to another, the end goal of Missiology is to equip ministers and future missionaries for the work of missions in the world.

Inequalities present in Missiology

As a study, Missiology is relatively new. It is an attempt to apply methodology to missions work. In and of itself, there is nothing wrong with that. What is overwhelming from the outside looking in is the way that women and people of color are notably absent from the scholarship and study of Missiology. There are a few men of color, here and there, and no women, making the overall missiology landscape thoroughly male and Caucasian. This means that the perspectives, ideals, and lens by which Missiology is often filtered comes through the eyes of Caucasian men. There is nothing wrong with men or Caucasians involved in missions or the study of missions, but there is a problem with a notable absence of women and people of color involved in discussion on missions. This is problematic for three main reasons:

- Missions do not just involve Caucasian individuals but largely involve people of color and minorities; thus, the needs that exist cannot be fathomed by Caucasian minds, exclusively;

- Women have historically held an overwhelming presence in missions work, and the exclusion of them from the study of missions means the perspectives of women on the mission field that have often been quite successful are not considered from the female perspective;

- The ways that women and people of color have handled mission work have often been extremely successful.

If the church herself is universal, we cannot ignore the beautiful diversity present in God's people, the world over. If the church herself is feminine, we cannot ignore the role or perspective of women in missions expansion and study. Women and people of color can offer a unique vision, purposed role and approach to missions that are needed and necessary for missions to be effective. If we only look at a Caucasian male perspective on missions, we are only seeing half the purpose and half the vision God has for the church. To properly understand missions, we must see both male and female involvement in missions and all racial involvement, to see what all have to offer to the greater missions picture.

Missions and culture

Missions are an interesting point of interest and study for people because missions hit directly where faith and culture meet and the ways that both impact lives. Faith and religious belief often dictate culture, and culture often dictates religious belief and perception of faith. The two are interwoven in ways we cannot easily divide, and that means mission work often deals with the deep complications that a religion – any religion – plays in the way that people perceive the Gospel and their willingness to receive it.

Missions training often revolves around theology and the ability to implement a certain denomination's understanding of church within a region. This is fine, to a certain point. It is understandable that any training institution wants to see to it that their information and understanding is a part of the work a missionary does. The problem with this is that little time is spent developing cultural appreciation or understanding. Working in missions is not a simple matter of knowing a lot about theology or about having a lot of textbook knowledge as pertains to book knowledge of Bible information or theology. Missions also relates to showing people how God can work for them, right where they are, while refocusing and building on the things within their culture that support their spiritual reeducation. This is more difficult than it sounds, and it is something that hits home at the way we understand faith for ourselves as much as how we understand evangelism and spiritual education. If we want to be successful in missions, we need to understand where we are going, the people who live where we are going, and the culture, economics, and spirituality that those people live and dwell within.

What do missions require?

Mission work requires an individual to either permanently or temporarily visit or relocate to an area to do foundational building or social gospel ministry in that area. To qualify as a mission, the following conditions must be met:

- One must be called of God to go into the missions field.

- The heart of missions is always the Gospel. While it's great to go overseas and do humanitarian work, that is not the heart of missions work; it is a common, or secondary result.

- The primary purpose of missions is to go with the Gospel to establish the church in a place where it does not already exist, or where it exists and needs such help to organize it, it requires outside intervention to offer to it what it cannot do for itself. This is not in the limited understanding of financial assistance (whereby an outside source comes and hands over resources to someone else), but in the understanding that an outside minister, teacher, instructor, or team is needed to come in and help establish the foundation that is not present.

- One cannot reside in that area, nor can it be that individual's hometown.

- The work must expand beyond basic evangelism and delve into the realm of foundational church establishment on any level. We will discuss this more later.

- It does not qualify as a mission if you are a speaker at an exclusive church event in that region that is already established (such as a convocation, church conference, etc.). One can go and do missionary work while they are somewhere for a conference or a speaker, but it is not the same as going somewhere specifically for a conference or event that does not expand beyond a church body or that does not address church issues.

There are five different types of missions activity:

- **Mission trip:** Lasting anywhere from a few days to four weeks, a mission trip seeks to meet a specific need or needs within a city, nation or region wherein a mission is set.

- **Short-term mission:** Lasts anywhere from four weeks to six months where a specific need or needs are met.

- **Long-term mission:** Lasts anywhere from six months to a period of years where a specific need or needs are met.

- **City/regional mission:** When an individual is specifically commissioned to move to city or limited region or to work within an area on a regular basis for the purpose of Christian ministry that they are not already living in or are not from originally.

- **Community/ethnic mission:** As part of being called to nations, there are those who may be called to work with a community or group of people that is different from them or what may be familiar to them, for the purpose of Christian ministry.

It is very possible that the different types of missions activity may overlap, intersect, or otherwise change with time. A mission trip may easily turn into a short-term mission, and long-term missions often turn into shorter ones, depending on politics or current events. City/regional missions often turn into local churches and church activities, and as a result, missionaries need to be prepared to make the commitment required to see through ministry work to the end or, at the same time, have their existing plans easily disrupted. Missionaries and those who assist need to expect flexibility, be prepared and willing to travel, and to have the good foresight and insight to know what is needed, and when. This comes through experience.

Availability

The major mark of a missionary or one who is sent to do the work of missions is availability. It is one thing to believe that one has an international call, and another thing entirely to meet the demands of that call. The reason for this is simple: the sound of having a large ministry with an international presence sounds more glamorous than it, in reality, is. People dream of luxury jets and flying first class around the world, eating in four-star restaurants and staying in five-star hotels. When fundraising, low financial commitments, average accommodations, and the stresses of ministry life come knocking, many abandon the idea of missions or other work all together. It doesn't help that the pursuit of average life, such as trying to have what everyone else is perceived to have, marriage and family life consuming every moment, and debt also push away the possibility of missions availability.

I understand the mentality many of us go into ministry with, because I have been there, myself. We have certain preconceived notions about what being in ministry will be like and we anticipate that going around the world will take the format we envision. The longer we are in ministry and things don't come to fruition as we had hoped, we have two choices for response. The first is to continue to wait on what we hope to materialize, the second is to return to God's Throne and examine our existing concepts.

It is also relevant to state that many ministers have compounded so many responsibilities unto themselves, they render themselves unavailable for missions. If God has given us the vision to go, that may mean letting go of some responsibilities, expenses, people, and downsizing the vision to make room for missions in our lives. If our entire existence revolves around a few key people, places, or things, missions will never become a viable reality.

Being a missionary means that moving forward with the Gospel into unknown territory is our priority, at least during the time when the mission comes to us. When we resume our normal standard of living, we must prepare for the next assignment, the next mission. Ministry building, establishment, and foundations must come before other things that we might like and hope for, because obeying God in the form of forward motion is the meaning of and essence of our very lives.

Wishing, hoping, and talking about an intended interest in missions does not make one a missionary, nor does it make missions possible. Most churchgoers will probably not be called to missions, although everyone has the opportunity and purpose to move forward with the Gospel through evangelism and should take the opportunity to assist a missionary or missions team at least once in their lifetimes.

The church and modern missions

For most of the church's history, missions were a primary focus of church life and of church participation. If an average churchgoer was not personally interested in missions, they were expected to give to missions. Mission Sundays, missions speakers, missions reports, and activities encouraging missions were all a part of the regular church member's life, and they were able to tangibly touch and see the work of missions and the purpose of missions, even if they never set foot on a boat to cross a sea to join in mission work.

This standard concept of missions – people go and then report back via their denominations – sounds simple enough. Most missions existed with the support of denominations that either partially or entirely funded their projects, with the expectations that the churches or outreaches they started would be affiliated with the denomination that sponsored the individual missionary.

As money started to wane and interest in missions went with it, many Protestant denominations started to develop what is known as a more "ecumenical" model for missions. Instead of focusing so much on the sponsorship and establishment of a denomination, they started emphasizing the commonalities of Protestant believers and encouraging those interested in missions to focus on missions within pre-established communities or working on humanitarian ecumenical efforts with groups of churches. The reason for this is simple: denominations were unable to sponsor missionaries like they used to, increased emphasis on seminary or denominationally sponsored education prior to missions (rather than a simple training course, and an emphasis on politics and political advocacy rather than proper training in ministry and Gospel work. These different factors have combined with the standard missionary

11

concepts have increased teams of missions, created shorter mission terms, and also reduced missions costs for denominations who expect participants to raise their own funds.

Neither the traditional mission structure or the more ecumenical model for missions works well in modern society. It excludes more modern church structures, including the non-denominational church, which are often independent and too small structurally to support their own missions. The traditional structure teaches denominational hierarchy, while the ecumenical model acts as if none of that exists. The important Biblical and structural foundations for a solid church lack in both models is often absent, and churches are seldom, if ever, equipped to establish self-sufficiency in their operation.

The more typical missions model appeared to work well for the church, at least on the surface. It made denominations grow larger, but with growth came incredible responsibility. It's not a secret that much of the international church deals with severe maintenance, growth, and financial issues. Many foreign churches claim alliance or allegiance to a denomination, and that denomination may have no idea who that church is or what they teach. There is also question as to the doctrine and spiritual understanding in many of those churches because their autonomy and independence equate to something different than it does in western mindsets (where such is often a revolt against state churches or state control). While the basic principle that some are sent to take the Gospel to distant lands and expand the work of the church is still the basic, foundational concept of missions work today, it is not without its issues, especially when we consider history and the role that denominationalism has often placed in missions structure.

Down to today, the peripherals of that traditional, denominational concept and model of missions are often ill-equipped to meet the needs that exist for missions and to interest the modern church in missions support. Part of this rests in that church structure has changed, thus missions structure also must change. But what we hear in church is also different, causing us, as believers, to leave a mindset that considers missions and thinks more about ourselves. Some call it selfish, some call it the church of me, but theologically speaking, it relates to an over-emphasis on want and personal need rather than on God or spiritual interest.

Once upon a time, we were all taught the importance of

contentment and satisfaction in our lives. God never promised our lives would be perfect, but we recognized that it was a divine principle to find contentment with our overall lives. It's not that we won't ever want anything else again or aspire to be better in our lives, but we learned to trust God for what we had and follow a sense of divine providence when it came to discerning our futures. We didn't think that what we wanted to happen was a guarantee it would, and we had a better sense of distinguishing ourselves from God. We were a part of the church because we knew God had done something for us that we could not do for ourselves, and we wanted others to receive of that. Even though we didn't have much, we found something to give from what we had because we knew there was someone out there who had less.

Today much of what we hear in church is the opposite of contentment: it is insatiable greed. It is not uncommon to go into a church and hear message after message or teaching after teaching about the needs we have, the wants we have, and about believing God to meet those needs and wants. There's nothing wrong with this in concept, except that the focus is on our need being met rather than on God, the source of all provision. The more we need and want, the bigger the hole gets between contentment and where we stand. The deeper message in this is lack, and that we need God to forever fix our lack wherever it lies before we can do anything for anyone else. If we are in lack, right where we are, then we can't be the ones God uses to make a difference. Our entire spiritual lives exist to fill this lack, this void, and we will not budge until that lack is met. The mentality of eternal lack seldom, if ever, has an end. There is always something else we want, something else we need to accomplish, something that we must start believing for, all over again. We are so busy waiting for our own perceived needs to be met, we don't ever reach the point where we care about anyone else's.

This may sound harsh, but the reality is that if we think we are lacking, we don't have the time or interest to care about others. The severe financial disparities, lack of volunteers, and closing church doors show us that many churchgoers don't even see their way to care about the local church they attend or the local leader that teaches them, let along care about the state of souls or the church halfway around the world. This goes both ways, as well. If a pastor in another country is only worried about raising money for the work they are doing, no matter how good it may be, and uses tactics of manipulation, dishonesty, or turns his ear to the needs of the church somewhere else, they have not learned the principle of true contentment, either.

No matter where you are in the world, a true heart of missions requires giving. It is a worldwide cause that as we go one place, others support it; then those in turn are able to support others, going on and over, and beyond. If we desire to turn the tide on missions, we need to change our foundational aspects of church education and turn those teachings toward God. When we are focused on Him, our sites of missions and our desire to impact the lives of others will change.

The spirituality of missions

The work of missions has a unique spirituality, all its own. Going forth with the Gospel into unknown territory reminds us of Christ's mission to come from heaven into this world for the purposes of salvation. In many ways, missionaries walk His footsteps in a literal way. They experience time and space away from their family and friends, they forsake all they know to proclaim the Gospel, they discipline themselves to learn the Word and hear from the Father, and to deal with the isolation of missions life. The entire missions experience changes the relationship that a missionary has with God, with the church, with those that he or she knows, and to grow as an individual in the character and will that God desires for each and every one of us to have.

The basics of missions spirituality taps into a few poignant and important areas of spiritual development, all of which relate to the Great commission of Matthew 28:16-20:

BUT THE ELEVEN DISCIPLES PROCEEDED TO GALILEE, TO THE MOUNTAIN WHICH JESUS HAD DESIGNATED. WHEN THEY SAW HIM, THEY WORSHIPED HIM; BUT SOME WERE DOUBTFUL. AND JESUS CAME UP AND SPOKE TO THEM, SAYING, "ALL AUTHORITY HAS BEEN GIVEN TO ME IN HEAVEN AND ON EARTH. GO THEREFORE AND MAKE DISCIPLES OF ALL THE NATIONS, BAPTIZING THEM IN THE NAME OF THE FATHER AND THE SON AND THE HOLY SPIRIT, TEACHING THEM TO OBSERVE ALL THAT I COMMANDED YOU; AND LO, I AM WITH YOU ALWAYS, EVEN TO THE END OF THE AGE." (NASB)

- **Designation:** To be designated means to be assigned for a purpose that we are not yet doing but are preparing to do. Our purpose as believers is to discover our God-assigned designation, prepare for it, and ultimately, walk in it.

- **Overcoming doubt:** There will always be reasons why we suspect God did not command us to do whatever He designates us to do. There will always be reasons to think God should call someone else, that it's not really for us, or God should send someone else. Doubt is doubt is doubt. We must overcome our doubts so we can freely and fully worship God.

- **Authority:** The authority a minister of the Gospel has is not their own. No true minister of God is called of themselves, and no true missionary goes of their own accord. God is the final authority. As true servants, the authority we have is given from the Father. Keeping this in mind brings us to a place of true humility, where it is clear our ministry is endowed to go forth with power, one we have not earned.

- **Go:** Christianity is not a static belief system. The Holy Spirit, present everywhere and in all time, is often compared to forces that move: wind, breath and water. These forces have a notable presence – you know when they are there, or when they are not – and they have a movement that goes along with them. If we are endowed and filled with the Holy Spirit, our desire should be to move, to go, to engage and flow, transforming the world with the power and presence of God.

- **Discipleship:** Nowhere in the Bible does it say that we should go into the world and get everyone saved. This mentality creeps in when we allow the ideal of evangelism to define the church rather than allowing God to build a sense of evangelism in each of us through understanding of the apostolic. It is not God's desire we have one experience with Him, but an ongoing relationship with Him by which He teaches us, through the Holy Spirit and His church, and that we grow into the fullness of life and purpose He has for every one of us. God desires we become lifelong students.

- **Obedience:** Obedience is a big word with complex implications. It is difficult enough to abide by obedience in this world, let alone maintain and operate divine obedience when we cannot see God. Such is evident by the rampant disobedience we see in the world and in the church, as people try to sidestep the will of God. Obedience is a matter of priority. How obedient we are to God – especially with the difficult things – is a powerful testimony of how much we believe in Him. If we love God, we will keep His commands to us, which extend to any direct word He gives that is specifically and directly for us, even if it is not written.

- **Baptism:** The debates about whether baptism is relevant today defy true belief in the Great Commission. If the Great Commission, the great sending, is something we understand to be for us, then water baptism is an essential part of that. As we go forth and make disciples, we are commanded to literally immerse new disciples into Christ, burying them into His death through water baptism, then raising them to life. This prepares the believer for their life in Christ but also connects them to missionary life in a special way. For a missionary to do missions they must die to themselves. They must die to their concepts and ideals of what church or ministry are like. They often risk their lives so others can live and believe in Christ. Baptism is, thus, an important part of every missions experience. It brings not just the baptismal candidate, but also the missionary, full circle in their journey.

- **Relationship:** I truly believe the Father, Son, and Holy Spirit are specifically mentioned in Matthew 28:19 because it is an expression of relationship and in relationship, unity. A missionary's relationship with God extends from them to those they teach, and from those they teach, the church continues to move forward, into eternity. Missions remind us of the importance of divine relationship and relationship with one another in the Body of Christ.

- **Teaching:** Disciples cannot grow without proper teaching, and a big portion of missions is teaching, rather than standard preaching alone. The difference between preaching and teaching is the level of instruction and the overall tone of what is taught. Preaching catches an audience, causes people to take note, and may appear more entertaining that teaching, which seeks to impart essential information. Where preaching catches the ear and is somewhat entertaining, teaching disciplines.

- **Omnipresence:** God is with us, through until the end of time. One who is brave enough to take whatever they have and go forth with the Gospel, sometimes against what might seem to be sound reason, with everything pointing to the contrary, is someone who understands the presence of Christ as with them throughout eternity. If God can be with them at home, God can be with them wherever He commands them to go. This unique perspective on the divine touch of the eternal comforts the missionary as well as provides assurance to all who encounter a missionary that God is really there, truly eternal, and truly involved with His creation.

Chapter 1 Summary

- Missions are the specific sending work by which an individual or individuals are called by God and sent into different nations, regions, areas, or lands for the purpose of proclaiming the Gospel and establishing foundational roots for the spread of the church. They may be quick, short-term, or long-term in their duration. They may also relate to city or regional commissions or relate to community or ethnic work.

- In the bigger picture of church evangelism, missions may or may not be successful.

- An individual who goes on a mission or is involved in missions is known as a missionary. The major mark of a missionary is availability.

- Individuals who assist in missions should receive proper training and instruction. Believers who do not travel with missionaries should still assist in missions through prayer, financial giving, and interest.

- Missiology is the study of missions, missionary function, and the impact of missions in Christianity. There are many inequalities present in missiology work, which means we should strive for greater universal representation in the study of missions.

- Missions hit the point where faith and culture meet, and the way that both impact lives. All missionaries should strive to develop cultural appreciation and understanding.

- Missions require a call, a heart for the Gospel, church establishment or assistance, a willingness to be sent outside of one's present location and delve beyond basic evangelism.

- Traditional forms of mission models often do not work in modern times. The true heart of missions requires giving, and a central focus for missions to impact a lasting purpose in regions with the work of the church.

- The spirituality of missions reminds us of important components for our own spiritual lives: designation, overcoming doubt, authority, go, and discipleship.

Chapter 1 Assignments

- Write an essay (minimum 5-8 sentences) telling why you are interested in missions. What do you feel you have to offer to missions work? What do you feel you can offer to the mission field? How do you understand the view of missionary activity in your own life? What are you prepared to give up in your own life to pursue missions?

- Look up a current event in the world's scope (beyond that of the United States) and write a few short sentences on what role missions can play in helping that situation which exists. Please include reference information for that current event, including where the article can be found.

CHAPTER TWO:
THE NEEDS OF THE INTERNATIONAL CHURCH

—————————⌇—————————

The average pastor views his church as a local church with a missions program;
while he ought to realize that if he is in fact pastoring a church,
it is to be a global church with a missions purpose.
(Unknown[1])

WHEN you think of church, what comes to mind? Most of us think of the neat white buildings on the street corner. Somehow, we connect that image to the first century church, to Jesus Christ and His followers, and we expect all churches to meet with this same image. If a church is a little different or doesn't look quite like we imagine, we classify it as sub-par or not really church.

It shouldn't need to be said that our romanticized images of church are not an accurate picture of the church, nor is it in any sense all the church is ever to hope to become. The church is a big ball of everything transformed by the touch of Christ's love and the impact of God's hand. It is you; it is me; it is the face and value of every believer, the world over, who has come in to take their place in God's Body. The bigger we see the church, the smaller we see ourselves, and we hear the true echo that *HE MUST INCREASE AND I MUST DECREASE.* (John 3:30).

In missions work, an individual takes on a nature of the church and a perspective of it that is unlike anything they have ever experienced before. Seeing the church through new eyes will help us gain a better perspective of what is needed in missions work. To be in missions, one must see the church as a missionary, as well as seeing the world through the eyes of international church missions.

The church...in the beginning

When it comes to understanding the exact nature of the church in the world, we often trip up because there are so many disagreements as to just what purpose the church has in this world. If we don't properly understand the role of the church, we will never properly understand the nature of the people who make up the church, of believers, and of their role in the world.

The church is not something that is arbitrarily here, nor is it an accident. The church is not here to make up for Israel's failings, as some might teach. The church is a part of prophecy, something that God foresaw before the foundations of the world. Simply put, the work of the church has been something on the heart and mind of God, within His foresight and His purpose, from the very beginning.

The Book of Ephesians properly displays the role that the church plays in eternity, namely, an eternal purpose. This might sound obvious, but it is amazing how often we overlook the fact that the church has existed from the beginning, something outside of the boundaries of natural identity or means. In my book, *Touching The Church in Eternity: A Journey Through the Book of Ephesians* (Righteous Pen Publications, 2016), I state the following:

I WILL MAKE YOU AND THE WOMAN
   ENEMIES TO EACH OTHER [PLACE HOSTILITY/ENMITY BETWEEN YOU AND THE WOMAN].
YOUR DESCENDANTS [SEED] AND HER DESCENDANTS [SEED]
   WILL BE ENEMIES.
ONE OF HER DESCENDANTS [HE] WILL CRUSH YOUR HEAD,
   AND YOU WILL BITE [STRIKE; BRUISE; CRUSH] HIS HEEL [ROM. 16:20; REV. 12:9]."

THEN GOD SAID TO THE WOMAN,
"I WILL CAUSE YOU TO HAVE MUCH TROUBLE [OR INCREASE YOUR PAIN]
   WHEN YOU ARE PREGNANT [IN CHILDBEARING],
AND WHEN YOU GIVE BIRTH TO CHILDREN,
   YOU WILL HAVE GREAT PAIN.
YOU WILL GREATLY DESIRE [THE WORD IMPLIES A DESIRE TO CONTROL; 4:7]
YOUR HUSBAND,
   BUT HE WILL RULE OVER YOU." (Genesis 3:15-16, EXB)

This prophecy, more than any other specified passage in the early chapters of Genesis, proves that the plan of the church was always present within the mind and plan of God. While mankind has officially moved into sin, both Adam and Eve moving away from God via sin and deception, God made a promise to Eve and to all who would come after her. God was not going to leave humanity in a lost state, alienated from Him. God had a better plan, a better purpose, something more incredible to unite all of us to than just a man and woman in paradise. The prophecy reveals a few key things to us about the church, because as with many Biblical prophecies, she is hiding in the words of the text:

- *The woman and the serpent are automatic enemies from this point on:* All that is represented within the woman, and those who are the descendants of this woman, have an automatic response to evil and to manipulation. The hostility placed there, often instinctual in women, is God-given.

- *The descendants of the woman are automatic enemies with the serpent:* I shall discuss this in detail paralleling with the next point.

- *One descendant shall come from the woman, who shall be begotten without the assistance of a natural man, the "seed" of a woman:* Biology tells us that it takes a male and a female to create life, with the man offering seed. This prophecy speaks of a child's birth from the seed of a woman, Who will crush the head (or authority) of the enemy, and the enemy shall bruise His heel. We know this to be a prophecy of the birth, death, and resurrection of Jesus Christ, all in a few words. By His birth, Jesus would be born via a divine conception that did not involve a man; by His death, the serpent struck the heel of Christ, bruising or wounding him; by His resurrection, Christ crushed the head of the serpent, destroying his power, influence, and authority.

- *The woman, Eve, here is not just a representation of women, but of the church, as well:* The type present here is not just of Eve as a woman, but Eve as a prefigure of the church to come. The church herself is feminine, as was Eve. Even though those *in the church may be beguiled and charmed by Satan, the ultimate authority goes to her new Adam, Christ, because the church is the new Eve. Her descendants, those that are produced by the church, fight the battle and war with Satan, experiencing the intense odds and occasional bruising attacks that he brings our way. The ultimate victory, however, shall belong to the descendants (the church members).*

- ***The labor of the church shall be difficult:*** *The term "labor" here does not exclusively imply childbirth in the original Hebrew language. It is automatically associated with birth, however, because it is spoken of in terms of women. The "labor" spoken of to Eve and the "work labor" spoken of to Adam are the same exact word, and indicate a difficulty in life. This side of heaven, the work of the church will be difficult and will be done in a labor of love.*

- ***The church shall desire her husband (Christ) and He will lead and guide us:*** *The natural aspect of this prophecy that men would rule over women is not spoken of as being the ideal relationship or of a relationship built on godly principles. It simply states that this is what would happen, and this distortion causes us to misunderstand the relationship and love that the church would have with Christ. The control and confusion that has resulted from abuse of power and vying for control has caused us to miss the powerful submission that Christ extended toward His bride in His death on the cross. In Eve, we see the promise to come: that we will desire our Lord, and He will rule in His rightful authority over the church, leading us into all truth. We see fulfillment of this teaching expounded greater in Ephesians 5:21-33.*

- ***Every time we do something in connection with the church, we are connected all the way back to our original roots of Adam and Eve:*** *In their very lives, in their very work, in their very relationship, Adam and Eve show us a picture of the church. We can see its struggles, its difficulties, its challenges and temptations, and we can also see its redemption. Nothing and no one, not even the gates of hell, would overcome it. They were the first to come along, the first to teach us about the church,* *and the first to believe and hope for a promise that they probably didn't even understand in their lifetimes.*

Hearing the words spoken by God to Eve should give us a greater awareness of what we are a part of as the church. Though Eve was fallen, through seed that would come from her own stock (a woman), she would see restoration. Being here, in this time and place, within the eternal picture of the church, is not an accident. If the church is a part of the purpose of God from eternity past to eternity future, then our place within the church has a purpose, too. We are one of many, one who has united with Christ and is now also united with our brothers and sisters around the world, brought together as enemies of Satan, to do the work of God in this world.

The pre-Israelite call

IN GOD'S SIGHT, THE EARTH HAD BECOME CORRUPT AND WAS FILLED WITH VIOLENCE. GOD SAW THAT THE EARTH WAS CORRUPT, BECAUSE ALL CREATURES BEHAVED CORRUPTLY ON THE EARTH.

GOD SAID TO NOAH, "THE END HAS COME FOR ALL CREATURES, SINCE THEY HAVE FILLED THE EARTH WITH VIOLENCE. I AM NOW ABOUT TO DESTROY THEM ALONG WITH THE EARTH, SO MAKE A WOODEN ARK. MAKE THE ARK WITH NESTING PLACES AND COVER IT INSIDE AND OUT WITH TAR. THIS IS HOW YOU SHOULD MAKE IT: FOUR HUNDRED FIFTY FEET LONG, SEVENTY-FIVE FEET WIDE, AND FORTY-FIVE FEET HIGH. MAKE A ROOF FOR THE ARK AND COMPLETE IT ONE FOOT FROM THE TOP. PUT A DOOR IN ITS SIDE. IN THE HOLD BELOW, MAKE THE SECOND AND THIRD DECKS.

"I AM NOW BRINGING THE FLOODWATERS OVER THE EARTH TO DESTROY EVERYTHING UNDER THE SKY THAT BREATHES. EVERYTHING ON EARTH IS ABOUT TO TAKE ITS LAST BREATH. BUT I WILL SET UP MY COVENANT WITH YOU. YOU WILL GO INTO THE ARK TOGETHER WITH YOUR SONS, YOUR WIFE, AND YOUR SONS' WIVES. FROM ALL LIVING THINGS—FROM ALL CREATURES—YOU ARE TO BRING A PAIR, MALE AND FEMALE, INTO THE ARK WITH YOU TO KEEP THEM ALIVE. FROM EACH KIND OF BIRD, FROM EACH KIND OF LIVESTOCK, AND FROM EACH KIND OF EVERYTHING THAT CRAWLS ON THE GROUND—A PAIR FROM EACH WILL GO IN WITH YOU TO STAY ALIVE. TAKE SOME FROM EVERY KIND OF FOOD AND STOW IT AS FOOD FOR YOU AND FOR THE ANIMALS."

NOAH DID EVERYTHING EXACTLY AS GOD COMMANDED HIM. (Genesis 6:11-22)

It is atypical to trace spiritual history back further than Abram, but every example of an individual's life holds some relevance or spiritual education for us. All of them hold some picture into salvation history and the way God works among the choices and decisions of individuals. We've already discussed Eve, and now we are going to briefly look at the call of Noah before we start looking at the most obvious example of the way God called out the nations.

Let's understand that nobody in the early chapters of Genesis met the qualifications to be classified as a "Hebrew" people. That designation came later, and along with that designation came the identity. What becomes important about this fact is simple: God did call people, prior to this designation, who did His work within the world. The handful of people serving God gives the phrase "remnant" a whole new meaning. If we consider the wickedness of Noah's day, or the way in which Cain and Abel picked obvious sides as pertain to right and wrong, it is obvious that those who sought out God and heard from Him enough to follow Him were individuals that were few and far between.

The type that is created, therefore, shows us the price of being called; that few would, in the generations of millions and millions of people, the numbers of those who make the true commitment to God are, indeed, not many; and that being willing to stand out as a believer in a world full of non-believers is a brave endeavor, no matter what time frame such occurs in history.

It also shows us the missionary character present in those who dared to do right in a world that did not understand them, or their qualities. They were lone individuals or lone families in societies that had no idea where they were coming from or what they spoke of, because there was no theological evolution or explanation for God so early on in history. This, in no way, invalidates their message; in fact, it raises it up and raises their commitment to proclaim a message to a hostile and intolerable environment.

Noah is almost treated as an oddity among scholars. I suspect this is because there are many who believe Noah was nothing more than a story, something to fill pages and relate imaginary legends. This treatment of Noah as a story leads to treating his experience as theologically irrelevant, and the byproduct of that is he is not properly studied when it comes to his own experience.

We will look at a study of Noah from a missions perspective in a later chapter, but for now, we are going to examine his own call, his own experience as an individual who was called by God that did not fit into the "norm." He wasn't like anyone around him, and this made him explicitly different. It is not an accident he was the one picked in his day to stand against his culture and offer salvation. The ark that he built represented protection as the world was destroyed in a divine cleansing from the evil that plagued it, and the man and his floating ark promised redemption and a new day for those limited few who were spared. In Noah's call, we see the role of obedience in salvation: that following God means not following everyone else; and that the promise of salvation is for those who are willing to follow God, no matter who they are or where that call will lead.

The "calling out" of the nations

When we read the Bible, especially if we read through the lens of doctrinal teaching, it is easy for us to think that multicultural inclusion in the church is a radical thing, something that never existed before the work of Christ on the cross. The reality, however, is that such inclusion is the very foundation of Israel, of leading a people to do the work of God in this world and stand set apart from the rest.

THE LORD SAID TO ABRAM, "LEAVE YOUR LAND, YOUR FAMILY, AND YOUR FATHER'S HOUSEHOLD FOR THE LAND THAT I WILL SHOW YOU. I WILL MAKE OF YOU A GREAT NATION AND WILL BLESS YOU. I WILL MAKE YOUR NAME RESPECTED, AND YOU WILL BE A BLESSING.

I WILL BLESS THOSE WHO BLESS YOU,
    THOSE WHO CURSE YOU I WILL CURSE;
        ALL THE FAMILIES OF THE EARTH
            WILL BE BLESSED BECAUSE OF YOU."

ABRAM LEFT JUST AS THE LORD TOLD HIM, AND LOT WENT WITH HIM. NOW ABRAM WAS 75 YEARS OLD WHEN HE LEFT HARAN. ABRAM TOOK HIS WIFE SARAI, HIS NEPHEW LOT, ALL OF THEIR POSSESSIONS, AND THOSE WHO BECAME MEMBERS OF THEIR HOUSEHOLD IN HARAN; AND THEY SET OUT FOR THE LAND OF CANAAN. WHEN THEY ARRIVED IN CANAAN, ABRAM TRAVELED THROUGH

THE LAND AS FAR AS THE SACRED PLACE AT SHECHEM, AT THE OAK OF MOREH. THE CANAANITES LIVED IN THE LAND AT THAT TIME. THE LORD APPEARED TO ABRAM AND SAID, "I GIVE THIS LAND TO YOUR DESCENDANTS," SO ABRAM BUILT AN ALTAR THERE TO THE LORD WHO APPEARED TO HIM. FROM THERE HE TRAVELED TOWARD THE MOUNTAINS EAST OF BETHEL, AND PITCHED HIS TENT WITH BETHEL ON THE WEST AND AI ON THE EAST. THERE HE BUILT AN ALTAR TO THE LORD AND WORSHIPPED IN THE LORD'S NAME. THEN ABRAM SET OUT TOWARD THE ARID SOUTHERN PLAIN, MAKING AND BREAKING CAMP AS HE WENT. (Genesis 12:1-9)

Religious traditions conveniently paint Abram as belonging to any number of belief systems: Jews believe he was a Jew, Christians think of him as a Christian, Jehovah's Witnesses think he was a Jehovah's Witness, Muslims think he was a Muslim, Mormons think he was a Mormon, and so on and so forth. None of these assertions are true. Abram was a pagan man living in a pagan society, comfortable and accustomed to pagan ways. He wasn't a young, punk kid trying out Wicca or alternative religion. He was a 75-year-old man who lived with ancient pagan belief and custom throughout his entire life. It was his way of being and his way of reasoning with the spiritual world. In other words, our faith tradition and that of all three major world religions began with a pagan man who was called by God to venture out into something new, to do something different, to stand apart from everything that he knew to follow the true God, Who he had never directly encountered before in His life.

If we view the foundations of our spiritual understanding in this way, it proves that God did a "new thing" (Isaiah 43:19) in terms of Gentile inclusion within the church in the belief of restorative understanding, that the church is a part of the restoration of all things (Acts 3:21). It's not an accident that the Scriptures ask us if we notice what it is God is doing. We should recognize it because it has been done before, and if we are as spiritual we claim to be, we should see it clearly as it comes to pass. Abram followed God and became the foundation of a people Who were to be uniquely for God, obeying Him and dwelling with Him, We aren't doing something new here, so much as understanding what has been done since the beginning. We are re-presenting something ancient in a way that is new to those who hear, those who begin again with God and come out of where they are. We herald the voice of God to those who have never heard Him call out to them, and in that process, we become agents of change, sent with a mission in this world to make sure that all know God is real and that He desires true and lasting relationship with Him.

AFTER THESE EVENTS, THE LORD'S WORD CAME TO ABRAM IN A VISION, "DON'T BE AFRAID, ABRAM. I AM YOUR PROTECTOR. YOUR REWARD WILL BE VERY GREAT."

BUT ABRAM SAID, "LORD GOD, WHAT CAN YOU POSSIBLY GIVE ME, SINCE I STILL HAVE NO CHILDREN? THE HEAD OF MY HOUSEHOLD IS ELIEZER, A MAN FROM DAMASCUS." HE CONTINUED, "SINCE YOU HAVEN'T GIVEN ME ANY CHILDREN, THE HEAD OF MY HOUSEHOLD WILL BE MY HEIR."

THE LORD'S WORD CAME IMMEDIATELY TO HIM, "THIS MAN WILL NOT BE YOUR HEIR. YOUR HEIR WILL DEFINITELY BE YOUR VERY OWN BIOLOGICAL CHILD." THEN HE BROUGHT ABRAM OUTSIDE AND SAID, "LOOK UP AT THE SKY AND COUNT THE STARS IF YOU THINK YOU CAN COUNT THEM." HE CONTINUED, "THIS IS HOW MANY CHILDREN YOU WILL HAVE." ABRAM TRUSTED THE LORD, AND THE LORD RECOGNIZED ABRAM'S HIGH MORAL CHARACTER.

HE SAID TO ABRAM, "I AM THE LORD, WHO BROUGHT YOU OUT OF UR OF THE CHALDEANS TO GIVE YOU THIS LAND AS YOUR POSSESSION."

BUT ABRAM SAID, "LORD GOD, HOW DO I KNOW THAT I WILL ACTUALLY POSSESS IT?"

HE SAID, "BRING ME A THREE-YEAR-OLD FEMALE CALF, A THREE-YEAR-OLD FEMALE GOAT, A THREE-YEAR-OLD RAM, A DOVE, AND A YOUNG PIGEON." HE TOOK ALL OF THESE ANIMALS, SPLIT THEM IN HALF, AND LAID THE HALVES FACING EACH OTHER, BUT HE DIDN'T SPLIT THE BIRDS. WHEN VULTURES SWOOPED DOWN ON THE CARCASSES, ABRAM WAVED THEM OFF. AFTER THE SUN SET, ABRAM SLEPT DEEPLY. A TERRIFYING AND DEEP DARKNESS SETTLED OVER HIM.

THEN THE LORD SAID TO ABRAM, "HAVE NO DOUBT THAT YOUR DESCENDANTS WILL LIVE AS IMMIGRANTS IN A LAND THAT ISN'T THEIR OWN, WHERE THEY WILL BE OPPRESSED SLAVES FOR FOUR HUNDRED YEARS. BUT AFTER I PUNISH THE NATION THEY SERVE, THEY WILL LEAVE IT WITH GREAT WEALTH. AS FOR YOU, YOU WILL JOIN YOUR ANCESTORS IN PEACE AND BE BURIED AFTER A

GOOD LONG LIFE. THE FOURTH GENERATION WILL RETURN HERE SINCE THE AMORITES' WRONGDOING WON'T HAVE REACHED ITS PEAK UNTIL THEN."

AFTER THE SUN HAD SET AND DARKNESS HAD DEEPENED, A SMOKING VESSEL WITH A FIERY FLAME PASSED BETWEEN THE SPLIT-OPEN ANIMALS. THAT DAY THE LORD CUT A COVENANT WITH ABRAM: "TO YOUR DESCENDANTS I GIVE THIS LAND, FROM EGYPT'S RIVER TO THE GREAT EUPHRATES, TOGETHER WITH THE KENITES, THE KENIZZITES, THE KADMONITES, THE HITTITES, THE PERIZZITES, THE REPHAIM, THE AMORITES, THE CANAANITES, THE GIRGASHITES, AND THE JEBUSITES." (Genesis 15:1-21)

Genesis 15 contains references of particular disdain among scholars, for one reason: they can't figure out why they are included in the Bible. The ritual and sacrifice present herein doesn't reflect Jewish ritual or Old Testament sacrifice, because the details within its contents were never replayed in history. What this passage does reflect is ancient pagan ritual: splitting the animals in two, leaving the birds whole, using a smoking pot and flaming torch to catch the sacrifices on fire, all reflect ancient pagan ritual. If this is the case, and Abram has been called out of paganism, why is this recount in the Bible? The reason is simple: it remains in the Bible because Abram was a pagan, and it shows the way that God reached out to him, right where he was. He didn't reach out to Abram using methods that Abram would have found disconcerting or confusing, but He sent him a message using something familiar to him.

When God seeks to call us into His church, especially when the church is an unfamiliar agency to us, God will use that which we know and that which is familiar to move us from a place of ignorance to knowledge, enough to get us on the right track and to learn what we need to about our lives in Him. This doesn't mean we understand it all when we are first called and means a great deal of patience is involved in the process from call to true understanding. It is the nature of the church, however, to facilitate this process through discipleship.

It is worth noting that discipleship is, indeed, a process. Very few testimonies exist of individuals who are so convinced of Christianity and all it has to offer that they discard, burn, or destroy any shadow of their former lives. Involvement with church is often challenging, people don't always respond the way that we might hope and expect them to do so, information can be confusing, and family and friends often create intense ties that are not so easily discarded. Discipleship has steps forward and back, processes that don't always look like progress, and an integral way that learning and life are often interconnected.

Missions work requires the missionary to view discipleship in a full perspective, seeing the reality that people do not always instantly convert, but are transformed, one step at a time, one victory at a time. Every one of us is working out and walking through our salvation process, transforming more and more into the image of divine reflection God calls us to be, and that means working with those who are newly discipled or on different phases of discipleship cause us to examine those aspects of our own character, being, and spiritual life that are not as redeemed as we might hope them to be. This is different from backsliding or walking away from the faith, all together in that we are acknowledging that the narrow path isn't always a straight line from point A to point B.

Types and shadows in the pagan's experience with God

Sometimes we believe in a polarity between ourselves and the world: we are good, and the world (and everything in it) is inherently evil. I am not sure how we can adopt such a position if we believe the world and all that is in it has been created by God (Genesis 1:1). Yes, sin is in this world and is an active aspect of the governance of the world in this present age, but it does not mean that the world, in its basic creation, is evil. It also does not mean God is uninvolved or distant. The evil that exists in this world points out the severe realities of sin. While the contents of the world may not always reflect the grandeur of their Creator and we certainly acknowledge that people have free will and choose which way they go in their lives, we cannot deny that, when we look out over salvation history, God has a purpose and a plan, even in the present day.

Our look at the call of Abram ties into our work with non-believers as missionaries. Looking at Abram as first one who was called out of something should give us insight into what, as missionaries, we do for others. It should also reveal to us what was done for us in a spiritual perspective. We were all taken from something, redeemed from something, brought out of something and placed into something.

SO REMEMBER THAT ONCE YOU WERE GENTILES BY PHYSICAL DESCENT, WHO WERE CALLED "UNCIRCUMCISED" BY JEWS WHO ARE PHYSICALLY CIRCUMCISED. AT THAT TIME YOU WERE WITHOUT CHRIST. YOU WERE ALIENS RATHER THAN CITIZENS OF ISRAEL, AND STRANGERS TO THE COVENANTS OF GOD'S PROMISE. IN THIS WORLD YOU HAD NO HOPE AND NO GOD. BUT NOW, THANKS TO CHRIST JESUS, YOU WHO ONCE WERE SO FAR AWAY HAVE BEEN BROUGHT NEAR BY THE BLOOD OF CHRIST.

CHRIST IS OUR PEACE. HE MADE BOTH JEWS AND GENTILES INTO ONE GROUP. WITH HIS BODY, HE BROKE DOWN THE BARRIER OF HATRED THAT DIVIDED US. HE CANCELED THE DETAILED RULES OF THE LAW SO THAT HE COULD CREATE ONE NEW PERSON OUT OF THE TWO GROUPS, MAKING PEACE. HE RECONCILED THEM BOTH AS ONE BODY TO GOD BY THE CROSS, WHICH ENDED THE HOSTILITY TO GOD.

WHEN HE CAME, HE ANNOUNCED THE GOOD NEWS OF PEACE TO YOU WHO WERE FAR AWAY FROM GOD AND TO THOSE WHO WERE NEAR. WE BOTH HAVE ACCESS TO THE FATHER THROUGH CHRIST BY THE ONE SPIRIT. SO NOW YOU ARE NO LONGER STRANGERS AND ALIENS. RATHER, YOU ARE FELLOW CITIZENS WITH GOD'S PEOPLE, AND YOU BELONG TO GOD'S HOUSEHOLD. AS GOD'S HOUSEHOLD, YOU ARE BUILT ON THE FOUNDATION OF THE APOSTLES AND PROPHETS WITH CHRIST JESUS HIMSELF AS THE CORNERSTONE. THE WHOLE BUILDING IS JOINED TOGETHER IN HIM, AND IT GROWS UP INTO A TEMPLE THAT IS DEDICATED TO THE LORD. CHRIST IS BUILDING YOU INTO A PLACE WHERE GOD LIVES THROUGH THE SPIRIT. (Ephesians 2:11-22)

When we talk about being "taken out" of something, just what is it that we are talking about? When we talk vaguely about being taken from the "world," I am not sure we understand just what that means. We might think of being taken from drugs, alcohol, promiscuous sex, or any host of other things that seem to cloud our judgment and render bad behavior. The Bible isn't being that simplistic when it talks about moving from one thing to another. Behavior might be the subject matter that offends or bothers people, but the issue that lies underneath is what God seeks to address in each of us.

GOD'S WRATH IS BEING REVEALED FROM HEAVEN AGAINST ALL THE UNGODLY BEHAVIOR AND THE INJUSTICE OF HUMAN BEINGS WHO SILENCE THE TRUTH WITH INJUSTICE. THIS IS BECAUSE WHAT IS KNOWN ABOUT GOD SHOULD BE PLAIN TO THEM BECAUSE GOD MADE IT PLAIN TO THEM. EVER SINCE THE

CREATION OF THE WORLD, GOD'S INVISIBLE QUALITIES—GOD'S ETERNAL POWER AND DIVINE NATURE—HAVE BEEN CLEARLY SEEN, BECAUSE THEY ARE UNDERSTOOD THROUGH THE THINGS GOD HAS MADE. SO HUMANS ARE WITHOUT EXCUSE. ALTHOUGH THEY KNEW GOD, THEY DIDN'T HONOR GOD AS GOD OR THANK HIM. INSTEAD, THEIR REASONING BECAME POINTLESS, AND THEIR FOOLISH HEARTS WERE DARKENED. WHILE THEY WERE CLAIMING TO BE WISE, THEY MADE FOOLS OF THEMSELVES. THEY EXCHANGED THE GLORY OF THE IMMORTAL GOD FOR IMAGES THAT LOOK LIKE MORTAL HUMANS: BIRDS, ANIMALS, AND REPTILES. SO GOD ABANDONED THEM TO THEIR HEARTS' DESIRES, WHICH LED TO THE MORAL CORRUPTION OF DEGRADING THEIR OWN BODIES WITH EACH OTHER. THEY TRADED GOD'S TRUTH FOR A LIE, AND THEY WORSHIPPED AND SERVED THE CREATION INSTEAD OF THE CREATOR, WHO IS BLESSED FOREVER. AMEN.

THAT'S WHY GOD ABANDONED THEM TO DEGRADING LUST. THEIR FEMALES TRADED NATURAL SEXUAL RELATIONS FOR UNNATURAL SEXUAL RELATIONS. ALSO, IN THE SAME WAY, THE MALES TRADED NATURAL SEXUAL RELATIONS WITH FEMALES, AND BURNED WITH LUST FOR EACH OTHER. MALES PERFORMED SHAMEFUL ACTIONS WITH MALES, AND THEY WERE PAID BACK WITH THE PENALTY THEY DESERVED FOR THEIR MISTAKE IN THEIR OWN BODIES. SINCE THEY DIDN'T THINK IT WAS WORTHWHILE TO ACKNOWLEDGE GOD, GOD ABANDONED THEM TO A DEFECTIVE MIND TO DO INAPPROPRIATE THINGS. SO THEY WERE FILLED WITH ALL INJUSTICE, WICKED BEHAVIOR, GREED, AND EVIL BEHAVIOR. THEY ARE FULL OF JEALOUSY, MURDER, FIGHTING, DECEPTION, AND MALICE. THEY ARE GOSSIPS, THEY SLANDER PEOPLE, AND THEY HATE GOD. THEY ARE RUDE AND PROUD, AND THEY BRAG. THEY INVENT WAYS TO BE EVIL, AND THEY ARE DISOBEDIENT TO THEIR PARENTS. THEY ARE WITHOUT UNDERSTANDING, DISLOYAL, WITHOUT AFFECTION, AND WITHOUT MERCY. THOUGH THEY KNOW GOD'S DECISION THAT THOSE WHO PERSIST IN SUCH PRACTICES DESERVE DEATH, THEY NOT ONLY KEEP DOING THESE THINGS BUT ALSO APPROVE OTHERS WHO PRACTICE THEM. (Romans 1:18-32)

Romans 1 is used to justify all sorts of political positions and personal opinions, but the context that it is often used is incorrect. The chapter was not included in the Bible to justify various political positions or to berate groups of people over the head but is here to teach us about the way that God revealed Himself to the Gentiles – or pagan groups – to build a clear way to see to their eventual salvation now through Christ.

"Gentile" is a designation meaning "nations," and comes about in contrast between Israel and other nations. After the call of Abram, his ancestors progressively moved to become the Hebrew nation that was poised to take the Promised Land. By the time the Israelites were enslaved by Egypt, it is obvious they had taken on a certain nature or character that noted them as different from other tribes or nations, but there were no formal regulations by which to identify them. After God redeemed His people from slavery in Egypt, the Hebrews spent forty years in the wilderness. While they were there, they received the specific codes and conducts that would define them as a nation, a set apart people.

In keeping with national identities of those times, the Israelites observed a code of law that encompassed six hundred and thirteen different rules and regulations that extended to most areas of life. Some of those codes were spiritual, some were hygienic, some were social, and some were political, extending to the way in which they would interact with other nations. These laws were what defined the nation of Israel, setting it apart from Gentiles, and establishing it as special or unique.

We know about Israel, how Israel came to regard itself, and the reality that Israel seldom, if ever, met up to the standards of its written law. Israel thought the Gentile nations surrounding them were their problem, when Israel's problem was itself. Disobedience is a part of all of us, every single one of us, and it was Israel's problem, too. They might have blamed the influences of all their neighbors, but Israel was ultimately responsible for itself. They had the law, so they should have known better.

What the Apostle Paul expresses in Romans 1, therefore, is in contrast with the issues that Israel faced. Israel's self-righteousness and improper application of the law was no worse than the sins of the Gentiles. That is expounded in Romans 2, which means Romans 1 is about how God reached out to the pagan, and how the pagan avoided or disregarded God.

We can see from Romans 1 that the pagan had knowledge of God through nature: through watching times and seasons, through seedtime and harvest, by watching and interacting with the natural elements, and in the general course of monitoring creation. The Gentiles did not have the law, but they had nature, a natural law, of sorts, and from that, they encountered the reality of created order and that some greater spiritual force must be behind all that exists. The passage goes on to state that the Gentiles lost their way by idolizing creation. Instead of worshipping the Creator, they elevated nature to a status of worship, and worshipped it instead. The passage shows the consequences of idolatry and magic, of people doing things under spells that they would not do otherwise, and that, above all, the Gentiles were without excuse for disobeying God, just as the Jews were without excuse for disobeying God, because all had enough experience with God to know better.

If we carefully examine pagan religion, we can see that the pagans of old did have enough knowledge to recognize something spiritually important was present within natural order. They developed various forms of types and shadows, seeing something to come, but worshipping the type instead of seeing those things as a promise of the coming of Christ. Throughout paganism, their gods turned water into wine, had twelve disciples, were born of virgins, performed many miracles, multiplied loaves and fishes, and other commonalities that pointed to the reality and promise of the Messiah to come. Their error was turning these types and shadows into gods and objects of worship.

From reading Romans 1, we can discover what Gentiles were known for:

- **Idolatry**: An idol is anything put in the place of God and worshipped as God in one's life. One may deliberately worship something in defiance of God or may gradually work their way up to an admiration, need, or exaltation of something in the place of or beyond God. In Biblical times, idols were associated with actual gods that had various identities and were believed to control the different forces of nature or natural happenings.

- **Witchcraft**: Today we associate witchcraft with Disney movies, Halloween spells, and fanciful tales of good or bad witches. From a Biblical understanding, true witchcraft is far more sinister than what we might see depicted in fairy tales or movies for children. Witchcraft is based on the belief that the natural world reflects the spiritual world, and things in the natural realm can be manipulated or aligned in a certain way to change or influence the spiritual world. The manipulation of elements occurs through spellcasting, which pagans believe starts the spiritual process to whatever result they seek. For example, if a woman desires another person to fall in love with her, she would cast a specific spell to attract that person to her. Witchcraft takes many forms; there are many different strains of paganism (most parallel or overlap at points), there are many types of spells, and there are many different gods or forces identified within the various pagan theologies, but all witchcraft has two things in common: It is about exerting control for a personal purpose by using natural elements to accomplish something spiritual, and it involves the manipulation of those elements, forces, or people involved to bring about its goal.

- **Nature worship:** Even though nature worship is a form of idolatry, I am mentioning it separately because it is notable enough to have its own specific identification in Romans 1. To define it briefly, nature worship is the worship of anything found in nature, especially that which relates to the life process. More specific forms of nature worship include pantheism (the belief that the divine is in all, and all is, therefore the divine), animism (the belief that people, objects, animals, or places can possess divine or spiritual qualities), or shamanism (the belief that other spiritual worlds are accessible through the shaman, who is able to obtain these worlds through altered states of consciousness). Most, if not all, of these different aspects of nature worship are found in places throughout the Old Testament, although they may not be identified by their identifying names.

- **Ancestral worship:** Worship of ancestors is found throughout the world and is based in the belief that the dead can influence the living, either positively or negatively. It was believed that keeping the dead happy equated to a happier life for those who are living, and ignoring the dead would result in hauntings, curses, or other negativity inflicted upon the living from beyond the grave. Offerings of prayer, food, incense, or other items might be given in homage to the dead.

- **Sexual rites:** Biblical prostitution falls into two categories: that which was done for pagan fertility rites in connection with pagan temples, and that which was done for profession outside of religious purposes or ties. When we read about New Testament prohibitions on sexual practices, prostitution, or sexual interactions, they are almost always in reference to pagan fertility rites in which a man or woman would engage in sex with a temple prostitute for a desired spiritual result. Whether heterosexual sex, homosexual sex, bisexual sex, or any other form of sexual activity, the purpose was to manipulate elements and start something in the natural that would spill over into the spiritual. This means temple prostitution served the purpose of casting a spell, and the result of such was witchcraft.

Rescued from self-righteousness

Before we go pointing all fingers at the Gentiles, let's remember that both Jew and Gentile have the opportunity to become a part of the church. Jesus did not just die to save the Gentile; He also died to save the Jew. The written law never had the power to save, but it existed to make us aware of sin and make us aware of ourselves. Its purpose was to make us aware that we need a savior. Instead of adopting this humbling mindset, the Israelites became arrogant, feeling the law made them superior, even though they never followed the law in totality.

SO EVERY SINGLE ONE OF YOU WHO JUDGE OTHERS IS WITHOUT ANY EXCUSE. YOU CONDEMN YOURSELF WHEN YOU JUDGE ANOTHER PERSON BECAUSE THE ONE WHO IS JUDGING IS DOING THE SAME THINGS. WE KNOW THAT GOD'S JUDGMENT AGREES WITH THE TRUTH, AND HIS JUDGMENT IS AGAINST THOSE WHO DO THESE KINDS OF THINGS. IF YOU JUDGE THOSE WHO DO THESE KINDS OF THINGS WHILE YOU DO THE SAME THINGS YOURSELF, THINK ABOUT THIS: DO YOU BELIEVE THAT YOU WILL ESCAPE GOD'S JUDGMENT? OR DO YOU HAVE CONTEMPT FOR THE RICHES OF GOD'S GENEROSITY, TOLERANCE, AND PATIENCE? DON'T YOU REALIZE THAT GOD'S KINDNESS IS SUPPOSED TO LEAD YOU TO CHANGE YOUR HEART AND LIFE? YOU ARE STORING UP WRATH FOR YOURSELF BECAUSE OF YOUR STUBBORNNESS AND YOUR HEART THAT REFUSES TO CHANGE. GOD'S JUST JUDGMENT WILL BE REVEALED ON THE DAY OF WRATH. GOD WILL REPAY EVERYONE BASED ON THEIR WORKS. ON THE ONE HAND, HE WILL GIVE ETERNAL LIFE TO THOSE WHO LOOK FOR GLORY, HONOR, AND IMMORTALITY BASED ON THEIR PATIENT GOOD WORK. BUT ON THE OTHER HAND, THERE WILL BE WRATH AND ANGER FOR THOSE WHO OBEY WICKEDNESS

INSTEAD OF THE TRUTH BECAUSE THEY ARE ACTING OUT OF SELFISHNESS AND DISOBEDIENCE. THERE WILL BE TROUBLE AND DISTRESS FOR EVERY HUMAN BEING WHO DOES EVIL, FOR THE JEW FIRST AND ALSO FOR THE GREEK. BUT THERE WILL BE GLORY, HONOR, AND PEACE FOR EVERYONE WHO DOES WHAT IS GOOD, FOR THE JEW FIRST AND ALSO FOR THE GREEK. GOD DOES NOT HAVE FAVORITES.

THOSE WHO HAVE SINNED OUTSIDE THE LAW WILL ALSO DIE OUTSIDE THE LAW, AND THOSE WHO HAVE SINNED UNDER THE LAW WILL BE JUDGED BY THE LAW. IT ISN'T THE ONES WHO HEAR THE LAW WHO ARE RIGHTEOUS IN GOD'S EYES. IT IS THE ONES WHO DO WHAT THE LAW SAYS WHO WILL BE TREATED AS RIGHTEOUS. GENTILES DON'T HAVE THE LAW. BUT WHEN THEY INSTINCTIVELY DO WHAT THE LAW REQUIRES THEY ARE A LAW IN THEMSELVES, THOUGH THEY DON'T HAVE THE LAW. THEY SHOW THE PROOF OF THE LAW WRITTEN ON THEIR HEARTS, AND THEIR CONSCIENCES AFFIRM IT. THEIR CONFLICTING THOUGHTS WILL ACCUSE THEM, OR EVEN MAKE A DEFENSE FOR THEM, ON THE DAY WHEN, ACCORDING TO MY GOSPEL, GOD WILL JUDGE THE HIDDEN TRUTH ABOUT HUMAN BEINGS THROUGH CHRIST JESUS.

BUT,
IF YOU CALL YOURSELF A JEW;
IF YOU RELY ON THE LAW;
IF YOU BRAG ABOUT YOUR RELATIONSHIP TO GOD;
IF YOU KNOW THE WILL OF GOD;
IF YOU ARE TAUGHT BY THE LAW SO THAT YOU CAN FIGURE OUT THE THINGS THAT REALLY MATTER;
IF YOU HAVE PERSUADED YOURSELF THAT YOU ARE:

> *A GUIDE FOR THE BLIND;*
> *A LIGHT TO THOSE WHO ARE IN DARKNESS;*
> *AN EDUCATOR OF THE FOOLISH;*
> *A TEACHER OF INFANTS (SINCE YOU HAVE THE FULL CONTENT OF KNOWLEDGE AND TRUTH IN THE LAW);*

THEN WHY DON'T YOU WHO ARE TEACHING OTHERS TEACH YOURSELF?
IF YOU PREACH, "NO STEALING," DO YOU STEAL?
IF YOU SAY, "NO ADULTERY," DO YOU COMMIT ADULTERY?
IF YOU HATE IDOLS, DO YOU ROB TEMPLES?

IF YOU BRAG ABOUT THE LAW, DO YOU SHAME GOD BY BREAKING THE LAW? AS IT IS WRITTEN: THE NAME OF GOD IS DISCREDITED BY THE GENTILES BECAUSE OF YOU.

CIRCUMCISION IS AN ADVANTAGE IF YOU DO WHAT THE LAW SAYS. BUT IF YOU ARE A PERSON WHO BREAKS THE LAW, YOUR STATUS OF BEING CIRCUMCISED HAS CHANGED INTO NOT BEING CIRCUMCISED. SO IF THE PERSON WHO ISN'T CIRCUMCISED KEEPS THE LAW, WON'T HIS STATUS OF NOT BEING CIRCUMCISED BE COUNTED AS IF HE WERE CIRCUMCISED? THE ONE WHO ISN'T PHYSICALLY CIRCUMCISED BUT KEEPS THE LAW WILL JUDGE YOU. YOU BECAME A LAWBREAKER AFTER YOU HAD THE WRITTEN LAW AND CIRCUMCISION. IT ISN'T THE JEW WHO MAINTAINS OUTWARD APPEARANCES WHO WILL RECEIVE PRAISE FROM GOD, AND IT ISN'T PEOPLE WHO ARE OUTWARDLY CIRCUMCISED ON THEIR BODIES. INSTEAD, IT IS THE PERSON WHO IS A JEW INSIDE, WHO IS CIRCUMCISED IN SPIRIT, NOT LITERALLY. THAT PERSON'S PRAISE DOESN'T COME FROM PEOPLE BUT FROM GOD. (Romans 2:1-29)

The Apostle Paul wrote Romans 2 to go along with Romans 1, not to leave Romans 1 as a distant entity that doesn't make much sense. If we take it out of context, Romans 1 can sound like any number of criticisms or confusions. Our foundational understanding of the church is unity: unity with God and with one another, and that means we must overcome sin through Christ to that end.

Romans 2 is an uncomfortable chapter when we start looking to deal with the international church. In many ways, our limited view of church has turned us into the Israelites, thinking we have a persecution complex because adhere to right when, in reality, we are doing things all wrong and completely ineffectively. In missions, we must adopt an inclusive mindset: one that embraces the principle of "Gentiles" that we embody today, that looks down upon believers of other nations or of non-believers who do not interact or engage in the same way that we do, and stop hoping that our isolationist belief systems are going to be enough to change hearts and minds. Through the work of Christ, the entire world was opened up before the Jewish community. The principles of separateness and holiness that were designed to embolden them toward doing right towards God and others had broken down into a sense of self-righteousness that had no power to save them. In looking at ourselves and at the church today, how much of that has rubbed off to right where we are right now, and how is it hurting our view of the international church, their needs, and the needs of the world, at large, that we are called to meet through missions?

From reading Romans 2, we can discover what the Jews were known for and cause us to consider:

- **Self-righteousness:** Romans 2 addresses many characteristics that the Jews had in the first century...that we also see among believers today. Pomposity, self-righteousness, doing things to be seen of men, hearing the law without doing, and overtly breaking the law when they knew what it taught. God's point in such revelation was to show us that self-righteousness or relying on one's own definition of righteousness through oneself, was just as bad as idolatry. Being pompous or doing things to be praised of others without any heart behind them was just as bad as ancestral worship. Hearing the law and not doing what it stated (or even trying) was just as bad as sexual rites. Disobeying God was just as bad as witchcraft or nature worship. Sin is sin is sin, and the sins of Israel were not worse than the sins of the Gentiles.

- **Having the right things and falling into wrong, time and time again:** Let's consider the experience that Israel had with God: Israel had God Himself as their teacher. He is the best leadership imaginable. There were times when the entire nation heard from God Himself. God sent them wonderful individuals who did their very best to lead the nation rightly...and they still failed. They failed over and over and over again, no matter who was sent to them or what was done for them.

- **Dysfunctional relationship with God:** Some people talk about a relationship with God, as if any relationship is sufficient. It is completely possible to have a relationship with God that is disordered or dysfunctional, not because of God, but because of one's perception of God and what He should or should not do for them. The Israelites had a completely dysfunctional relationship with God: they only did what they had to do to keep favor with Him until they reached the point where they felt they could get away with doing wrong because they had a relationship with Him that others did not.

- **Learning doesn't substitute for doing**: The scribes and Pharisees of Israel were the most learned people in all of Israel. They knew the laws backwards and forwards, they knew the ins and outs, and they knew them so well that they were able to contrive and twist them into something other than their intention. Having all the knowledge in the world about salvation, about the Bible, or about any aspect of spirituality does not compensate for not following what we know God desires us to do.

- **Holding on to a written code was never going to save them**: We read the Bible from the Hebrew perspective, but have we ever considered what the Israelites looked like to the Gentiles? Here they were, claiming to have all this information, knowledge, insight, and perspective, they thought themselves better than everyone else...and they still kept falling into the same issues and traps, time and time again. Israel longed for a tangible code, something they could see and adopt, that would make sense to their need for a visual spirituality. Israel claimed to be saved and to have salvation, but it was obvious to the Gentiles looking in that their written code was not enough to save, nor separate, them.

- **Our influences might matter, but they do not make our choices**: Israel was influenced by the vast number of Gentile nations that surrounded them. Yes, they might have influenced Israel, but they did not make the decision for Israel to follow the actions of these Gentile nations. In the end, Israel had the knowledge to do right, and they chose not to do what they knew they were supposed to do. Yes, influences matter. Israel was supposed to separate itself from such influences, so Israel already did the wrong thing by placing its people in a position to be influenced. At the end of the day, however, each individual Israelite made their own choice to do what the pagan nations around them were doing. Nobody forced them, nor did anyone sway the influences in that direction. Yes, influences are relevant, but they are not to blame for the decisions anyone makes.

- **Supremacy is supremacy is supremacy**: By the time of the New Testament, the Hebrews of the Bible believed themselves superior to everyone else, even though they did the things everyone else did. They believed themselves to be a superior race, superior nation, and superior people. Thinking you are better than anyone else is still a sin, for whatever the reason you believe supremacy to be relevant.

- **We really don't accept that all sin is the same before God**: No matter how much we might want to stand back and think that stealing is the same as murder or adultery is the same as lying before God, we all partition sin in our own minds as "greater" or "lesser." By trying to examine our motives or the root cause of our reasoning, we try to lessen the view of sin before God's eyes by reducing it within our own. The self-righteousness of the Jews was just as equally displeasing to God as the idolatry of the pagans, but the Jews didn't see what they did in that way. This means we must all examine ourselves, each before God, because our sins are just as bad as someone else's, no matter how big or small they seem to us.

Seeing both the Jews and Gentiles in ourselves and the church at large

I believe the Jew-Gentile distinction has been made in Romans 1 and 2 for one reason: no matter how we categorize ourselves or our sin, at the end of the day, we are all the same. Whether we are born Jew or Gentile, every one of us has both Jew and Gentile within us. We are all self-righteousness in some way, seeing ourselves as superior to someone else, or succumbing to practices of idolatry, witchcraft, sexual vice, or natural or ancestral worship...or all the above. Israel succumbed to both, and I have no doubt the Gentiles succumbed to both, as well. Both the practices of the Jews and the Gentiles were present in both groups, even though neither side might have wanted to admit or deal with that. In Christ, in the church, find redemption from these characteristics, which are international by nature. They are found in all groups and all nations, no matter what a group may believe or embrace from a doctrinal perspective.

And now, we find all of us in the church: those who are self-righteous, those who rely on the letter of the law to save them, those who have been idolaters, those who worshipped everything but the true God, those who are forever learning but never coming to a place of doing, those who've been influenced improperly, those who've engaged in sexual magic, those who've played around with witchcraft, and those who have sinned...which is all of us. Jesus has redeemed us from those things which held us bound, those ideals and concepts which were a part of our identity, the ingrains of our culture and our teaching, to bring us to where we are, in Him, today.

Missions work deals with these different issues head-on, both within the missionary, who must constantly check themselves for the tendency to be self-righteous or self-imposing through spirituality, to refrain from judgment and isolated thinking, and into a place where those the missionary reaches are ready and able to come into this wonderful thing that now defines us: the church.

The Kingdom of God is within you

I've been teaching on the Kingdom for almost twenty years, but it never gets old. There are so many things to learn about the Kingdom because the Kingdom of God is within us. The more we learn about the Kingdom, the more we learn about God and ourselves. It is a discovery process as we work out our salvation with fear and trembling, seeing what God brought us through and where we are going.

AND WHEN HE WAS DEMANDED OF THE PHARISEES, WHEN THE KINGDOM OF GOD SHOULD COME, HE ANSWERED THEM AND SAID, THE KINGDOM OF GOD COMETH NOT WITH OBSERVATION: NEITHER SHALL THEY SAY, LO HERE! OR, LO THERE! FOR, BEHOLD, THE KINGDOM OF GOD IS WITHIN YOU. (Luke 17:20-21, KJV)

WE ARE GOD'S COWORKERS, AND YOU ARE GOD'S FIELD, GOD'S BUILDING. (1 Corinthians 3:9)

When we talk about Kingdom, we are talking about the work and the church of God that builds it. The Kingdom of God is God's governance within the church, within those who choose to be a part of what He is doing. The church is not a distant building, nor is it a denomination, nor is it a Sunday morning service. The church is us, who are a part of the Kingdom governance God has established. It is every believer, every believer who is found in Him, and who has grabbed hold of what He has to offer in a way that has changed them. If there is one key facet we can see from our examination of who is in the church because of what Jesus has redeemed us from, it is change. There is a difference in us: within us, among us, and around us. The Kingdom cannot be observed, nor seen as we build physical buildings unto ourselves or surround ourselves with those who flock to what we have to say. Seeing the Kingdom within us in a personal way means that the nature of the church is a part of who we are. It's not far away or distant, it is not something we arbitrarily do to make others happy, but if we are transformed and changed...it is who we are.

As a missionary, carrying the Kingdom is essential. Missions have faltered because the grand denominations we have built to ourselves have fallen apart. All we have left to examine is whether or not the Kingdom of God is truly within us. We answer that as we examine the nature of the church.

The nature of the church

- **Eternal:** *AND I TELL YOU, YOU ARE PETER, AND ON THIS ROCK I WILL BUILD MY CHURCH, AND THE GATES OF HADES WILL NOT PREVAIL AGAINST IT.* (Matthew 16:18, NRSV)

- **The Body:** *NOW I'M HAPPY TO BE SUFFERING FOR YOU. I'M COMPLETING WHAT IS MISSING FROM CHRIST'S SUFFERINGS WITH MY OWN BODY. I'M DOING THIS FOR THE SAKE OF HIS BODY, WHICH IS THE CHURCH.* (Colossians 1:24)

  CHRIST IS JUST LIKE THE HUMAN BODY—A BODY IS A UNIT AND HAS MANY PARTS; AND ALL THE PARTS OF THE BODY ARE ONE BODY, EVEN THOUGH THERE ARE MANY. (1 Corinthians 12:12)

- **One:** *I'VE GIVEN THEM THE GLORY THAT YOU GAVE ME SO THAT THEY CAN BE ONE JUST AS WE ARE ONE. I'M IN THEM AND YOU ARE IN ME SO THAT THEY WILL BE MADE PERFECTLY ONE. THEN THE WORLD WILL KNOW THAT YOU SENT ME AND THAT YOU HAVE LOVED THEM JUST AS YOU LOVED ME.* (John 17:22-23)

- **A relationship counterpart**: *AS FOR HUSBANDS, LOVE YOUR WIVES JUST LIKE CHRIST LOVED THE CHURCH AND GAVE HIMSELF FOR HER. HE DID THIS TO MAKE HER HOLY BY WASHING HER IN A BATH OF WATER WITH THE WORD. HE DID THIS TO PRESENT HIMSELF WITH A SPLENDID CHURCH, ONE WITHOUT ANY SORT OF STAIN OR WRINKLE ON HER CLOTHES, BUT RATHER ONE THAT IS HOLY AND BLAMELESS.* (Ephesians 5:25-27)

- **Enduring**: *WHOEVER HAS EARS MUST LISTEN: IF ANY ARE TO BE TAKEN CAPTIVE, THEN INTO CAPTIVITY THEY WILL GO. IF ANY ARE TO BE KILLED BY THE SWORD, THEN BY THE SWORD THEY WILL BE KILLED. THIS CALLS FOR ENDURANCE AND FAITHFULNESS ON THE PART OF THE SAINTS.* (Revelation 13:9-10)

- **Apostolic**: *HE GAVE SOME APOSTLES, SOME PROPHETS, SOME EVANGELISTS, AND SOME PASTORS AND TEACHERS. HIS PURPOSE WAS TO EQUIP GOD'S PEOPLE FOR THE WORK OF SERVING AND BUILDING UP THE BODY OF CHRIST UNTIL WE ALL REACH THE UNITY OF FAITH AND KNOWLEDGE OF GOD'S SON. GOD'S GOAL IS FOR US TO BECOME MATURE ADULTS—TO BE FULLY GROWN, MEASURED BY THE STANDARD OF THE FULLNESS OF CHRIST.* (Ephesians 4:11-13)

- **Pentecostal**: *WHEN PENTECOST DAY ARRIVED, THEY WERE ALL TOGETHER IN ONE PLACE. SUDDENLY A SOUND FROM HEAVEN LIKE THE HOWLING OF A FIERCE WIND FILLED THE ENTIRE HOUSE WHERE THEY WERE SITTING. THEY SAW WHAT SEEMED TO BE INDIVIDUAL FLAMES OF FIRE ALIGHTING ON EACH ONE OF THEM. THEY WERE ALL FILLED WITH THE HOLY SPIRIT AND BEGAN TO SPEAK IN OTHER LANGUAGES AS THE SPIRIT ENABLED THEM TO SPEAK.* (Acts 2:1-4)

- **Something we experience**: *AND THEY SAID TO THE WOMAN, "WE NO LONGER BELIEVE BECAUSE OF WHAT YOU SAID, FOR WE HAVE HEARD FOR OURSELVES AND KNOW THAT THIS ONE IS TRULY THE SAVIOR OF THE WORLD."* (John 4:42)

- **Communal**: *THE GRACE OF THE LORD JESUS CHRIST, THE LOVE OF GOD, AND THE COMMUNION OF THE HOLY SPIRIT BE WITH ALL OF YOU.* (2 Corinthians 13:13, NRSV)

- **Worldwide** - *SO NOW YOU ARE NO LONGER STRANGERS AND ALIENS. RATHER, YOU ARE FELLOW CITIZENS WITH GOD'S PEOPLE, AND YOU BELONG TO GOD'S HOUSEHOLD. AS GOD'S HOUSEHOLD, YOU ARE BUILT ON THE FOUNDATION OF THE APOSTLES AND PROPHETS WITH CHRIST JESUS HIMSELF AS THE CORNERSTONE. THE WHOLE BUILDING IS JOINED TOGETHER IN HIM, AND IT GROWS UP INTO A TEMPLE THAT IS DEDICATED TO THE LORD. CHRIST IS BUILDING YOU INTO A PLACE WHERE GOD LIVES THROUGH THE SPIRIT.* (Ephesians 2:19-22)

Universal church vs. local church

If there is one common theme that all of us have heard of, at one point in time, it is about the nature of the "local church." Most of us were told, at some point in time, that we need to find ourselves a local church and set ourselves up there - staying there consistently, under the same pastor or leader, to receive what we need from God. Some individuals go to the vast extreme to discourage anyone and everyone from ever leaving that church, no matter what error or wrong may occur there; and we also see the extremes of people being told they have to go to a local church and "settle" on one, even though they may disagree on part of what is taught doctrinally. We also have the experience that people are often so into the concept of a local church that they forget about the bigger church picture, failing to realize Christians are found all over the world, not just in a local community within the United States. I've personally experienced the testimony of many who found themselves so wounded by an immediate local church that they lost all sight of faith in Christ and the bigger Christian picture - and simply abandoned Christianity all together. Others see the displays of some churches as an opportunity to mock and defame Christ because the representation of such religiosity is so poor that one can't help but believe something has to be wrong.

These varied responses about the local church tell us two things about it. The first is that the local church can represent Christianity in a powerful way to those who are immediately impacted by its presence. The second is that the local church, while receiving many such opportunities to represent Christianity, must represent that balance between local and universal. This balancing act of presenting both a universal faith and response to both universal and immediate need is a delicate one, and not to be taken lightly. It is why, as Christians, we must take a serious look at the local church and examine its place within the universal body of Christ rather than seeing the universal church as a larger extension of the local community.

There is no doubt that the local church has always made up an important aspect of Christianity. As the church began to grow, history shows a struggle between the expanding church and the local church. We can see from church history that when universal control is implemented upon the local body, the local church becomes nothing more than a mouthpiece for religious politicians. When a small oligarchy emerged to battle over the entire worldwide church, the first thing that notably disappeared was the five-fold ministry. One of the most powerful purposes held for apostles, prophets, and evangelists alike is to remind local churches of the universality of the body. As these three offices have traditionally served itinerantly, we can clearly see the relevance they would play to constantly remind the local communities and churches they visited about the fact that there is more to recognize, do, and believe than what just may be immediately taught by local authorities. The apostle, prophet, and evangelist certainly did not and do not operate to lord control or intimidate others - but they do hold a powerful relevance to bridge the universal and local churches together. The notable absence of these offices in history should awaken us and make us all aware of the great importance in the fully functioning five-fold ministry. It also reminds local leaders that they indeed are not the end of the line as ultimate authorities and do likewise have to be accountable for what they teach beyond themselves.

Yet in modern times where the universal body is sometimes denounced, we see problems emerge that display the exact opposites of those created when the local church is ignored. One of the greatest emerging problems of the past fifty or so years has reared itself in the form of controlling local leaders. Numerous reports exist showing forth local leadership which takes upon itself the right to tell people who to marry, what gifts they may or may not walk in within the church, what jobs they can take, how many children they can have, and threaten church members with hellfire or disobedience to God if they decide to leave the church or disregard the dictates of the leaders. In my own life, I have experienced more local leaders like this than not; and it has been my own experience that these leaders are often one of the biggest oppositions to the modern rise in apostles (and the five-fold, by extension) today. I don't question whether there are many sincere local church leaders who seek the best for their congregations and lead as tender shepherds. We likewise can't pretend that individuals do not exist who are out there, giving local church a bad name. It is such leaders who create the thousands of victims of spiritual abuse walking around among us today; people who have grown so scarred by their images of defective leadership that they find themselves unable to face God in a personal and life-changing way.

Another common problem we see is the over-emphasis of the local church in which members lose sight of everyone else. We have reduced persecution to a trite expression uttered when someone at work doesn't want to attend church with us and completely forgot that people still intensely suffer for their faith. Somewhere in the world right now, there is a man, woman, or child dying for their faith in Christ. In many countries in this world, someone can risk losing their job, their housing, their children, and their very life because they are a Christian. There are believers everywhere in the world - and there are Christian apostles, prophets, and evangelists laboring for the Gospel in other cities, countries, and territories beyond a local church for the pursuit of the Gospel. Such workers can never be forgotten, even when somebody attends a local church.

There is also the issue of local churches which try to be universal on their own, with a pastor or leader that tries to fill the role of the five-fold ministry in one man or woman. In so doing, the church often becomes about reaching more people without meeting their needs. It is possible for a local church to be so impersonal and distant that the church can become totally void of teaching substance. There are many churches today which pride themselves in such; they claim to be about reaching non-believers yet ignore the needs of developing and growing Christians to walk as the mature sons and daughters of God. The local church has the job of responding to the immediate needs of its community - including spiritual needs. This means that there is something for everyone in the church at any stage of spiritual growth; those who are new believers are not ignored, and neither are those who have been walking with the Lord for a long time.

It is also a frequent problem that local churches provide nothing but, as they would say, "teaching" to the community. The church has a spiritual call, which cannot be ignored; but the local church can neither deny its call by Jesus to meet the practical needs of those who are hurting (Matthew 25:31-46). This balance is achieved by recognizing that by meeting practical needs we open the door to meet spiritual needs; even Jesus Himself used common, ordinary means of practical means to meet and illustrate spiritual needs (Luke 9:14-17).

It is important to understand how the church fits into the definition of universal to recognize it is not merely a local body, but a universal one. How is the church universal?

- The body of Christ is universal because Christ died not just for the immediate handful of believers who followed Him through His earthly ministry, but for every person in the world who might come to repent and believe in Him (John 3:16). The church is not just for a certain ethnicity, group, or organization, but is open to everybody; it is not exclusive. Universality emphasizes inclusivity; an over-emphasis on locality emphasizes exclusivity.

- The church exists everywhere because the New Testament tells us the Kingdom of God is within us and among us (Luke 17:21). We are the building of God, and the temple of the Holy Spirit (1 Corinthians 3:9,16). Anywhere there is a believer, there is the church. The church exists under all sorts of conditions, situations, and cultures worldwide; and it is still the church, with the same God operating in believers (Ephesians 4:6). We can believe in what is true despite our cultural, language, or societal differences.

- The church is universal because it is not based on economic status. Anyone from any class, category, or income status can believe in Christ and is equal in the sight of Christ (James 2:1-12).

- The church challenges traditional notions of sexism and racism. It is religion which builds these walls solid, but God truly reveals there is neither male nor female, slave nor free, Jew or Gentile, but a true oneness among believers who have died to themselves and risen to life in Him (Galatians 3:26-29).

Thus, the church is universal because it is the one new humanity born in Christ. It is a Kingdom, not a mere earthly society; and it shall never end. And what we must recognize is that the local church does indeed have a place in the universal body of Christ; however, the universal body is not the extension of the local church. The local church is a small, immediate body of the larger body of believers. It is a type, or reflection, of that larger glory which we can recognize transcends cultures, languages, and barriers through the eternal Spirit of God.

In looking at the church as a universal entity, the local church functions for the following:

- **Meeting:** Hebrews 10:25 tells us not to forsake the assembling of ourselves together. Understanding the church to be the "called out" ones recognize we must do something now that we are called out. The local church functions for believers to gather, meet, fellowship, worship, pray, praise, and learn. It is a powerful forum for learning and teaching. The local church, however, does not have to be a group that formally meets on Sundays in a building and promptly ends at 12 PM. Communities in the New Testament met a wide variety of needs; we see communities that met in homes (Romans 16:5), local groups that seemed to have assembled in buildings specifically for the churches (Romans 16:16), and individuals who were even taught by individuals in their own homes (Acts 18:26). Fellowship in the New Testament likewise went far beyond a Sunday morning meeting; the church of Acts seems to have met daily and engaged in the sharing of communion, breaking bread in the form of meals, sharing items, and giving in collections (Acts 2:42-47).

- **Having *"all things in common"* (Acts 2:44):** The biggest facets in religion today are the disagreements of men (2 Timothy 2:14). Denomination after denomination rises with the intent to establish rules or regulations which disagree with someone else's rules or regulations. One thing we often do not see when examining the history of such disagreements is a turning to God's Word for the answers. Often, what we find instead are history's mistakes where the opinions of men are passed off as the Word of God (Matthew 15:1-9). Having "all things in common" does not mean we have to agree about everything; the Word doesn't require us to hold to the same politics, have the same world views about current events, or even the same opinions about most social customs; but it does require that we all adhere to certain beliefs: one body, one Spirit, one hope, one Lord, one faith, one baptism, one God and Father of us all (Ephesians 4:4-6). We learn as we continue in Ephesians 4 that these essential teachings and proper understanding of them are held through God-inspired and ordained leadership in the five-fold ministry (Ephesians 4:7-16). This means there are going to be a lot of times where we have to put aside the non-essential and grow out of the notion that church is getting people to agree with us. Church is not a political forum to push candidates or agendas. It is about introducing people to Christ!

- **Attending or fellowshipping with a local church is not a matter of choosing the "church of your choice":** Years ago, at the end of Billy Graham crusades, those who prayed the sinner's prayer were advised to join the "church of your choice." Belonging to church - both local and universal - is not about us! While we do belong by our choice, we must follow where God leads us and seek to uphold, grow, and develop a greater sense of God's truth as we do so. God commands us to be where we are spiritually fed and supported on the foundation of the apostles and prophets (Ephesians 2:19-22). We are also commanded to turn aside from false teachers and not simply attend somewhere because the teaching appeals to us on a fleshly level (1 Timothy 4:1-5). If a church does not meet these criteria, it is not where God would have us to be. Attending a church can't be about following wherever seems to be the most crowded, liking the pretty music, or showing off church clothes. A church that is no more than superficially deep in this sense is truly not the church of Christ and is not for true followers to attend.

- **The local church is to grow:** Local churches that seem more like an unwelcoming family reunion (the pastor's wife plays the organ, the pastor's son takes the collection, the pastor's cousins teach Sunday school, etc.) than an environment where anyone is welcome are not reflecting the growth that is to take place within the church. Local churches aren't supposed to be topping out at a certain membership roster and then ceasing to grow. I certainly acknowledge the challenges churches face today and the competitions of secular events; but the New Testament era also had its own entertainments and competitions which the first century churches faced, fought, and won. We aren't facing something new and revolutionary today. How does the church grow? *SO THE CHURCHES WERE STRENGTHENED IN THE FAITH AND GREW DAILY IN NUMBERS.* (Acts 16:5, NIV) Churches must be strengthened in faith to grow in numbers! The answer isn't to turn everything into a seeker-friendly hot spot; it is to strengthen the faith of the church. This takes everyone's participation!

- **By the gifts of the Spirit**: Every member mature and operational in the Spirit must be free to walk in their gifts within the command of order and peace in the churches. Church isn't a free-for-all, but at the same time, it is a participation of every member (1 Corinthians 12:1-30) because every member is a part of the body of Christ and given necessary gifts for the building up of the church.

- **Serve as the hands and feet of Christ to the community**: Never forget the opportunity to witness the Gospel not just through evangelism and teaching but also through feeding the hungry, providing drink to the thirsty, clothing the naked, visiting the sick and imprisoned, and meeting other necessary practical needs (Matthew 25:31-46). Such provides an important grounding because it makes spiritual teaching practical, real, and applicable.

- **A spot for community evangelism**: A lot of churches teach evangelism to be about handing out tracts. I don't remember handing out tracts in the New Testament, and I have yet to meet anyone who came to know Christ through a tract. Let us never forget that the most powerful witness is found through the lives, actions, and testimonies of church members who are living the Christian call to be "little Christs" to everyone they meet (Romans 1:16-17, Colossians 1:9-14). The local church is the training center to equip Christians for this task.

- **Provide Christians in every city, nation, and part of this world with practical assistance to spiritual and life issues**: In life, we encounter situations that call for advice, guidance, and support. The local church is there to provide this to its members - to give guidance, assistance, teaching, counseling, and support in every situation (Matthew 16:13-19, Matthew 18:15-17, James 5:13-16).

The bottom line of the division between the local and universal church is one of control between leadership. Local pastors and leaders do not want to feel subject to universal leadership, especially when centuries of abuses have incurred at the hands of individuals who sought universal control. Yet in pursuit of avoiding universal control, too many local church leaders have in turn become the monsters they sought to avoid. It is understandable that a local church leader with many years invested in a congregation may be inclined to resist the changes of an apostle or the prophetic words of a prophet; however, that doesn't mean it is acceptable to reject such to maintain absolute control. The local church can only get better by letting in the universal church and its ministerial representatives.

The local church and universal church are called not to co-exist, but to be one with the other. There is still a division in the hearts and minds of many, a competition, if you will, between the local church and the universal church. The local church is a miniature version of the universal one body which exists in Christ. They are not to be antithetical, nor are they to become problematic to the other. A local church which divides itself from the universal body has need of either education among its leaders or removal from their positions until they learn God's plan for the local church. It is only when the local church begins to connect itself again with a universal understanding that the true oneness God intends for us - that we be one as Christ and the Father are one - begins to emerge and we find ourselves able to proclaim the Gospel to the nations as Christ's original command to us becomes a possibility once again (Mark 16:15-20).

- **The universal offices**: Apostle and prophet

- **The "bridge" offices:** Evangelist and teacher

- **Local offices:** Pastor and teacher (much of the time)

Overall needs in diverse places

Having looked at the church conceptually, realistically, spiritually, and universally, we need to examine the needs that the universal church has. These needs sometimes overlap with the local churches you may be more familiar with, and many times they are quite different or needed in a different way or for a different reason. These needs exist, they are a valid part of the church experience, and if we are called to be missionaries, we are called to rise to those spiritual needs and bring forth what is needed in due season.

- **Teaching:** There is an overall lack of teaching in the church, both at home and abroad. If the church emphasizes entertainment, then it does not advocate teaching. Lack of proper teaching and doctrinal emphasis, focusing more on everyday life applications of Scripture frequently taken out of context have made it so the average person is unable to understand the Bible and the Christian life in a way that can help them overcome and persevere. Couple this with the fact that teaching has taken on a first-world characteristic, concerned with materialism and financial prosperity, has led to a church led by blind teachers who do not have the proper thoughts and instruction to offer. This leads to Bible misunderstanding.

- **Leadership:** Looking on social media definitely clarifies there is no shortage of people who think they are leaders, but there is a serious disparity in those who are called to do real leadership in real time. This becomes especially true in countries with developing churches who look to any leadership model they can get, thus often confusing the true with the false and mixing the two. Leaders often take on the responsibility of leadership too early in their spiritual process, leaving them unequipped to properly lead. They then seek the guidance of anyone willing to teach them, causing complete spiritual confusion.

- **Finances:** There are many churches without basic finances to maintain rent or mortgages, do necessary repairs, or handle day-to-day expenses. Many of these congregations also deal with personal lack, unable to meet personal housing, food, clothing, or medical needs. These churches often try to be heavy-handed on outreach as they attempt to meet practical needs but are unable to meet any long-term needs as members live in poverty and churches and ministries close.

- **Healing the cultural clash:** The place where culture and religion meet often causes frustration. This becomes especially true in nations hostile to Christianity or who are hostile period, such as war zones or civil conflicts. Christian conversions can be perceived as cultural or familial rebellions, hostility towards the government, or turning one's back on culture.

- **Leadership training:** Leaders need training, no matter how gifted they may be. Without access to proper ministry training, many international churches falter. The few who do get some training often receive a confused and faltering theology that will help more than heal ministry.

- **Western church interest and understanding:** Politics have divided the world. We too succumb to the idea that the church "over there" is the wrong church or that it doesn't exist. We need to take an interest in the international church because they are part of us, and we are part of them.

Chapter 2 Summary

- The church is a part of prophecy, something foreseen before creation. The work of the church has been something on the heart and mind of God, within His foresight and purpose, from the very beginning. Genesis chapter 3 reveals important things about this prophecy: The woman and her descendants are enemies of the serpent; a descendant to come would be born without the assistance of a natural man; Eve is a representation of the church; the labor of the church shall be difficult; the church shall desire Christ, and He will lead and guide us; and every time we do something in connection with the church, we are connected back to the beginning.

- God called people prior to the designation of the Hebrews, who did God's work within the world. Noah is an example of such. The work of the few who were called proves the price of being called; few would make the commitment to God; being a believer is brave, no matter what time it comes in history. Abram was an example of such, a pagan man called by God to do something new.

- If we view the foundations of our spiritual understanding in this way, it proves that God did a "new thing" (Isaiah 43:19) in terms of Gentile inclusion within the church in the belief of restorative understanding, that the church is a part of the restoration of all things (Acts 3:21). It's not an accident that the Scriptures ask if we notice what it is God is doing. We should recognize it because it has been done before.

- When God calls us into His church, especially when church is unfamiliar to us, God will use what we know to move us from a place of ignorance to knowledge. Discipleship is a process.

- "Gentile" is a designation meaning "nations," and comes about in contrast between Israel and other nations.

- The pagan had knowledge of God through nature: through watching times and seasons, through seedtime and harvest, by watching and interacting with the natural elements, and in the general course of monitoring creation. The Gentiles did not have the law, but they had nature, a natural law, of sorts, and from that, they encountered the reality of created order and that some greater spiritual force must be behind all that exists. The Gentiles lost their way by idolizing creation.

- Gentiles were known for idolatry, witchcraft, nature worship, ancestral worship, and sexual rites. The Jews were known for self-righteousness, having the right things and falling into wrong repeatedly. They hoped the written code would save them, but it existed to make us aware of sin and ourselves before God. Whether Jew or Gentile, every one of us has Jew and Gentile within us; in Christ, we find redemption.

- When we talk about the Kingdom, we talk about the work and the church if God that builds it up. The Kingdom is God's governance within the church. The church is eternal, the body, one, a relationship counterpart, enduring, apostolic, Pentecostal, something we experience, communal, and worldwide.

- The local church is an extension of the universal church, and neither should be in competition with the other. It functions for meeting, having things in common, growth, community service, and providing Christians everywhere with assistance for spiritual and life matters.

- The universal offices: Apostle and prophet; the "bridge" offices: Evangelist and teacher; local offices: Pastor and teacher.

- Needs in the church today are teaching, leadership, finances, healing the cultural clash, leadership training, and western church interest and understanding.

Chapter 2 Assignments

- What nation interests you for missions? Research the worship customs of that nation, including Christian activity (if any) and create a summary report on the spiritual situation in that nation.

- Write an essay (5-8 sentences minimum) about the light of salvation and church existence as discussed in this chapter in terms of missions and missions interest.

- Write a summary (3-5 sentences) on the interest of the local church in missions. Given what we have discussed in this chapter, why do you think there is limited – or a lot – of emphasis on missions?

The Madras Indian Mission, 1892-1908

CHAPTER THREE:
MISSIONS AND EVANGELISM

——————————⌒—————————

In the vast plain to the north I have sometimes seen, in the morning sun,
the smoke of a thousand villages where no missionary has ever been.
(Robert Moffat[1])

WHENEVER missions come up, most people (especially established leaders) shy away from them. We think that to be a missionary, one must be a proficient evangelist. We always assume missions work is all about evangelizing in some foreign land where we do not speak the language and no one has ever heard the Name "Jesus." It sounds exotic...it sounds sacrificial...let's be real, it sounds intimidating. We picture missionaries trekking on foot across mountains and sitting alone in cabins without electricity to read the Bible by candlelight, as they try to interpret the Bible into the language of wherever they are.

One would think from the outset that living up to our fantasies about mission life is impossible. Yes, there are missionaries who work as I just described, but this is not the only way that missions work takes form. There are many experiences and dimensions that make up the cross-cultural impact of missions work.

In this chapter, we will look at the connection between missions and evangelism and the different ways both take form for the edification of the church. There is a difference between evangelism and missions. Understanding the commonalities and differences will help us grow as believers preparing for missions work.

Two types of missions activity

There are two main categories of missions activity: Evangelistic and foundational.

- **Evangelistic missions** are about spreading the Gospel to unreached populations. They may or may not involve church contact in that specific region, but will, most likely, move heavily in areas of outreach, instructing native populations, basic Christian education, and helping establish home church until the time comes when enough members exist to have a separate church (if such is an option in that area or region).

- **Foundational missions** relate to churches in an area or region that need assistance to establish, continue, build, or flourish. Such relates to interacting with a church, group of churches, or network of churches in a region for the purpose of addressing issues, establishing leadership, training where it's needed, teaching, and building upon solid foundations so individuals who experience the Gospel call through evangelism have somewhere to go. This way, churches can maintain their work without relying on the western church to provide for them.

The difference between evangelism and missions

Evangelism and missions overlap, but this does not mean they are the same thing. Yes, evangelism is a part of missions, but missions are not necessarily a part of everyone's evangelism or the way that everyone evangelizes. There is nothing wrong with either one, but it is important to recognize and affirm different evangelism styles.

Let's start by acknowledging that evangelism is a fundamental call of all Christians. Every single believer, no matter who they are, what level of spiritual interest they have, and what their greater life calling may be, is called to evangelism. To break this down simply:

- Every believer has the responsibility of living their faith in their everyday life, through their choices and pursuits, and in how they interact with others.

- Every believer has the responsibility of telling others about their faith, as the opportunity arises.

- The responsibility of spreading the faith does not just belong to ordained clergy. This means every believer has the duty to attend to their faith, learn more about it, take an interest in it, and connect with leaders who can properly teach them about belief, life, and expressions of faith, in all forms.

- Every believer must experience faith for themselves and see themselves as a part of the Kingdom. This is an active participation, not just looking out over crowds and thinking there is nothing for them to do.

- Evangelism is something that stirs within each believer. All of us should have the deep desire to share our faith with others because we recognize what God has done in our lives. We might not know the best way to do that or might experience shyness or insecurity, but we should want to share the greatness of God with others. Our lives might not resemble that of a millionaire, and we may never have it all together, but because of what God has done for us, there is a change in us that moves from glory to glory and faith to faith.

- Evangelism can be done right where we are, at any time and place, any time the moment hits. We don't have to move far away, go overseas, live in a big city, have a lot of money, or have a team of people to assist with the work. We can evangelize with our friends, neighbors, coworkers, family, and we can do good every day of our lives, reaching out to all of those who are right where we are.

Missions often take the form of evangelistic work. When we think of missions, evangelism is usually what we associate with their pursuits. Missions are not exclusively about evangelism, however. Missions are about going forth with the Gospel in the hopes that lives will change and the church will be built up wherever one goes. It is not as simple as going into an area, preaching, and then leaving everyone to fend for themselves. Missions is about taking the effort and turning evangelism into discipleship where the tools and teachers to do so are not available, thus the missionary or missions team introducing that area to church, the way it should be done, with the vision and foresight of creating self-sustaining spirituality within those people.

Missions may also exist without the primary focus of evangelism in an area, at all. It is a great thing to build up a church or Christian community in a region, but the primary purpose of evangelism is to introduce people to the world of discipleship, not to get them saved and leave them to their own devices. If we approach missions as nothing more than an evangelistic outreach in another city, we are doing nothing more than trying to do something that we could do right at home.

Missions work may also seek to help correct existing issues within an existing Christian community. If the focus on evangelism overtakes the needed balance for church establishment and order, churches will suffer, and so will believers. Church maintenance is a careful balance of Kingdom workers, with everyone doing their part and ensuring pastors and congregations are not overwhelmed with more believers than they can handle or train for Kingdom life.

Exponential worldwide evangelism has led to the problem of which I just spoke. Crusades draw crowds, but lack of church infrastructure has left many believers to their own devices or to unite with various doctrinal systems that might be available, but do not teach truth as we know it. Ministers, both local and abroad, might brag of starting hundreds of churches, but those churches quickly close or falter because they are not equipped to function as they should and cannot rise to meet the needs of the people.

Untrained leaders equate to churches that either barely stay afloat or sink. Proper leadership training is not one of evangelism, but one of ensuring discipleship can continue. A missions team can go into an area and train leaders and establish order and structure among a church, and it still be a mission if they never go beyond those walls to evangelize a community.

It is a fundamental mistake of many Missiology programs to treat all evangelism as if it is missions. Missions are no less important if they are not specifically evangelistic by nature, because they are engaging the church to establish and build up disciples as they evangelize. Evangelism is no less important than missions, and we should stop crossing lines and confusing things to try and build up our own platforms. Both evangelism and missions are needed to build the church, evangelism is needed in missions, and church development is needed within missions. All are important, essential aspects to the fundamentals of life and work of the Kingdom, and no matter what we do, we do for the glory of God.

Constructive evangelism in missions

THE FRUIT OF THE RIGHTEOUS IS A TREE OF LIFE; AND HE THAT WINNETH SOULS IS WISE. (Proverbs 11:30, KJV)

Both evangelism and foundational missions are necessary to continue the work of the church anywhere in the world. The church will not survive without individuals who are willing to do the hard work of evangelism, but the church will also not survive if there is no local church to attend. Great churches get their start through great evangelism, which consists of the following in missions:

- **Connecting to the audience**: Different cultures regard and respect teachers and leaders in different ways. As a conduit of the Gospel, you may need to adapt methods, styles of dress, language, or word usage in such a manner that will help your audience listen to what you have to say.

- **Consistency**: Some missionaries stay in a region for years before they see church growth. When planning evangelistic missions, it is important to make sure the work can continue if a missionary can't remain in a region long-term.

- **Materials or distribution in the native language (if no one speaks English)**: Learning about the languages of the world is a fascinating process, because with the more than 6,000 languages spoken throughout the world, there are a handful of languages that are spoken worldwide. Depending on the region where one takes an interest in missions work, it is prudent to learn a language that can suffice in that area.

- **Promotes church growth**: Evangelism shouldn't serve to just get people to believe, but to get them to believe and take an interest in discipleship, learning about their faith, and connecting to other believers.

Why foundational missions work helps continue the church

If we only think of missions in terms of evangelism, we are missing an important balance needed in the continuity and continuation of the work of local or smaller churches worldwide. Traditionally speaking, mission churches were founded by denominations that funded them for a period, depending on the structure and governance of the denomination. Most churches affiliated with denominations, however, held to local church structures that were autonomous in nature or required the local churches to send funds back to headquarters in a specified, fixed amount each year. Given either situation, the churches, which started because of missions, often lose the support of their denominational founders and are expected to maintain a certain level of autonomy and function on their own. The organizations pull out, the missionaries or long-term individuals assigned to that territory or work either die or leave, and even if they are replaced, the string of missionaries often falls flat at some point in time or another. It sounds great to say the churches are supposed to function autonomously, but it has a long history of not working to completion. The churches either die or fail to survive, usually due to lack of internal governance.

International cultures do not follow the same structural or social guidelines of ministries in the west. That means cultural overflow tends to overtake how these churches try to maintain their operations. In keeping with this structure, they will probably go and seek out churches and missions that are in the west, expecting them to fund their projects, assist and teach them as their denominations did or they see denominations doing, and finding themselves hostile and intolerant when a minister tells them they are not approaching the matter properly or with right order.

In the end, many of these missions churches or outgrowth ministries influenced by missions falter because they do not have the proper structure within their organizations to maintain their work independently of a denomination or dependency organization. It is no question to the relevance of missions, but if missions create dependents rather than individuals prepared to continue the Gospel whether someone is there to help them all the time or not, then the missions work has not been successful.

For these reasons, foundational missions are as essential as evangelistic missions. Just because a church exists or a ministry exists does not mean it is established for success. Foundational missions open the door for the needed education, leadership training, and structural purposes to maintain churches worldwide. Evangelism is great, but it doesn't produce fruit if we cannot offer solid churches for new converts and spiritual maintenance for long-term believers. There are many churches who need the expertise of solid ministers and their teams to go and help implement structure, train leadership, educate, teach doctrinal matters that are often confused, muddled, or lacking, provide budgeting and business advice, and help continue to build church projects long-term.

When involved in these missions projects, the goal is to create relationships, not just seminar-style leadership. Foundational missions projects should exist to create dialogue and discussion, and to connect the international church. This means three possible things should come forth from foundational missions:

- Covering or other long-term association between ministries

- Link for long-distance education or connection (not specifically financial in nature)

- Program continuation, including a return missions trip or long-term missionaries

Missions and counterfeit religious groups

When it comes to defining a "counterfeit religious group," things become complicated. Not everyone defines a counterfeit religion in quite the same way. This means what I might define as counterfeit, someone else might consider legitimate. Most of the time, the term "counterfeit" is meant to imply that a religious group adheres to or follows a doctrinal set that an individual or a group of people do not regard as legitimate. This sounds leading; in many ways, it is. Virtually any group with any doctrinal deviation from the officiating organization can fall into the category of "counterfeit." Others use it more to define an organization that somehow looks legitimate (i.e., it looks Christian), but it does not follow the same foundational pattern of doctrine and ethics of standard church organizations.

Counterfeit religious groups are not standard non-Christian religions that are active in witnessing and spread of their faith. For example, even though Christians may not accept Hindu or Islamic belief, they are not "counterfeit." They are exactly what they claim to be, which are non-Christian organizations who desire to proclaim their faith. They are upfront about their motive and are upfront about their belief system. This is not to say that all Hindus or Muslims are upfront or honest in their methods, but their agenda is obvious, regardless of their methods. When I refer to a group being "counterfeit," such basis is not made on the doctrine of a group alone. It is made by examining a group's methodology and the way in which they proclaim themselves to be a church that is Christian on the surface, but does not adhere to a Scriptural understanding of belief. They proclaim their message, Bible in hand, but what they are pushing is not Christian, even though it might look like it.

Counterfeit religion has taken the stage for missions work over the past 50 years because counterfeit groups are eager and willing to send individuals as missionaries. With missions at the seat of their work, they provide elaborate missions training and programs and expect so many of their members to engage in missions annually. Missions are a part of their lives, because that is how they are able to maintain converts.

This is a cross-examination of what the missions field looks like:

- In 2014, more than 82,000 missionaries working in 400 missions were from the Church of Jesus Christ of Latter-day Saints (Mormons).[2]

- Jehovah's Witnesses spent 1,841,180,235 hours in field ministry between 2012-2013.[3]

- 419,000 foreign missionaries classify themselves as specifically "Christian" missionaries, not aligning with other-stated organizations.[4]

The numbers alone indicate that true Christian missionaries are largely outnumbered. From the general statistic of 419,000 missionaries, we can assume that many of those are from missions organizations or denominations. Yet within that number, we also find many missionaries who may themselves represent denominations or churches that fall into the "counterfeit" category.

If there is one thing we can say for counterfeit groups, it is that they are active and involved in evangelism and missions. Their organizations have the money and the vision to assist their missionaries, and they make missions a priority. Their missionaries are often zealous, reasonably well-versed in the beliefs of their organization, and they are ready, willing, and able to do missions work in a way that many nominative Christian believers and even ministers are often unwilling. Yet, at the same time, their work makes the work of true missionaries that much more difficult.

What we tend to see among international churches are a doctrinal mix of beliefs that reflect both true and counterfeit Christianity, along with an occasional tribal or primitive cultural religion in some regions. A church may claim to believe in Jesus, spiritual gifts, five-fold leadership, or refer to itself by a traditional denomination's name while holding strains of Jehovah's Witnesses teaching, refer to the Book of Mormon, or claim certain Sabbatarian strains of belief, or hold to unique eschatology that reflects such of end-time groups. As the denominations have left, the missions from counterfeit religious groups have filled the void, to the detriment of the spiritual development of such churches.

The churches of the world need the intervention of properly trained missionaries who know the value of ministry service and have the skill and ability to develop them beyond a denominational outgrowth that went awry. Creating lasting relationships from missions becomes of the utmost importance considering what we have just discussed. Churches all over the world need the long-term support and interest to grow into the churches they are destined to become, and they cannot become such without the involvement and commitment of interested and dedicated missionaries.

Mission works that do not specifically relate to evangelism

It should be said that all the examples mentioned below may very well lead to evangelism among the local church. It is, most likely, the foundation of doing something incredible within the area where the work takes place. The difference is that the purpose of the missions project is not for the missionary to engage in evangelism themselves, but to work with the existing believers who are already a part of the church.

- **Leadership training:** A common lament on social media is the way in which leaders are thoughtlessly placed in our churches today. We cannot believe untrained individuals are put in positions of authority, whether they are too young, too inexperienced, or too newly saved. In other countries, however, untrained leaders are not always placed because someone wants to say they have so many leaders under them (although this does sometimes happen because western leaders want to say they have international ministers). Many untrained leaders exist in overseas churches simply because there is no one to train them, although the continuation of a church or ministry depends on their positioning. They may mimic what they see other leaders do or pick up bits and pieces of leadership roles from the different religious groups that have come in to influence the church, but odds are good they do not know what they are doing or how to do it well. Leadership training needs to be specific and structured, clear and direct, and exact in its Biblical nature and direction.

- **Church teaching:** As we discussed in the last chapter and earlier in this one, proper teaching is a commodity in the international church. There are many who sound Christian but adhere to a mixture of different beliefs and systems, many of which are not a part of true teaching. It doesn't make someone a non-believer, it just means they have not had proper teaching to inspire a full understanding of spiritual belief. Just as Priscilla and Aquila took a man aside to make the way clearer to him (Acts 18:26), so too this may happen within a missions context. When a minister goes to teach churches in another country, they must consider the way teaching is done within that nation and what is considered proper or improper conduct to teach others. The message must be presented in a way that can be easily understood and implemented by the church at hand.

- **In-church project:** Sometimes we need help launching projects or project initiatives. An in-church project may take many forms but might relate to establishing something like a Bible institute or school, leadership training structured within the church itself, the beginnings of a Sunday school program, or an evangelistic outreach. Assistance for such may happen through teaching or instruction but may even involve up-close-and-personal assistance where a missionary rolls up his or her sleeves and helps to see that the necessary job is done.

- **Administrative instruction:** Administrative instruction relates to disciplinary issues or problems a church may experience on the inside that clearly reflect on the outside. It's not uncommon to meet individuals who are uncertain of how to handle such administrative problems, because they are new to a situation or were handled by higher-ups in a denominational setting. Administrative instruction may also relate to the way leadership and assistance in ministry interact with one another, such as appointments, assistant leadership, and general day-to-day administration. For such work, a missionary needs to get involved in restructuring and help establish what needs to be done, where.

- **Edification:** Sometimes mission work exists for fellowship, to experience cultural diversity, or mutual edification. Edification is more than just giving a pat on the back; it is also about building up proper structure and encouraging believers to continue in their foundations.

Missions and crusades

I can't mention missions work without commenting on crusades. There is a notable absence of commentary on how to do a crusade in this book in connection with missions activity, for one simple reason: I don't believe that crusades accomplish much. The concept of crusade activity appeals to the ideals that bigger is always better, and the more people we reach at one time, the more effective the event is.

It is my own personal opinion that crusade mentality appeals to our vanity, which is why we see so much of it these days in connection with overseas work. We love the idea that a group of poor, unfortunate souls come to our meeting and now profess Christ. We also love the idea that once the crusade is over, we don't have to think another thing about it. It looks good, it looks like something has been done, but in the long run...it often creates problems.

If you live in a nation or region with limited churches, getting "saved" is an awesome thing...but how will salvation be maintained? If there are no churches or getting to the church is a hardship, it's likely that individual will not move toward discipleship and will have difficulty maintaining their faith (if they keep it, at all).

There is nothing wrong with the concept of a crusade as long as it is done for the right reason and with the right mentalities in mind. It should never be done as something to justify a ministry's experience or to say someone is doing something with their work. Having large events are fine as long as provision is made to connect individuals to churches and patterns of discipleship to enhance their spiritual lives. In such a mission activity, a missionary must prepare not just for the immediate event, but the long-term work that must also accompany it.

Outlining the essentials of faith

This chapter would not be complete if we did not discuss the essentials of faith. The essentials of faith are the very foundation by which believers can teach and instruct others, whether our work relates to evangelism, foundational missions, or both. Despite many different statements of faith throughout the centuries, the basics of faith can be found in Ephesians 4 in three different sections: Ephesians 4:1-6 is about essential doctrine, Ephesians 4:7-16 is about essential leadership, and Ephesians 4:17-32 is about living the Christian life.

THEREFORE, AS A PRISONER FOR THE LORD, I ENCOURAGE YOU TO LIVE AS PEOPLE WORTHY OF THE CALL YOU RECEIVED FROM GOD. CONDUCT YOURSELVES WITH ALL HUMILITY, GENTLENESS, AND PATIENCE. ACCEPT EACH OTHER WITH LOVE, AND MAKE AN EFFORT TO PRESERVE THE UNITY OF THE SPIRIT WITH THE PEACE THAT TIES YOU TOGETHER. YOU ARE ONE BODY AND ONE SPIRIT, JUST AS GOD ALSO CALLED YOU IN ONE HOPE. THERE IS ONE LORD, ONE FAITH, ONE BAPTISM, AND ONE GOD AND FATHER OF ALL, WHO IS OVER ALL, THROUGH ALL, AND IN ALL. (Ephesians 4:1-6)

The Apostle Paul wrote this chapter with the intent of clarifying the essentials of unity. In the ministry of the Apostle Paul, unity was a central focus. He worked with the nations, including Jews who lived in the Diaspora, and it was his deepest desire that the church would come together and work as one Body of Christ. To Paul, unity wasn't just a catchy phrase used to tug at heartstrings or make people feel warm and fuzzy; it was something that drove him, something that he felt could identify the church among other belief systems and prove our doctrinal understanding to be true.

We don't look at unity in quite this way today, but we should. One of the major reasons missions projects fail is due to disunity in the ranks. Whether disunity comes with those we work to evangelize or edify, among our own missions team, or within leadership ranks, disunity is a major reason missions work has failed in modern history. Our ability to interact and work with one another, whether on a missions project or any other work of the church, says a lot about what we believe. If we believe as we claim to believe, working with others who have the same foundational beliefs should not be a problem for us. Unity challenges us at the heart of our realities; are they true, are they false, and do we apply them to ourselves? In summary, unity is the heart of our doctrine; it is what we believe, it is the essence of our faith in practice, and it is proof that the Kingdom we speak of so often lives in us.

Unity is also at the very heart of missions, which is why missions fail without unity. As the church expands, it grows, and with growth comes unity. Unity is a part of working one to another, having spiritual things in common, and being willing to set aside the selfishness we each carry to serve God. All of us desire to take care of ourselves and to see to it that ourselves and those closest to us have the best. It is a part of fallen nature, that instinctive trait that tells us we should not trust other people. In Christ, we move from distrust to trust; following the discernment of the Holy Spirit to work with one another in Christian love for the growth of the church and the Gospel's advance through the nations.

The Apostle Paul opens his statement – which quickly turns doctrinal – with a plea, asking us to live lives worthy of the calling to which we have been called. This establishes that no matter what we believe, if God is in it, it wasn't our idea. We were called to this system, to our faith, hearing the voice of God speak to us through the truth, and we recognize Him therein. Our first union is with God, becoming one with Him through Christ, and in walking whatever direction He calls us to go. Our lives are no longer our own. Christ is with us, and the Spirit directs us. We are to live as we are called to live, putting aside selfishness and personal intention, and consider our place in this body of Christ, this place where we are not only in love with the Lord, but we are also a part of Him this side of heaven. Not only are we to live rightly, but we are also to do it with a good attitude, humility and gentleness, never forcing our beliefs on anyone, nor trying to use our beliefs to manipulate or contrive. We are to be patient, understanding and bearing with our brethren of believers. After all, they have become a part of us, and us with them, and we see salvation's process at work with them, in all they do and advance to become.

The Apostle also shows us that the unity of the Spirit must be maintained through a bond of peace. Unity comes from the Spirit. We cannot manufacture unity because we all attempt to do so by using human methods and means. This means unity does not:

- Dress alike
- Look alike
- Sound alike
- Talk alike
- Do all the same things all the time

You could form the most efficient denomination, have the most elaborate statement of faith and force every member of the church to submit to it, you could even make it so that everyone knows what to say and when, all the time – but none of these things will mark unity. Without the Holy Spirit, you have nothing more than conformity, which does not lead to life.

Still, that root begins when we put on the love God commands us to have. The love of God is what transforms and changes all of us, and it is the very thing that touches the hearts of those we reach in missions. The language might be different, the culture might be different, the skin color might be different, but the love of God is what changes us from the inside out. The Kingdom of God is not possible without love: love from God, love for God, love of one another.

Unity is maintained through the bond of peace. This all sounds nice and poetic, but it means that unity is a concerted, deliberate effort that we must make every effort to maintain. The means by which we maintain it is a spirit of peace reigning in and among the churches. Working with other people is never easy, especially in the context of the church. We find ourselves at different maturity levels and levels of spiritual understanding, and God still expects us to find some way to unify for the goal and purpose of the Gospel. It sounds impossible, and by natural means, it certainly is. It is only by God's grace that we can maintain that unity through a peaceable bond.

Missionaries too must remember God's call to be peaceable. The Gospel itself is threatening enough without the added burden of a calculated, violent individual who comes to cause trouble. We call Jesus the "Prince of Peace" for a reason, and there is a reason why peace is still one of the most radical notions this world has ever seen: it requires spiritual maturity. Just as with unity, we can create any semblance of false, short-lived peace that changes nobody's lives and does nothing in the long-term to maintain a spiritual semblance of wholeness. Missionaries are called to bring wholeness to people's lives, to offer them something they cannot receive somewhere else and model that reassurance, that inward trust that God can and do all things through Christ (Philippians 4:13).

The Apostle Paul moves to his series of "one" statements: one body, one Spirit, one hope, one Lord, one faith, one baptism, one God and Father of all. The fact that there are seven of them points to perfection, to the wholeness of God and the perfect completion found when the church resides in Him. This is not just an ordinary mission we are on as churchgoers; this is divine, something united by seven key unities:

- **One body:** We sometimes look, by our nature, for there to be only one true church, but what we look for through this lens is wrong. We are many parts in one body. The church, therefore, that rests its belief system on Ephesians 4 is that one body, wherever it is in the world, no matter its name or position.

- **One Spirit, the Holy Spirit:** This is in contrast with polytheism, which recognized different spirits for each universal force in existence. Via magic, each individual practitioner of witchcraft desired to summon their desired spirit for their desired purpose. This is not how true faith operates, and our belief system contrasts with such a spiritual outlook. We recognize though there are many of us and many gifts bestowed, there is only one Spirit, the Holy Spirit of God.

- **One hope, to which we were called:** The calling we spoke of earlier relates to each hope of salvation, the ultimate promise of faith that we hold dear. No matter what we may see in this world, we know the true hope, the hope of all God has promised, is what we hold to in trial and difficulty.

- **One Lord, Jesus Christ:** We do not serve many lords, but only One, Jesus Christ. He is our Savior, our Redeemer, our true friend, and is with us forever. Though we do not see Him with our eyes, He remains our Lord, because He is truly present wherever two or three of us gather (Matthew 18:20).

- **One faith:** There is only one faith that we have, not multiple faiths. We all individually believe in God, and we have different ways of expressing our experience with God and our experience of faith, there is only one faith that saves and leads to eternal life with God.

- **One baptism:** In ancient cultures, baptism was used to signify one had achieved a certain level of belief within a philosophy or cultural school of thought. There were many baptisms done in the name of a group's founder or teacher, with individuals claiming to belong, or be one, with any number of teachers and systems (1 Corinthians 1:10-17). To say there is one baptism indicates we are born again to new life, dead in our sin through the water of baptism and then raised to life again, and that such only comes through Christ.

- **One God and Father of all:** I've heard it said that we are all the children of God; everyone does not know it yet. It is true to say that God is our Creator, our originator, the source of our being, and One Who desires us to recognize His roll in our lives. To be an effective missionary, we must see all as God's creation, at work in us and our lives even if we don't recognize Him and trusting that God to be the foundation for everywhere we go as we follow Him for the Gospel.

BUT EACH OF US WAS GIVEN GRACE ACCORDING TO THE MEASURE OF CHRIST'S GIFT. THEREFORE IT IS SAID,

*"WHEN HE ASCENDED ON HIGH HE MADE CAPTIVITY ITSELF A CAPTIVE;
HE GAVE GIFTS TO HIS PEOPLE."*

*WHAT DOES THE PHRASE "HE CLIMBED UP" MEAN IF IT DOESN'T MEAN THAT HE
HAD FIRST GONE DOWN INTO THE LOWER REGIONS, THE EARTH? THE ONE
WHO WENT DOWN IS THE SAME ONE WHO CLIMBED UP ABOVE ALL THE
HEAVENS SO THAT HE MIGHT FILL EVERYTHING.*

*HE GAVE SOME APOSTLES, SOME PROPHETS, SOME EVANGELISTS, AND SOME
PASTORS AND TEACHERS. HIS PURPOSE WAS TO EQUIP GOD'S PEOPLE FOR THE
WORK OF SERVING AND BUILDING UP THE BODY OF CHRIST UNTIL WE ALL
REACH THE UNITY OF FAITH AND KNOWLEDGE OF GOD'S SON. GOD'S GOAL IS
FOR US TO BECOME MATURE ADULTS—TO BE FULLY GROWN, MEASURED BY THE
STANDARD OF THE FULLNESS OF CHRIST. AS A RESULT, WE AREN'T SUPPOSED
TO BE INFANTS ANY LONGER WHO CAN BE TOSSED AND BLOWN AROUND BY
EVERY WIND THAT COMES FROM TEACHING WITH DECEITFUL SCHEMING AND
THE TRICKS PEOPLE PLAY TO DELIBERATELY MISLEAD OTHERS. INSTEAD, BY
SPEAKING THE TRUTH WITH LOVE, LET'S GROW IN EVERY WAY INTO CHRIST,
WHO IS THE HEAD. THE WHOLE BODY GROWS FROM HIM, AS IT IS JOINED AND
HELD TOGETHER BY ALL THE SUPPORTING LIGAMENTS. THE BODY MAKES
ITSELF GROW IN THAT IT BUILDS ITSELF UP WITH LOVE AS EACH ONE DOES ITS
PART.* (Ephesians 4:7-16)

The Apostle Paul then moves to expound about leadership and the
proper leadership necessary to build the church. In chapter 6 of this
book, we will examine the specific role that the Ephesians 4:11
ministry plays in missions. For now, we are going to look at why
leadership is foundational to the spiritual edification of the church,
and why believing in such leadership is essential to successful
church function.

It's great to think we can follow any old model we like to make
churches work, but we can't. We can't do this, for one simple reason:
we are all given grace according to the measure of Christ's gift.
From that grace, gifts are given. Leadership – divine leadership – is
a gift from God, because it is directly from Him. All have a measure
of grace to do whatever He has called us to do. In that grace is the
call to leadership for those He appoints for that purpose. Those in
leadership, those called to equip the Body until He returns, are there
by His grace to do that difficult and challenging job.

The leadership positions listed in Ephesians 4 are apostles, prophets, evangelists, pastors, and teachers. These offices exist for the work of ministry, to act in service to the church and the world. Some are sent, some speak for God, some proclaim Christ, some shepherd, and some instruct. Put that entire picture together and you find maintenance of God's vision for unity, promote faith and knowledge in spiritual things, maturity, and the measure of Christ in our midst. Such will keep us from being thrown about by every strain of teaching that comes our way, every ideal that sounds brilliant but is just more mess, and from the schemes and wiles of evil individuals. No, we can speak truth in love, from a motive of love rather than vengeance, building us all up into the body we are called to be, modeling the head, Christ.

SO I'M TELLING YOU THIS, AND I INSIST ON IT IN THE LORD: YOU SHOULDN'T LIVE YOUR LIFE LIKE THE GENTILES ANYMORE. THEY BASE THEIR LIVES ON POINTLESS THINKING, AND THEY ARE IN THE DARK IN THEIR REASONING. THEY ARE DISCONNECTED FROM GOD'S LIFE BECAUSE OF THEIR IGNORANCE AND THEIR CLOSED HEARTS. THEY ARE PEOPLE WHO LACK ALL SENSE OF RIGHT AND WRONG, AND WHO HAVE TURNED THEMSELVES OVER TO DOING WHATEVER FEELS GOOD AND TO PRACTICING EVERY SORT OF CORRUPTION ALONG WITH GREED.

BUT YOU DIDN'T LEARN THAT SORT OF THING FROM CHRIST. SINCE YOU REALLY LISTENED TO HIM AND YOU WERE TAUGHT HOW THE TRUTH IS IN JESUS, CHANGE THE FORMER WAY OF LIFE THAT WAS PART OF THE PERSON YOU ONCE WERE, CORRUPTED BY DECEITFUL DESIRES. INSTEAD, RENEW THE THINKING IN YOUR MIND BY THE SPIRIT AND CLOTHE YOURSELF WITH THE NEW PERSON CREATED ACCORDING TO GOD'S IMAGE IN JUSTICE AND TRUE HOLINESS.

THEREFORE, AFTER YOU HAVE GOTTEN RID OF LYING, EACH OF YOU MUST TELL THE TRUTH TO YOUR NEIGHBOR BECAUSE WE ARE PARTS OF EACH OTHER IN THE SAME BODY. BE ANGRY WITHOUT SINNING. DON'T LET THE SUN SET ON YOUR ANGER. DON'T PROVIDE AN OPPORTUNITY FOR THE DEVIL. THIEVES SHOULD NO LONGER STEAL. INSTEAD, THEY SHOULD GO TO WORK, USING THEIR HANDS TO DO GOOD SO THAT THEY WILL HAVE SOMETHING TO SHARE WITH WHOEVER IS IN NEED.

DON'T LET ANY FOUL WORDS COME OUT OF YOUR MOUTH. ONLY SAY WHAT IS HELPFUL WHEN IT IS NEEDED FOR BUILDING UP THE COMMUNITY SO THAT IT

BENEFITS THOSE WHO HEAR WHAT YOU SAY. DON'T MAKE THE HOLY SPIRIT OF GOD UNHAPPY—YOU WERE SEALED BY HIM FOR THE DAY OF REDEMPTION. PUT ASIDE ALL BITTERNESS, LOSING YOUR TEMPER, ANGER, SHOUTING, AND SLANDER, ALONG WITH EVERY OTHER EVIL. BE KIND, COMPASSIONATE, AND FORGIVING TO EACH OTHER, IN THE SAME WAY GOD FORGAVE YOU IN CHRIST. (Ephesians 4:17-32)

The remainder of chapter 4 deals with the way we live as Christians. As ministers, we know instruction in practical life application is one of the most important things we can offer to our congregations, conference attendees, and fans who follow our work. It is also one of the most important aspects of instruction in the mission field.

Perhaps the thing I love the most about Paul's instructions is the nature of their practicality. The advice Paul gives to believers can be followed and embraced no matter where someone lives in the world. No matter what someone experiences, the words of the Apostle Paul provide applicable insight into right now. It means we must sometimes dig a little deeper than surface words to make sure we understand them, but there is always something in there that we can walk away with, knowing how we can live in our day and time.

It is vitally essential that Christians worldwide adopt proper conduct and interaction not just with other Christians, but with their neighbors of all belief systems. We have been called out of the thinking of worldly nations, which operate by violence and hardness of heart (stubbornness, unwillingness to love others). We are not given selfishness or greedy gain. We are renewed; set apart; and willing to put on the nature of Christ. This, as an essential part of the Christian walk, must also become a part of the manner by which we are called.

It all comes down to believing – or not believing – the things we spoke of earlier in this chapter. The apostle provides great contrast between the unbelieving and the believing and clarifies the believer to be one who does not behave as the unbelieving. Putting off all falsehood, we love our neighbor, and we act like we love our neighbor. We do not deliberately seek to wrong other people. We share with one another; we watch our mouths and what come out of them; and we uphold honor for the Spirit, Who is not only our ensign for the day of redemption, but for all we do, speak, and believe right now.

Missions is a world of unity; of the truth and essentials of faith played out, moving in unison with leadership that is purposed by God to set it forth, establish it, and move in it. The more we understand this, the more we will grow to understand the true way that Jesus, as the heart of missions, is present whether we go to start the church or to clean it up.

Chapter 3 Summary

- There are two main categories of missions activity: evangelistic and foundational. Evangelistic missions are about spreading the Gospel to unreached populations. Foundational missions relate to churches in a region that need assistance to establish, continue, build, or flourish.

- Evangelism is a fundamental call of all Christians.

- Missions do often take the forms of evangelistic works, but missions are not exclusively about evangelism. Missions are about going forth with the Gospel in the hopes that lives will change and the church grow. They are no less important if they are not specifically evangelistic by nature, because they engage the church to establish and build up disciples as they evangelize.

- Constructive points of evangelism in missions include connecting to the audience, consistency, materials or distribution in the native language, and promoting church growth.

- Foundational missions are important because they help churches worldwide to establish the proper beliefs, leadership, and teaching to flourish and move forward. They also create relationships between churches on an international level.

- Counterfeit religious groups often do the most evangelizing because their followers are trained and prepared to go forth with their doctrine. The result, however, is a mix of belief systems that may be partially true and partially false.

- Some mission works that do not relate to evangelism are leadership training, church teaching, in-church projects, administrative instruction, fellowship, and the edification of the saints.

- Crusades do not work, nor do the results last, without discipleship and churches to attend.

- When teaching, do not forget the essentials of faith: Unity, right interactions with one another, one body, one Spirit, one hope, one Lord, one faith, one baptism, and one God and Father of all.

- The proper leadership structure for the church is apostles, prophets, evangelists, pastors, and teachers.

- Never ignore practical teaching for everyday living. We must all learn how to conduct and interact not just with other Christians, but with all neighbors of all belief systems.

Chapter 3 Assignments

- Write an essay (5-8 sentences) on the role you see yourself playing in missions. Do you see yourself working more in an evangelistic role, or more of a foundational role? How can you contribute your role to missions, and how can your work help a mission to flourish?

- Create an infographic on the needs of the church in the country that interests you for missions activity. Do they need more foundational help, evangelistic help, or a mixture of both? What suggestions do you have to address the issues of the church present in that nation in a missions situation?

- Create a brief presentation (using Microsoft PowerPoint or an equivalent program) on the essentials of faith and how you would teach on them in a missions capacity (10 slides maximum).

Staff and students at Chefoo School, Yantail, China

CHAPTER FOUR:
MISSIONS IN THE OLD TESTAMENT

———————— ⌇ ————————

If the Great Commission is true, our plans are not too big; they are too small.
(Pat Morley[1])

MISSIONS are usually thought of as a New Testament endeavor, but that is not where missions originated. The work of going forth with a specified message for a specific purpose shows up in the Old Testament as well as the new, often in places we would never suspect.

It has always been God's desire to bless every family of the world, right from the very beginning. Thus, from the very beginning, we see the work and desire of missions activity and purpose active and alive even before the formal foundation of God's church. In this chapter, we will look at these missions activities as found in the Old Testament, their success and failures, and what God desires to show us about missions from an Old Testament perspective.

A lone guy on a difficult mission

THE LORD SAW THAT HUMANITY HAD BECOME THOROUGHLY EVIL ON THE EARTH AND THAT EVERY IDEA THEIR MINDS THOUGHT UP WAS ALWAYS COMPLETELY EVIL. THE LORD REGRETTED MAKING HUMAN BEINGS ON THE EARTH, AND HE WAS HEARTBROKEN. SO THE LORD SAID, "I WILL WIPE OFF OF THE LAND THE HUMAN RACE THAT I'VE CREATED: FROM HUMAN BEINGS TO LIVESTOCK TO THE CRAWLING THINGS TO THE BIRDS IN THE SKIES, BECAUSE I REGRET I EVER MADE THEM." BUT AS FOR NOAH, THE LORD APPROVED OF HIM.

THESE ARE NOAH'S DESCENDANTS. IN HIS GENERATION, NOAH WAS A MORAL AND EXEMPLARY MAN; HE WALKED WITH GOD. NOAH HAD THREE SONS: SHEM, HAM, AND JAPHETH. IN GOD'S SIGHT, THE EARTH HAD BECOME CORRUPT AND WAS FILLED WITH VIOLENCE. GOD SAW THAT THE EARTH WAS CORRUPT, BECAUSE ALL CREATURES BEHAVED CORRUPTLY ON THE EARTH.

GOD SAID TO NOAH, "THE END HAS COME FOR ALL CREATURES, SINCE THEY HAVE FILLED THE EARTH WITH VIOLENCE. I AM NOW ABOUT TO DESTROY THEM ALONG WITH THE EARTH, SO MAKE A WOODEN ARK. MAKE THE ARK WITH NESTING PLACES AND COVER IT INSIDE AND OUT WITH TAR. THIS IS HOW YOU SHOULD MAKE IT: FOUR HUNDRED FIFTY FEET LONG, SEVENTY-FIVE FEET WIDE, AND FORTY-FIVE FEET HIGH. MAKE A ROOF FOR THE ARK AND COMPLETE IT ONE FOOT FROM THE TOP. PUT A DOOR IN ITS SIDE. IN THE HOLD BELOW, MAKE THE SECOND AND THIRD DECKS.

"I AM NOW BRINGING THE FLOODWATERS OVER THE EARTH TO DESTROY EVERYTHING UNDER THE SKY THAT BREATHES. EVERYTHING ON EARTH IS ABOUT TO TAKE ITS LAST BREATH. BUT I WILL SET UP MY COVENANT WITH YOU. YOU WILL GO INTO THE ARK TOGETHER WITH YOUR SONS, YOUR WIFE, AND YOUR SONS' WIVES. FROM ALL LIVING THINGS—FROM ALL CREATURES—YOU ARE TO BRING A PAIR, MALE AND FEMALE, INTO THE ARK WITH YOU TO KEEP THEM ALIVE. FROM EACH KIND OF BIRD, FROM EACH KIND OF LIVESTOCK, AND FROM EACH KIND OF EVERYTHING THAT CRAWLS ON THE GROUND—A PAIR FROM EACH WILL GO IN WITH YOU TO STAY ALIVE. TAKE SOME FROM EVERY KIND OF FOOD AND STOW IT AS FOOD FOR YOU AND FOR THE ANIMALS."

NOAH DID EVERYTHING EXACTLY AS GOD COMMANDED HIM.

THE LORD SAID TO NOAH, "GO INTO THE ARK WITH YOUR WHOLE HOUSEHOLD, BECAUSE AMONG THIS GENERATION I'VE SEEN THAT YOU ARE A MORAL MAN. FROM EVERY CLEAN ANIMAL, TAKE SEVEN PAIRS, A MALE AND HIS MATE; AND FROM EVERY UNCLEAN ANIMAL, TAKE ONE PAIR, A MALE AND HIS MATE; AND FROM THE BIRDS IN THE SKY AS WELL, TAKE SEVEN PAIRS, MALE AND FEMALE, SO THAT THEIR OFFSPRING WILL SURVIVE THROUGHOUT THE EARTH. IN SEVEN DAYS FROM NOW I WILL SEND RAIN ON THE EARTH FOR FORTY DAYS AND FORTY NIGHTS. I WILL WIPE OFF FROM THE FERTILE LAND EVERY LIVING THING THAT I HAVE MADE."

NOAH DID EVERYTHING THE LORD COMMANDED HIM.

NOAH WAS 600 YEARS OLD WHEN THE FLOODWATERS ARRIVED ON EARTH. NOAH, HIS SONS, HIS WIFE, AND HIS SONS' WIVES WITH HIM ENTERED THE ARK TO ESCAPE THE FLOODWATERS. FROM THE CLEAN AND UNCLEAN ANIMALS, FROM THE BIRDS AND EVERYTHING CRAWLING ON THE GROUND, TWO OF EACH, MALE AND FEMALE, WENT INTO THE ARK WITH NOAH, JUST AS GOD COMMANDED NOAH. AFTER SEVEN DAYS, THE FLOODWATERS ARRIVED ON THE EARTH. IN THE SIX HUNDREDTH YEAR OF NOAH'S LIFE, IN THE SECOND MONTH, ON THE SEVENTEENTH DAY—ON THAT DAY ALL THE SPRINGS OF THE DEEP SEA ERUPTED, AND THE WINDOWS IN THE SKIES OPENED. IT RAINED ON THE EARTH FORTY DAYS AND FORTY NIGHTS. THAT SAME DAY NOAH, WITH HIS SONS SHEM, HAM, AND JAPHETH, NOAH'S WIFE, AND HIS SONS' THREE WIVES, WENT INTO THE ARK. THEY AND EVERY KIND OF ANIMAL—EVERY KIND OF LIVESTOCK, EVERY KIND THAT CRAWLS ON THE GROUND, EVERY KIND OF BIRD — THEY CAME TO NOAH AND ENTERED THE ARK, TWO OF EVERY CREATURE THAT BREATHES. MALE AND FEMALE OF EVERY CREATURE WENT IN, JUST AS GOD HAD COMMANDED HIM. THEN THE LORD CLOSED THE DOOR BEHIND THEM.

THE FLOOD REMAINED ON THE EARTH FOR FORTY DAYS. THE WATERS ROSE, LIFTED THE ARK, AND IT RODE HIGH ABOVE THE EARTH. THE WATERS ROSE AND SPREAD OUT OVER THE EARTH. THE ARK FLOATED ON THE SURFACE OF THE WATERS. THE WATERS ROSE EVEN HIGHER OVER THE EARTH; THEY COVERED ALL OF THE HIGHEST MOUNTAINS UNDER THE SKY. THE WATERS ROSE TWENTY-THREE FEET HIGH, COVERING THE MOUNTAINS. EVERY CREATURE TOOK ITS LAST BREATH: THE THINGS CRAWLING ON THE GROUND, BIRDS, LIVESTOCK, WILD ANIMALS, EVERYTHING SWARMING ON THE GROUND, AND EVERY HUMAN BEING. EVERYTHING ON DRY LAND WITH LIFE'S BREATH IN ITS NOSTRILS DIED. GOD WIPED AWAY EVERY LIVING THING THAT WAS ON THE FERTILE LAND— FROM HUMAN BEINGS TO LIVESTOCK TO CRAWLING THINGS TO BIRDS IN THE SKY. THEY WERE WIPED OFF THE EARTH. ONLY NOAH AND THOSE WITH HIM IN THE ARK WERE LEFT. THE WATERS ROSE OVER THE EARTH FOR ONE HUNDRED FIFTY DAYS.

GOD REMEMBERED NOAH, ALL THOSE ALIVE, AND ALL THE ANIMALS WITH HIM IN THE ARK. GOD SENT A WIND OVER THE EARTH SO THAT THE WATERS RECEDED. THE SPRINGS OF THE DEEP SEA AND THE SKIES CLOSED UP. THE SKIES HELD BACK THE RAIN. THE WATERS RECEDED GRADUALLY FROM THE EARTH. AFTER ONE HUNDRED FIFTY DAYS, THE WATERS DECREASED; AND IN THE SEVENTH MONTH, ON THE SEVENTEENTH DAY, THE ARK CAME TO REST ON THE ARARAT MOUNTAINS. THE WATERS DECREASED GRADUALLY UNTIL THE

TENTH MONTH, AND ON THE FIRST DAY OF THE TENTH MONTH THE MOUNTAIN PEAKS APPEARED.

AFTER FORTY DAYS, NOAH OPENED THE WINDOW OF THE ARK THAT HE HAD MADE. HE SENT OUT A RAVEN, AND IT FLEW BACK AND FORTH UNTIL THE WATERS OVER THE ENTIRE EARTH HAD DRIED UP. THEN HE SENT OUT A DOVE TO SEE IF THE WATERS ON ALL OF THE FERTILE LAND HAD SUBSIDED, BUT THE DOVE FOUND NO PLACE TO SET ITS FOOT. IT RETURNED TO HIM IN THE ARK SINCE WATERS STILL COVERED THE ENTIRE EARTH. NOAH STRETCHED OUT HIS HAND, TOOK IT, AND BROUGHT IT BACK INTO THE ARK. HE WAITED SEVEN MORE DAYS AND SENT THE DOVE OUT FROM THE ARK AGAIN. THE DOVE CAME BACK TO HIM IN THE EVENING, GRASPING A TORN OLIVE LEAF IN ITS BEAK. THEN NOAH KNEW THAT THE WATERS WERE SUBSIDING FROM THE EARTH. HE WAITED SEVEN MORE DAYS AND SENT OUT THE DOVE, BUT IT DIDN'T COME BACK TO HIM AGAIN. IN NOAH'S SIX HUNDRED FIRST YEAR, ON THE FIRST DAY OF THE FIRST MONTH, THE WATERS DRIED UP FROM THE EARTH. NOAH REMOVED THE ARK'S HATCH AND SAW THAT THE SURFACE OF THE FERTILE LAND HAD DRIED UP. IN THE SECOND MONTH, ON THE SEVENTEENTH DAY, THE EARTH WAS DRY.

GOD SPOKE TO NOAH, "GO OUT OF THE ARK, YOU AND YOUR WIFE, YOUR SONS, AND YOUR SONS' WIVES WITH YOU. BRING OUT WITH YOU ALL THE ANIMALS OF EVERY KIND—BIRDS, LIVESTOCK, EVERYTHING CRAWLING ON THE GROUND—SO THAT THEY MAY POPULATE THE EARTH, BE FERTILE, AND MULTIPLY ON THE EARTH." SO NOAH WENT OUT OF THE ARK WITH HIS SONS, HIS WIFE, AND HIS SONS' WIVES. ALL THE ANIMALS, ALL THE LIVESTOCK, ALL THE BIRDS, AND EVERYTHING CRAWLING ON THE GROUND, CAME OUT OF THE ARK BY THEIR FAMILIES. (Genesis 6:5-8:19)

Noah is seldom, if ever, given much scholarship attention, let alone missions assessment. When we read Noah, we read a story of a righteous man in the midst of unrighteousness who was called to build a boat and sail on water as he and his family were protected from annihilation. It sounds simple enough, and too often we let Noah's story die right where we found it.

Noah's mission was not specifically building the ark; that was Noah's commission from God, or his notable purpose (direct assignment). The Bible indicates it took approximately 100 years to complete, which is unfathomable for most of us in terms of a long-term divine ministry or assignment. Noah prepared for 100 years to be ready to set sail for his mission and engage in the deeper work of ministry that was for him.

Within Noah's command to build a boat was the mission of creating an entirely new world. To do that, he had the job of protecting his family. It was Noah's work to navigate through the waters as God purified the world. He was a dedicated and prepared missionary, warning every person that impending consequences for sin was to come and the time for repentance was now. While he waited for his mission to take place, he evangelized; he witnessed; he stood as an ensign that God is good and that He gives all the same chance to get right with Him, while the time is now.

Once Noah was able to leave the ark, he literally forged an entirely new world. It was one that got a fresh start and needed the forging of truth and history to educate it again for the very first time. Noah's job was not just to repopulate, but to reeducate, as well. Just as missionaries go to lands they've never seen that are new to them, so too Noah took on this same role after he and his family left the ark. He was righteous amidst disorder and then was a part of a new order, of reestablishing hope and truth, in a whole new situation for the chance to lead all to life.

Woman on a mission

NAOMI SAID TO HER DAUGHTERS-IN-LAW, "GO, TURN BACK, EACH OF YOU TO THE HOUSEHOLD OF YOUR MOTHER. MAY THE LORD DEAL FAITHFULLY WITH YOU, JUST AS YOU HAVE DONE WITH THE DEAD AND WITH ME. MAY THE LORD PROVIDE FOR YOU SO THAT YOU MAY FIND SECURITY, EACH WOMAN IN THE HOUSEHOLD OF HER HUSBAND." THEN SHE KISSED THEM, AND THEY LIFTED UP THEIR VOICES AND WEPT.

BUT THEY REPLIED TO HER, "NO, INSTEAD WE WILL RETURN WITH YOU, TO YOUR PEOPLE."

NAOMI REPLIED, "TURN BACK, MY DAUGHTERS. WHY WOULD YOU GO WITH ME? WILL THERE AGAIN BE SONS IN MY WOMB, THAT THEY WOULD BE HUSBANDS FOR YOU? TURN BACK, MY DAUGHTERS. GO. I AM TOO OLD FOR A HUSBAND. IF I WERE TO SAY THAT I HAVE HOPE, EVEN IF I HAD A HUSBAND TONIGHT, AND EVEN MORE, IF I WERE TO BEAR SONS— WOULD YOU WAIT UNTIL THEY GREW UP? WOULD YOU REFRAIN FROM HAVING A HUSBAND? NO, MY

DAUGHTERS. THIS IS MORE BITTER FOR ME THAN FOR YOU, SINCE THE LORD'S WILL HAS COME OUT AGAINST ME."

THEN THEY LIFTED UP THEIR VOICES AND WEPT AGAIN. ORPAH KISSED HER MOTHER-IN-LAW, BUT RUTH STAYED WITH HER. NAOMI SAID, "LOOK, YOUR SISTER-IN-LAW IS RETURNING TO HER PEOPLE AND TO HER GODS. TURN BACK AFTER YOUR SISTER-IN-LAW."

BUT RUTH REPLIED, "DON'T URGE ME TO ABANDON YOU, TO TURN BACK FROM FOLLOWING AFTER YOU. WHEREVER YOU GO, I WILL GO; AND WHEREVER YOU STAY, I WILL STAY. YOUR PEOPLE WILL BE MY PEOPLE, AND YOUR GOD WILL BE MY GOD. WHEREVER YOU DIE, I WILL DIE, AND THERE I WILL BE BURIED. MAY THE LORD DO THIS TO ME AND MORE SO IF EVEN DEATH SEPARATES ME FROM YOU." WHEN NAOMI SAW THAT RUTH WAS DETERMINED TO GO WITH HER, SHE STOPPED SPEAKING TO HER ABOUT IT.

SO BOTH OF THEM WENT ALONG UNTIL THEY ARRIVED AT BETHLEHEM. WHEN THEY ARRIVED AT BETHLEHEM, THE WHOLE TOWN WAS EXCITED ON ACCOUNT OF THEM, AND THE WOMEN OF THE TOWN ASKED, "CAN THIS BE NAOMI?"

SHE REPLIED TO THEM, "DON'T CALL ME NAOMI, BUT CALL ME MARA, FOR THE ALMIGHTY HAS MADE ME VERY BITTER. I WENT AWAY FULL, BUT THE LORD HAS RETURNED ME EMPTY. WHY WOULD YOU CALL ME NAOMI, WHEN THE LORD HAS TESTIFIED AGAINST ME, AND THE ALMIGHTY HAS DEEMED ME GUILTY?"

THUS NAOMI RETURNED. AND RUTH THE MOABITE, HER DAUGHTER-IN-LAW, RETURNED WITH HER FROM THE TERRITORY OF MOAB. THEY ARRIVED IN BETHLEHEM AT THE BEGINNING OF THE BARLEY HARVEST. (Ruth 1:8-22)

It deeply bothers me that, as a church, we do not treat the book of Ruth with any intensity. It is almost as if we treat it like a fanciful tale, something that was about distant people living a long time ago, in a land far, far away. Ruth and Naomi are not considered central characters within any serious theology, and this means we don't take Ruth and Naomi seriously as Biblical figures. To me, this is just sad. There may only be four chapters in the book of Ruth, but they are central identities to us about Gentile inclusion in the church. This also means that one of the first examples of missions in the Bible comes through the work of Ruth.

The story of Ruth is an intriguing one: a Jewish woman married to a Moabite man who gave up her entire people, identity, and culture to assimilate into his world. That's what people often did through marriage in those days. Ruth was surrounded by pagans: her husband, mother-in-law, father-in-law, brother-in-law, and sister-in-law. Then, one day, the world that she'd joined crumbled around her. Famine and difficult times caused her father-in-law, brother-in-law, and husband to die. Then her sister-in-law left to return to her own people. Ruth, however, was compelled to do something different, and that was to remain with her mother-in-law, a woman who seemed soured by life's experiences and was gravely unhappy about the hand she'd been dealt.

Through Ruth's intervention, Naomi came to learn about God firsthand in a way she never would have experienced without Ruth. She saw her dedication, kindness, love and true faith that God could bring them to the results that they needed. She might not have been able to reach out to anyone else, but Ruth most definitely qualifies as a woman who, through the purpose of God, was a missionary to Naomi.

Ruth proves that women can do missions and can do them just as good and as well as any man can. Her work also proves that long-term missions involve extended dedication that many are unwilling to make. She had to stay with her family, adopt their culture and language, live among them, dress as they did, eat as they did, and live as they did to reach the point where the impact made was enough to intervene and become a full witness to her of the purpose and glory of God. Ruth shows us missionary process and progress; that it often does not happen overnight and the importance in a long-term missions plan.

A mission against idolatry

THE ASSYRIAN KING BROUGHT PEOPLE FROM BABYLON, CUTH, AVVA, HAMATH, AND SEPHARVAIM, RESETTLING THEM IN THE CITIES OF SAMARIA IN PLACE OF THE ISRAELITES. THESE PEOPLE TOOK CONTROL OF SAMARIA AND SETTLED IN ITS CITIES. BUT WHEN THEY BEGAN TO LIVE THERE, THEY DIDN'T WORSHIP THE LORD, SO THE LORD SENT LIONS AGAINST THEM, AND THE LIONS BEGAN TO KILL THEM. ASSYRIA'S KING WAS TOLD ABOUT THIS: "THE NATIONS YOU SENT INTO EXILE AND RESETTLED IN THE CITIES OF SAMARIA DON'T KNOW THE RELIGIOUS PRACTICES OF THE LOCAL GOD. HE'S SENT LIONS AGAINST

THEM, AND THE LIONS ARE KILLING THEM BECAUSE NONE OF THEM KNOW THE RELIGIOUS PRACTICES OF THE LOCAL GOD."

SO ASSYRIA'S KING COMMANDED, "RETURN ONE OF THE PRIESTS THAT YOU EXILED FROM THERE. HE SHOULD GO BACK AND LIVE THERE. HE SHOULD TEACH THEM THE RELIGIOUS PRACTICES OF THE LOCAL GOD." SO ONE OF THE PRIESTS WHO HAD BEEN EXILED FROM SAMARIA WENT BACK. HE LIVED IN BETHEL AND TAUGHT THE PEOPLE HOW TO WORSHIP THE LORD.

BUT EACH NATIONALITY STILL MADE ITS OWN GODS. THEY SET THEM UP IN THE HOUSES THAT THE PEOPLE OF SAMARIA HAD MADE AT THE SHRINES. EACH NATIONALITY DID THIS IN WHICHEVER CITIES THEY LIVED. THE BABYLONIAN PEOPLE MADE THE GOD SUCCOTH-BENOTH, THE CUTHEAN PEOPLE MADE NERGAL, AND THE PEOPLE FROM HAMATH MADE ASHIMA. THE AVVITES MADE NIBHAZ AND TARTAK. THE SEPHARVITES BURNED THEIR CHILDREN ALIVE AS A SACRIFICE TO ADRAMMELECH AND ANAMMELECH, THE SEPHARVITE GODS. THEY ALSO WORSHIPPED THE LORD, BUT THEY APPOINTED PRIESTS FOR THE SHRINES FROM THEIR WHOLE POPULATION. THESE PRIESTS WORKED IN THE HOUSES AT THE SHRINES. SO THEY WORSHIPPED THE LORD, BUT THEY ALSO SERVED THEIR OWN GODS ACCORDING TO THE RELIGIOUS PRACTICES OF THE NATIONS FROM WHICH THEY HAD BEEN EXILED.

THEY ARE STILL FOLLOWING THEIR FORMER RELIGIOUS PRACTICES TO THIS VERY DAY. THEY DON'T REALLY WORSHIP THE LORD. NOR DO THEY FOLLOW THE REGULATIONS, THE CASE LAWS, THE INSTRUCTION, OR THE COMMANDMENT THAT THE LORD COMMANDED THE CHILDREN OF JACOB, WHOM HE RENAMED ISRAEL. THE LORD HAD MADE A COVENANT WITH THEM, COMMANDING THEM, DON'T WORSHIP OTHER GODS. DON'T BOW DOWN TO THEM OR SERVE THEM. DON'T SACRIFICE TO THEM. INSTEAD, WORSHIP ONLY THE LORD. HE'S THE ONE WHO BROUGHT YOU UP FROM THE LAND OF EGYPT WITH GREAT STRENGTH AND AN OUTSTRETCHED ARM. BOW DOWN TO HIM! SACRIFICE TO HIM! YOU MUST CAREFULLY KEEP THE REGULATIONS AND CASE LAWS, THE INSTRUCTION, AND THE COMMANDMENT THAT HE WROTE FOR YOU. DON'T WORSHIP OTHER GODS. DON'T FORGET THE COVENANT THAT I MADE WITH YOU. DON'T WORSHIP OTHER GODS. INSTEAD, WORSHIP ONLY THE LORD YOUR GOD. HE WILL RESCUE YOU FROM YOUR ENEMIES' POWER.

BUT THEY WOULDN'T LISTEN. INSTEAD, THEY CONTINUED DOING THEIR FORMER RELIGIOUS PRACTICES. SO THESE NATIONS WORSHIP THE LORD, BUT THEY ALSO SERVE THEIR IDOLS. THE CHILDREN AND THE GRANDCHILDREN ARE

DOING THE VERY SAME THING THEIR PARENTS DID. AND THAT'S HOW THINGS STILL ARE TODAY. (2 Kings 17:24-41)

Earlier in this text, I raised the point that we don't often think about what Israel looked like from the Gentile perspective. Here they were, a nation that was supposed to be set apart for the true God, and they were always falling into the sins and wrongdoing of everyone around them. Then the Gentile nations around them were given permission to occupy them because of their constant falls into idolatry, and we don't see much consideration for how Israel desired to look in their eyes once their falls and foreign occupations went on hiatus.

In 2 Kings 17:24-41, we get an idea of what Israel looked like to the Gentiles and an idea of a restorative plan to try and work with the Gentile nations. In it, the ideal was supposed to happen: the priests were called in, with government edict, to try and convert the pagans who they now lived with. This plan shows us exactly what the Israelites looked like to their neighbors: they appeared occupied, displaced, disorganized, and unprepared to handle their lives. In response, the King of Assyria called for the priests to come in, work with the people living there, and teach them the proper ways of worship.

The first formalized group of missionaries were Levites, the Hebrew priests who worked as the leaders of the people, operated and functioned within the temple, and offered the regular sacrifices for the people. They were selected due to their knowledge of the law and their obvious status within the community as experts on all things spiritual. The king's motive for doing such was probably two-fold: he sought to make the Israelites more comfortable in their situation and believed that by doing so, he could foster some cross-cultural insights. The priests went on this mission, did their work...and the Scriptures reveal to us that it was a complete and total failure. The various pagan cultures did not adhere to the statutes or teachings of God's commandments, and instead, maintained their own customs. Instead, they annexed worship of God along with their various other gods and reached out to Him in ways that were displeasing.

These priests had the difficult task of trying to evangelize a nation that had a convenient way of annexing religious beliefs on to their existing ones. They were not a nation of people who were going to quickly abandon their way of living for the true God. This meant the priests were immersed in a world unlike their own, forced to find balance between what they believed and how they could most effectively reach the people around them. In the end, they failed.

This story is found in the Bible to make us consider diverse factors when undertaking the work of missions. The first, and most obvious factor, is that a missions trip may very well be unsuccessful due to the circumstances of immersion in a missionary's experience. We are quick to blame unsuccessful endeavors on the way things are taught or presented, but that's not always the case, and such an assertion is not always fair. Not everyone is ready to accept the Gospel, and there are several factors involved in someone's reception to God's Word. Cultural influences, spiritual approaches to wisdom, a religion's theological viewpoints, the religious practices of the people, and the way that a missionary's nation is viewed from the outside looking in are all relevant factors in the way that missionary activities are received. We do not see anything in this passage that indicates the priests did anything culpable. They did not join in the worship of idols, they taught the people about God's precepts and what the people should do from a spiritual perspective, and they did what they did with government sanction. They weren't evil rebels with an evil agenda. Still, their mission was unsuccessful. It was difficult to experience, and probably even more difficult to walk away from.

Not every mission activity we undertake – even if it is God Who has appointed us to do it – will be successful. It's been said that "You win some, you lose some," and this is very applicable to missions. Sometimes circumstances aren't right, sometimes timing is off, and no matter how much you know are a great witness of God's truth, sometimes missions are just a big miss. This doesn't mean we should despair. The Hebrew priests were still priests, they were still leaders, and they still had ministry to operate. Just because one mission went awry did not mean they lost their ministerial call or position; it just meant they had a bad experience in missions.

Praising God Who calls us to all nations

Sing to the Lord a new song!
  Sing to the Lord, all the earth!
Sing to the Lord! Bless His Name!

SHARE THE NEWS OF HIS SAVING WORK EVERY SINGLE DAY!

DECLARE GOD'S GLORY AMONG THE NATIONS;
   DECLARE HIS WONDROUS WORKS AMONG ALL PEOPLE
   BECAUSE THE LORD IS GREAT AND SO WORTHY OF PRAISE.
HE IS AWESOME BEYOND ALL OTHER GODS
   BECAUSE ALL THE GODS OF THE NATIONS ARE JUST IDOLS,
    BUT IT IS THE LORD WHO CREATED HEAVEN!
GREATNESS AND GRANDEUR ARE IN FRONT OF HIM;
   STRENGTH AND BEAUTY ARE IN HIS SANCTUARY.

GIVE TO THE LORD, ALL FAMILIES OF THE NATIONS—
   GIVE TO THE LORD GLORY AND POWER!
GIVE TO THE LORD THE GLORY DUE HIS NAME!
   BRING GIFTS!
   ENTER HIS COURTYARDS!
BOW DOWN TO THE LORD IN HIS HOLY SPLENDOR!
   TREMBLE BEFORE HIM, ALL THE EARTH!

TELL THE NATIONS, "THE LORD RULES!
   YES, HE SET THE WORLD FIRMLY IN PLACE;
   IT WON'T BE SHAKEN.
   HE WILL JUDGE ALL PEOPLE FAIRLY." (Psalm 96:1-10)

It was uncommon for the Israelites to work with or minister to communities outside of their own at this point. Israel had the mentality that others should come to them, because they were a set apart people. To them, being set apart was enough of a witness in and of itself. It is unfortunate that Israel did not live up to its end of being set apart, but they, unfortunately, did not. Missions were not a focus of Old Testament life, but that doesn't mean there were never references to such activity or mention of such activity being done.

    Psalm 96 is a beautiful rendition praising God as the God of the whole world. Israel would have acknowledged Him as such, but would not have understood it in the sense of missions, of going forth and being a blessing to all nations and all peoples. Psalm 96, however, reveals to us key facets of mission work, of the work of missionaries among the nations and the important message missionaries carry as they go through the world with the Gospel.

Missionaries carry with them the good news of the Gospel, but they also herald everything that goes along with that Gospel promise. We know salvation is the best news we can provide, but along with salvation come other benefits. Salvation is a part of eternal life, and eternity is just as much a part of right now as it is after one's death. Missionary life is not just about proclaiming salvation, but teaching people how to live with God, how to interact with Him, and about the great grandeur that He alone is.

In Psalm 96, we see the command to sing to God a new song, proclaiming something new that the world has not sung before. All the world is to join in this powerful song, blessing God's Name, heralding His salvation, declaring His glory and works among all peoples. It even tells us why: Because God is great. He is greater than any false god, He is our Creator, and all is before Him.

If we are going to position ourselves in the middle of all families of the earth to call others to ascribe all that God is due, we must be worshippers ourselves. We need to know Who God is; we need to properly identify Him as Creator, Redeemer, and Sustainer; and we need to be unashamed to call out to other nations, telling them just Who God is and what He has to offer them. It also shows that missions call for us to teach people about God, specifically His goodness, glory, and what makes Him different from those idols that people chase due to heritage and cultural religious understandings.

Seeing the depths of God in the seas

SOME OF THE REDEEMED HAD GONE OUT ON THE OCEAN IN SHIPS,
  MAKING THEIR LIVING ON THE HIGH SEAS.
THEY SAW WHAT THE LORD HAD MADE;
  THEY SAW HIS WONDROUS WORKS IN THE DEPTHS OF THE SEA.
GOD SPOKE AND STIRRED UP A STORM
  THAT BROUGHT THE WAVES UP HIGH.
THE WAVES WENT AS HIGH AS THE SKY;
  THEY CRASHED DOWN TO THE DEPTHS.
THE SAILORS' COURAGE MELTED AT THIS TERRIBLE SITUATION.
  THEY STAGGERED AND STUMBLED AROUND LIKE THEY WERE DRUNK.
  NONE OF THEIR SKILL WAS OF ANY HELP.
SO THEY CRIED OUT TO THE LORD IN THEIR DISTRESS,
  AND GOD BROUGHT THEM OUT SAFE FROM THEIR DESPERATE
CIRCUMSTANCES.

GOD QUIETED THE STORM TO A WHISPER;
  THE SEA'S WAVES WERE HUSHED.
SO THEY REJOICED BECAUSE THE WAVES HAD CALMED DOWN;
  THEN GOD LED THEM TO THE HARBOR THEY WERE HOPING FOR.
LET THEM THANK THE LORD FOR HIS FAITHFUL LOVE
  AND HIS WONDROUS WORKS FOR ALL PEOPLE.
LET THEM EXALT GOD IN THE CONGREGATION OF THE PEOPLE
  AND PRAISE GOD IN THE ASSEMBLY OF THE ELDERS. (Psalm 107:23-32)

In the annals of history are numerous boat trips made by missionaries because no other forms of transportation were available. There is something in the experience we see here that provides for the experience of the missionary in the Old Testament, and that is seeing God through the trip and the experience of travel.

Missions are important for those who are reached, but as with all things in God, the missionary should also receive insight and revelation from God in the missions process. Being brought to another region, state, nation, or even continent by God means His hand is upon the trip. Through that process a missionary should see the hand of God. Seeing the world, creation, the way in which nature orders itself. Experiencing the world and the incredible diversity present within it should cause every missionary (or even well-traveled believer) should produce insight and a desire to learn more about the nature of God, thus bringing forth heaven-sent revelation.

A willingness to go

IN THE YEAR OF KING UZZIAH'S DEATH, I SAW THE LORD SITTING ON A HIGH AND EXALTED THRONE, THE EDGES OF HIS ROBE FILLING THE TEMPLE. WINGED CREATURES WERE STATIONED AROUND HIM. EACH HAD SIX WINGS: WITH TWO THEY VEILED THEIR FACES, WITH TWO THEIR FEET, AND WITH TWO THEY FLEW ABOUT. THEY SHOUTED TO EACH OTHER, SAYING:

"HOLY, HOLY, HOLY IS THE LORD OF HEAVENLY FORCES!
ALL THE EARTH IS FILLED WITH GOD'S GLORY!"

THE DOORFRAME SHOOK AT THE SOUND OF THEIR SHOUTING, AND THE HOUSE WAS FILLED WITH SMOKE.

I SAID, "MOURN FOR ME; I'M RUINED! I'M A MAN WITH UNCLEAN LIPS, AND I

LIVE AMONG A PEOPLE WITH UNCLEAN LIPS. YET I'VE SEEN THE KING, THE LORD OF HEAVENLY FORCES!"

THEN ONE OF THE WINGED CREATURES FLEW TO ME, HOLDING A GLOWING COAL THAT HE HAD TAKEN FROM THE ALTAR WITH TONGS. HE TOUCHED MY MOUTH AND SAID, "SEE, THIS HAS TOUCHED YOUR LIPS. YOUR GUILT HAS DEPARTED, AND YOUR SIN IS REMOVED."

THEN I HEARD THE LORD'S VOICE SAYING, "WHOM SHOULD I SEND, AND WHO WILL GO FOR US?"

I SAID, "I'M HERE; SEND ME."

GOD SAID, "GO AND SAY TO THIS PEOPLE:

LISTEN INTENTLY, BUT DON'T UNDERSTAND;
  LOOK CAREFULLY, BUT DON'T COMPREHEND.
MAKE THE MINDS OF THIS PEOPLE DULL.
  MAKE THEIR EARS DEAF AND THEIR EYES BLIND,
  SO THEY CAN'T SEE WITH THEIR EYES
  OR HEAR WITH THEIR EARS,
  OR UNDERSTAND WITH THEIR MINDS,
  AND TURN, AND BE HEALED."

I SAID, "HOW LONG, LORD?"

AND GOD SAID, "UNTIL CITIES LIE RUINED WITH NO ONE LIVING IN THEM, UNTIL THERE ARE HOUSES WITHOUT PEOPLE AND THE LAND IS LEFT DEVASTATED." THE LORD WILL SEND THE PEOPLE FAR AWAY, AND THE LAND WILL BE COMPLETELY ABANDONED. EVEN IF ONE-TENTH REMAIN THERE, THEY WILL BE BURNED AGAIN, LIKE A TEREBINTH OR AN OAK, WHICH WHEN IT IS CUT DOWN LEAVES A STUMP. ITS STUMP IS A HOLY SEED. (Isaiah 6:1-13)

One interesting contrast between Old and New Testament missions is the way in which Old Testament missions were frequently limited in their success rates. When God called many Old Testament leaders to missions, it seems as if there is a constant message that the people they would reach would either not understand or not receive the message.

Overall, being sent to deliver a message to anyone in the Old Testament, whether it was the Israelites or the nations, seems to have been an overall failure. This is not always the case, of course, as we will see in an example later in this chapter. It does seem that Israel's prophets and those who served as missionaries had a very difficult job, with many unknowns and an overall sense that while they served as prophets and had to do a work that they knew in the end would be unsuccessful. It must have put them in an awkward position with their family and friends, and we know it set them apart within the bigger picture of their spiritual communities. Being one who went forth with a specific message for a specific purpose was not glamorous, nor was it endlessly entertaining and fun.

The example of Isaiah's call and commission overlap into specified areas of ministry, including prophetic work. It also shows us the intensity of working in missions and answering God's call to go forth in missions. We should never approach missions work with the intent that it's going to be nothing but fun and entertainment. Missions is serious business and must be considered from the position that we are entrusted with a great, mighty and important message, the most important message of their lives.

Missionaries need to be prepared for any response they receive. Not only that, but they also must be prepared to deliver a message that while good, may not be perceived to be such. God's message of salvation is one of hope but also of change and difference, and ultimately, God calls every one of us to be different. Even if people refuse to hear, act like they don't understand, and the ultimate message delivered is one that foretells what will happen and the results are not pretty, the message must be delivered

Jeremiah, Ezekiel and missions

THE LORD'S WORD CAME TO ME:
"BEFORE I CREATED YOU IN THE WOMB I KNEW YOU;
  BEFORE YOU WERE BORN I SET YOU APART;
  I MADE YOU A PROPHET TO THE NATIONS."
"AH, LORD GOD," I SAID, "I DON'T KNOW HOW TO SPEAK
  BECAUSE I'M ONLY A CHILD."
THE LORD RESPONDED,
  "DON'T SAY, 'I'M ONLY A CHILD.'
    WHERE I SEND YOU, YOU MUST GO;

WHAT I TELL YOU, YOU MUST SAY.
DON'T BE AFRAID OF THEM,
  BECAUSE I'M WITH YOU TO RESCUE YOU,"
    DECLARES THE LORD.
THEN THE LORD STRETCHED OUT HIS HAND,
  TOUCHED MY MOUTH, AND SAID TO ME,
  "I'M PUTTING MY WORDS IN YOUR MOUTH.
THIS VERY DAY I APPOINT YOU OVER NATIONS AND EMPIRES,
  TO DIG UP AND PULL DOWN,
  TO DESTROY AND DEMOLISH,
  TO BUILD AND PLANT."

THE LORD ASKED ME, "WHAT DO YOU SEE, JEREMIAH?"

I SAID, "A BRANCH OF AN ALMOND TREE."

THE LORD THEN SAID, "YOU ARE RIGHT, FOR I'M WATCHING OVER MY WORD UNTIL IT IS FULFILLED."

THE LORD ASKED ME AGAIN, "WHAT DO YOU SEE?"

I SAID, "A POT BOILING OVER FROM THE NORTH."

THE LORD SAID TO ME, "TROUBLE WILL ERUPT FROM THE NORTH AGAINST THE PEOPLE OF THIS LAND."

I'M CALLING FOR ALL THE TRIBES OF GREAT NATIONS FROM THE NORTH, SAYS THE LORD, AND THEY WILL SET UP THEIR RULERS BY THE ENTRANCES OF JERUSALEM, ON ITS WALLS, AND IN EVERY CITY OF JUDAH. I WILL DECLARE MY JUDGMENT AGAINST THEM FOR DOING EVIL: FOR ABANDONING ME, WORSHIPPING OTHER GODS, AND TRUSTING IN THE WORKS OF THEIR HANDS. BUT YOU MUST PREPARE FOR BATTLE AND BE READY TO UTTER EVERY WORD I COMMAND YOU. DON'T BE FRIGHTENED BEFORE THEM, OR I WILL FRIGHTEN YOU BEFORE THEM. TODAY I HAVE MADE YOU AN ARMED CITY, AN IRON PILLAR, AND A BRONZE WALL AGAINST THE ENTIRE LAND—THE KINGS OF JUDAH, ITS PRINCES, ITS PRIESTS, AND ALL ITS PEOPLE. THEY WILL ATTACK YOU, BUT THEY WON'T DEFEAT YOU, BECAUSE I AM WITH YOU AND WILL RESCUE YOU, DECLARES THE LORD. (Jeremiah 1:4-19)

THE VOICE SAID TO ME: HUMAN ONE, STAND ON YOUR FEET, AND I'LL SPEAK TO YOU. AS HE SPOKE TO ME, A WIND CAME TO ME AND STOOD ME ON MY FEET, AND I HEARD SOMEONE ADDRESSING ME. HE SAID TO ME: HUMAN ONE, I'M SENDING YOU TO THE ISRAELITES, A TRAITOROUS AND REBELLIOUS PEOPLE. THEY AND THEIR ANCESTORS HAVE BEEN REBELLING AGAINST ME TO THIS VERY DAY. I'M SENDING YOU TO THEIR HARDHEADED AND HARD-HEARTED DESCENDANTS, AND YOU WILL SAY TO THEM: THE LORD GOD PROCLAIMS. WHETHER THEY LISTEN OR WHETHER THEY REFUSE, SINCE THEY ARE A HOUSEHOLD OF REBELS, THEY WILL KNOW THAT A PROPHET HAS BEEN AMONG THEM.

AND AS FOR YOU, HUMAN ONE, DON'T BE AFRAID OF THEM OR THEIR WORDS. DON'T BE AFRAID! YOU POSSESS THISTLES AND THORNS THAT SUBDUE SCORPIONS. DON'T BE AFRAID OF THEIR WORDS OR SHRINK FROM THEIR PRESENCE, BECAUSE THEY ARE A HOUSEHOLD OF REBELS. YOU'LL SPEAK MY WORDS TO THEM WHETHER THEY LISTEN OR WHETHER THEY REFUSE. THEY ARE JUST A HOUSEHOLD OF REBELS!

AS FOR YOU, HUMAN ONE, LISTEN TO WHAT I SAY TO YOU. DON'T BECOME REBELLIOUS LIKE THAT HOUSEHOLD OF REBELS. OPEN YOUR MOUTH AND EAT WHAT I GIVE YOU. THEN I LOOKED, AND THERE IN A HAND STRETCHED OUT TO ME WAS A SCROLL. HE SPREAD IT OPEN IN FRONT OF ME, AND IT WAS FILLED WITH WRITING ON BOTH SIDES, SONGS OF MOURNING, LAMENTATION, AND DOOM. (Ezekiel 2:1-10)

I reserved a special section for Isaiah because I feel the language and dedication of going for God rated a specific look. After this section, there is a look at the prophets Obadiah and Jonah, whose specific messages were for Gentile groups outside of Israel. Here we are going to look at some collective principles that relate to missions as found in two Old Testament prophets: Jeremiah and Ezekiel.

The Old Testament prophets were all missionaries. They were individuals called by God and sent with a specific message for a specific people. We don't have specific records of the call each one of them received. Especially in the case of many of the minor prophets, all we see are the messages they delivered. Most of the time, the words of the prophets were delivered to Israel, for one reason or another. The typical reason prophetic messages went forth to Israel were not for any of the reasons that people associate with prophetic word today. They did not promise endless material wealth or prosperity, but usually spoke words designed to bring about conviction. During Israel's history, the people of the nation had a sinking way of falling away from what they knew God told them to do, time and time again. The second things got better, or they got back into a place of spiritually good graces, they'd fall right back into their old ways. The Biblical prophets came forward to warn Israel about what would happen to them if they didn't obey God and do right, and the eventual consequences if they went ahead and fell into sin regardless of God's warning through the prophet.

The Old Testament prophets prove that one can go on a mission and work with and among churches in the process. There are as many among us who need to experience salvation as those outside of the church, but the way they need to experience it is different. Churches and church members need the experience of rebuke, correction, education, doctrinal understanding, and yes, to hear what God has to say.

Obadiah's mission of doom

THE VISION OF OBADIAH.
    THE LORD GOD PROCLAIMS CONCERNING EDOM:
    WE HAVE HEARD A MESSAGE FROM THE LORD—
        A MESSENGER HAS BEEN SENT AMONG THE NATIONS:
    "RISE UP! LET US RISE AGAINST HER FOR BATTLE!"
LOOK NOW, I WILL MAKE YOU OF LITTLE IMPORTANCE AMONG THE NATIONS;
    YOU WILL BE TOTALLY DESPISED.
YOUR PROUD HEART HAS TRICKED YOU—
    YOU WHO LIVE IN THE CRACKS OF THE ROCK,
    WHOSE DWELLING IS HIGH ABOVE.
  YOU WHO SAY IN YOUR HEART,
    "WHO WILL BRING ME DOWN TO THE GROUND?"
THOUGH YOU SOAR LIKE THE EAGLE,
    THOUGH YOUR NEST IS SET AMONG THE STARS,
    I WILL BRING YOU DOWN FROM THERE,
SAYS THE LORD.

IF THIEVES APPROACH YOU,
    IF ROBBERS BY NIGHT—HOW YOU'VE BEEN DEVASTATED!—
    WOULDN'T THEY STEAL ONLY WHAT THEY WANTED?
  IF THOSE WHO GATHER GRAPES CAME TO YOU,

WOULDN'T THEY LEAVE SOME GRAPES?
HOW ESAU HAS BEEN LOOTED,
HIS TREASURES TAKEN AWAY!
ALL THOSE WHO WERE YOUR ALLIES
HAVE DRIVEN YOU TO THE BORDER.
THOSE WHO WERE ON YOUR SIDE TRICKED YOU
AND TRIUMPHED OVER YOU.
THEY ARE SETTING YOUR OWN BREAD AS A TRAP UNDER YOU,
BUT YOU DON'T SEE IT COMING.
WON'T I ON THAT DAY, SAYS THE LORD,
DESTROY THE WISE FROM EDOM
AND UNDERSTANDING FROM MOUNT ESAU?
YOUR WARRIORS WILL BE SHATTERED, TEMAN,
AND EVERYONE FROM MOUNT ESAU WILL BE ELIMINATED.

BECAUSE OF THE SLAUGHTER AND VIOLENCE DONE TO YOUR BROTHER JACOB,
SHAME WILL COVER YOU,
AND YOU WILL BE DESTROYED FOREVER.
YOU STOOD NEARBY,
STRANGERS CARRIED OFF HIS WEALTH,
AND FOREIGNERS ENTERED HIS GATES
AND CAST LOTS FOR JERUSALEM;
YOU TOO WERE LIKE ONE OF THEM.
BUT YOU SHOULD HAVE TAKEN NO PLEASURE OVER YOUR BROTHER
ON THE DAY OF HIS MISERY;
YOU SHOULDN'T HAVE REJOICED OVER THE PEOPLE OF JUDAH
ON THE DAY OF THEIR DEVASTATION;
YOU SHOULDN'T HAVE BRAGGED
ON THEIR DAY OF HARDSHIP.
YOU SHOULDN'T HAVE ENTERED THE GATE OF MY PEOPLE
ON THE DAY OF THEIR DEFEAT;
YOU SHOULDN'T HAVE EVEN LOOKED ON HIS SUFFERING
ON THE DAY OF HIS DISASTER;
YOU SHOULDN'T HAVE STOLEN HIS POSSESSIONS
ON THE DAY OF HIS DISTRESS.
YOU SHOULDN'T HAVE WAITED ON THE ROADS
TO DESTROY HIS ESCAPEES;
YOU SHOULDN'T HAVE HANDED OVER HIS SURVIVORS
ON THE DAY OF DEFEAT.
THE DAY OF THE LORD IS NEAR

AGAINST ALL THE NATIONS.
AS YOU HAVE DONE, SO IT WILL BE DONE TO YOU;
  YOUR ACTIONS WILL MAKE YOU SUFFER!
JUST AS YOU HAVE DRUNK ON MY HOLY MOUNTAIN,
  SO WILL ALL THE NATIONS AROUND YOU DRINK;
  THEY WILL DRINK AND SWALLOW QUICKLY,
    AND THEY WILL BE LIKE THEY'VE NEVER BEEN BEFORE.

BUT ON MOUNT ZION THERE WILL BE THOSE WHO ESCAPE,
  AND IT WILL BE HOLY;
  AND THE HOUSE OF JACOB WILL DRIVE OUT THOSE WHO DROVE THEM
    OUT.
THE HOUSE OF JACOB WILL BE A FIRE,
  THE HOUSE OF JOSEPH A FLAME,
  AND THE HOUSE OF ESAU STRAW;
    THEY WILL BURN THEM UP COMPLETELY,
      AND THERE WILL BE NO ONE LEFT OF THE HOUSE OF ESAU,
FOR THE LORD HAS SPOKEN.
THOSE OF THE ARID SOUTHERN PLAIN WILL POSSESS MOUNT ESAU,
  AND THOSE OF THE WESTERN FOOTHILLS, THE LAND OF THE
    PHILISTINES;
  THEY WILL POSSESS THE LAND OF EPHRAIM AND THE LAND OF SAMARIA,
    AND BENJAMIN WILL POSSESS GILEAD.
THOSE WHO REMAIN OF THE ISRAELITES
    WILL POSSESS THE LAND OF THE CANAANITES AS FAR AS
      ZAREPHATH;
  AND THOSE LEFT FROM JERUSALEM AND WHO ARE NOW LIVING IN
    SEPHARAD
  WILL POSSESS THE CITIES OF THE ARID SOUTHERN PLAIN.
THE DELIVERERS WILL GO UP TO MOUNT ZION
  TO RULE MOUNT ESAU,
  AND THE KINGDOM WILL BE THE LORD'S. (Obadiah 1:1-21)

The prophecy of Obadiah is an example of an Israeli prophet receiving a prophetic word for a nation outside of Israel. In contrast with Jonah's experience where the people of Nineveh converted, Obadiah's prophecy is much heavier. It is a vivid, intense word that did not have a positive outcome.

Christian and Jewish tradition conflict on who Obadiah was and what he did in his life. What we do know is his prophecy was made in a post-exilic period, somewhere around the fifth century B.C.[2] We can also clearly see that the message of a mission may well relate to whatever is going on in a nation. This includes that which is dishonest or against God. Its goal may be to create accountability and repentance in the hearts of those who receive God's Word.

That having been said, missionaries must be very careful about what they take on as being a word from God versus an opinion or personal zeal on a particular issue. We live in a world loaded with opinions, politics, and personal convictions that can take over our influences and ideals if we think we are going to reach people and sway them to our perspective. The Prophet Obadiah did not do this. His message was one to oppressors, who were obviously oppressors, and he delivered a prophecy that ultimately promised hope to those who had been oppressed by Edom. He wasn't there to try and sway politics or become a social activist within this foreign nation. What he did was proclaim to them what was obviously wrong and what was going to happen because of that wrong.

A successful mission that bothered the missionary

THE LORD'S WORD CAME TO JONAH A SECOND TIME: "GET UP AND GO TO NINEVEH, THAT GREAT CITY, AND DECLARE AGAINST IT THE PROCLAMATION THAT I AM COMMANDING YOU." AND JONAH GOT UP AND WENT TO NINEVEH, ACCORDING TO THE LORD'S WORD. (NOW NINEVEH WAS INDEED AN ENORMOUS CITY, A THREE DAYS' WALK ACROSS.)

JONAH STARTED INTO THE CITY, WALKING ONE DAY, AND HE CRIED OUT, "JUST FORTY DAYS MORE AND NINEVEH WILL BE OVERTHROWN!" AND THE PEOPLE OF NINEVEH BELIEVED GOD. THEY PROCLAIMED A FAST AND PUT ON MOURNING CLOTHES, FROM THE GREATEST OF THEM TO THE LEAST SIGNIFICANT.

WHEN WORD OF IT REACHED THE KING OF NINEVEH, HE GOT UP FROM HIS THRONE, STRIPPED HIMSELF OF HIS ROBE, COVERED HIMSELF WITH MOURNING CLOTHES, AND SAT IN ASHES. THEN HE ANNOUNCED, "IN NINEVEH, BY DECREE OF THE KING AND HIS OFFICIALS: NEITHER HUMAN NOR ANIMAL, CATTLE NOR FLOCK, WILL TASTE ANYTHING! NO GRAZING AND NO DRINKING WATER! LET HUMANS AND ANIMALS ALIKE PUT ON MOURNING CLOTHES, AND LET THEM CALL UPON GOD FORCEFULLY! AND LET ALL PERSONS STOP THEIR EVIL BEHAVIOR AND THE VIOLENCE THAT'S UNDER THEIR CONTROL!" HE THOUGHT,

WHO KNOWS? GOD MAY SEE THIS AND TURN FROM HIS WRATH, SO THAT WE MIGHT NOT PERISH.

GOD SAW WHAT THEY WERE DOING—THAT THEY HAD CEASED THEIR EVIL BEHAVIOR. SO GOD STOPPED PLANNING TO DESTROY THEM, AND HE DIDN'T DO IT. (Jonah 3:1-10)

The story of Jonah gets me for several reasons. First, as pertains to this book, he is the most obvious and relatable story of a missionary that we have in the Old Testament. He was a prophet of Israel who was called to go beyond the comfortable borders of Israel and minister to the people of Nineveh. The call was one of repentance, because God was about to heavily judge the city due to their sins. This all sounds good and like the typical course of motion, right? Well, Jonah didn't see it that way. He was angry and hardened against the people of Nineveh and wanted them to suffer destruction for the way they treated Israel. He didn't want God to have mercy on them. That meant God sent him to complete a mission of which he had no interest. Instead of fulfilling it, Jonah went in the complete opposite direction, avoiding what God told him to do in complete disobedience.

After an encounter with God in the belly of a large fish, Jonah finally got his act together and went to Nineveh, dissatisfied but obeying God. When Nineveh repented, Jonah was angry to the point of being unreasonable. He argued with God, pouted, and waited for the destruction of the people to come, even though it never came.

Let's review: Jonah was angry because his mission was effective. We look over the other Old Testament individuals who worked in missions and the reality that much of what they did was ineffective, because the people of Israel remained in their sin, and now we have Jonah, who was angry because his mission was totally effective. It sounds weird and makes every one of us who has ever dealt with an unsuccessful mission want to pull our hair out, but Jonah raises a very important issue within missions: what happens when they turn out successful, but the overall result is not what we hoped for?

It's easy to want to judge Jonah, but I believe there's a little bit of Jonah in all of us. We have all run from assignments that were God-given because we didn't want to do them or deal with the ultimate results, and it wasn't always that the work would fail. Sometimes we just didn't want to obey God because we knew they would come together and work just the way God intended them. We always assume that doing what God asks us to do will be embraced by us readily and with excitement, but just as with anything else, God can ask some things of us that we would rather not do. We might be blessed to say yes as He calls us to go forth, but there are always going to be those tasks that bring results we could live without.

Missions bring about and bring out mixed feelings within missionaries, some of which we might never expect to feel or anticipate within our missions experience. We go into missions with an idea of what it is going to be like or feel like and despite our best successes, sometimes our sense of missions leaves us confused or bewildered, uncertain and questioning as to what we have always thought about God as true or untrue.

Jonah had his concepts of God and his experience with God because he didn't know God for himself in a way that transcended his doctrinal understanding. Jonah knew what he had been taught about God, he had some experience with God, he believed in God, and he knew what he perceived God to be, but he didn't know God, for all God is and can do. It's amazing to note how many missionaries throughout history have been stirred by doctrine, doctrinal ideas, and concepts created by men rather than a true discerning call from God. Through missions, the missionary comes face-to-face with God. This is true whether a mission seems successful as much as unsuccessful because in the process, the missionary develops a deeper sense and awareness of Who God is through their own personal experience.

Chapter 4 Summary

- From the very beginning, we see the work and desire of missions activity and purpose active and alive even before the formal foundation of God's church.

- Noah's mission was creating a new world. He navigated the waters as God purified the world. He stands as an ensign that God gives all the same chance to get right with Him.

- Ruth proves that women can do missions. Her work also proves that long-term missions involve extended dedication that many are unwilling to make.

- The first formalized group of missionaries were Levites, the Hebrew priests who worked as the spiritual leaders of Israel. They were selected due to their knowledge of the law and their status within the community. They were immersed in a world unlike their own, forced to find the balance between what they believed and how they could most effectively reach the people around them. In the end, they failed.

- A missions trip may very well be unsuccessful due to the circumstances which a missionary finds themselves immersed. We are quick to blame unsuccessful endeavors on the way things are taught or presented, but that's not always the case, and such an assertion is not always fair. Not everyone is ready to accept the Gospel, and there are several factors involved in someone's reception to God's Word.

- Missionaries carry with them the good news of the Gospel, but they also herald everything that goes along with that Gospel promise. Missionary life is not just about proclaiming salvation, but teaching people how to live with God, how to interact with Him, and about how great He is.

- Missions are important for those who are reached, but as with all things in God, the missionary should also receive insight and revelation from God in the missions process. Being brought to another region, state, nation, or even continent by God means His hand is upon the trip. Through that process, a missionary should see the hand of God.

- Israel's prophets and missionaries had a very difficult job, with many unknowns and an overall sense that while they had to do their work, in the end, they knew it would be unsuccessful.

- Missionaries need to be prepared for any response they receive. Not only that, they need to be prepared to deliver a message that while good, may not be perceived to be such.

- The Old Testament prophets were all missionaries: they were individuals called by God and sent with a specific message for a specific people. The Old Testament prophets prove that one can go on a mission and work with and among churches in the process.

- The message of a mission may well relate to whatever is going on in a nation that is dishonest or against God and may work to create accountability and repentance in the hearts of those who receive God's Word.

- Missionaries must be careful about what they take on as being a word from God versus an opinion or personal zeal. We live in a world loaded with opinions, politics, and personal convictions that can take over our ideals.

- Jonah is the most obvious and relatable story of a missionary that we have in the Old Testament. He was a prophet of Israel who was called to go beyond the comfortable borders of Israel and minister to the people of Nineveh. He was angry because his mission was effective.

- There's a little bit of Jonah in all of us. We have all run from assignments that were God-given because we didn't want to do them or deal with the ultimate results, and it wasn't always that the work would fail. Sometimes we just didn't want to obey God because we knew they would come together and work just the way God intended.

Chapter 4 Assignments

- Write an essay (5-8 sentences minimum) on what you have learned from exploring missions in the Old Testament. Which mission spoke to you most, and why?

- Create a PowerPoint or equivalent program slideshow on Missions in the Old Testament.

Missionary Mary Slessor with adopted children during her work in Nigeria (c. 1880)

CHAPTER FIVE:
MISSIONS IN THE NEW TESTAMENT

———————— ∼◟ ————————

To stay here and disobey God — I can't afford to take the consequence.
I would rather go and obey God than to stay here and know that I disobeyed.
(Amanda Berry Smith[1])

THE New Testament is missions central, especially in the essential heart of every matter that pertains to going forth with the Gospel. Most major New Testament figures classified as missionaries and are excellent inspirational examples for us in the work of missions within our own lives and ministries.

The beautiful examples we have of New Testament missions should cause us to desire to do more, to want more, to seek more out of our lives and our missions than just going somewhere, preaching, and going home. The examples we see of connection between people, churches, and the faith that inspired more than one generation of people to believe in God in a new way.

Jesus as a missionary

THE WORD [HE] WAS IN THE WORLD, AND THE WORLD WAS MADE [WAS CREATED; CAME INTO BEING] BY [THROUGH] HIM, BUT THE WORLD DID NOT KNOW [RECOGNIZE] HIM. HE CAME TO THE WORLD THAT WAS HIS OWN [OR HIS OWN COUNTRY; THAT WHICH WAS HIS OWN], BUT HIS OWN PEOPLE DID NOT ACCEPT [RECEIVE] HIM. BUT TO ALL WHO DID ACCEPT [RECEIVE] HIM AND BELIEVE IN HIM [IN HIS NAME; THE NAME INDICATING THE CHARACTER OF THE PERSON] HE GAVE THE RIGHT [POWER; AUTHORITY] TO BECOME CHILDREN OF GOD. THEY DID NOT BECOME HIS CHILDREN IN ANY HUMAN WAY [BY NATURAL DESCENT; BY PHYSICAL BIRTH; BY BLOOD]—BY ANY HUMAN PARENTS [HUMAN PASSION/DECISION; DESIRE/WILL OF THE FLESH] OR HUMAN DESIRE [A

HUSBAND'S DECISION; DESIRE/WILL OF A MAN/HUSBAND]. THEY WERE BORN OF GOD.

THE WORD BECAME A HUMAN [FLESH] AND LIVED [MADE HIS HOME; PITCHED HIS TABERNACLE; GOD'S GLORIOUS PRESENCE DWELT IN ISRAEL'S TABERNACLE IN THE WILDERNESS] AMONG US. WE SAW HIS GLORY [MAJESTY]—THE GLORY THAT BELONGS TO THE ONLY SON [ONE AND ONLY; ONLY BEGOTTEN] OF [WHO CAME FROM] THE FATHER—AND HE WAS FULL OF GRACE AND TRUTH [GOD'S GRACIOUS LOVE AND FAITHFULNESS; EX. 34:5–7]. JOHN TELLS THE TRUTH ABOUT [TESTIFIES CONCERNING; WITNESSES ABOUT] HIM AND CRIES OUT, SAYING, "THIS IS THE ONE I TOLD YOU ABOUT: 'THE ONE WHO COMES AFTER ME [IN TIME] IS GREATER THAN I AM, BECAUSE HE WAS LIVING [EXISTED] BEFORE ME [A REFERENCE TO CHRIST'S PREEXISTENCE].'"

BECAUSE HE WAS FULL OF GRACE AND TRUTH [FROM HIS FULLNESS; 1:14], FROM HIM WE ALL RECEIVED ONE GIFT AFTER ANOTHER [GRACE FOR GRACE; THIS COULD MEAN ABUNDANT GRACE OR THAT THE GRACE UNDER CHRIST REPLACED GRACE UNDER THE LAW]. THE LAW WAS GIVEN THROUGH MOSES [EX. 19–24], BUT GRACE AND TRUTH CAME THROUGH JESUS CHRIST. NO ONE HAS EVER SEEN GOD [GOD THE FATHER, WHO IS PURE SPIRIT; 4:24]. BUT GOD THE ONLY SON [GOD THE ONE AND ONLY; THE ONLY SON WHO IS HIMSELF GOD; GOD THE ONLY BEGOTTEN] IS VERY CLOSE TO [BY THE SIDE OF; CLOSE TO THE HEART OF; IN THE BOSOM OF] THE FATHER, AND HE HAS SHOWN US WHAT GOD IS LIKE [MADE HIM KNOWN]. (JOHN 1:10-18, EXB)

I ASSURE YOU THAT WE SPEAK ABOUT WHAT WE KNOW AND TESTIFY ABOUT WHAT WE HAVE SEEN, BUT YOU DON'T RECEIVE OUR TESTIMONY. IF I HAVE TOLD YOU ABOUT EARTHLY THINGS AND YOU DON'T BELIEVE, HOW WILL YOU BELIEVE IF I TELL YOU ABOUT HEAVENLY THINGS? NO ONE HAS GONE UP TO HEAVEN EXCEPT THE ONE WHO CAME DOWN FROM HEAVEN, THE HUMAN ONE. JUST AS MOSES LIFTED UP THE SNAKE IN THE WILDERNESS, SO MUST THE HUMAN ONE BE LIFTED UP SO THAT EVERYONE WHO BELIEVES IN HIM WILL HAVE ETERNAL LIFE. GOD SO LOVED THE WORLD THAT HE GAVE HIS ONLY SON, SO THAT EVERYONE WHO BELIEVES IN HIM WON'T PERISH BUT WILL HAVE ETERNAL LIFE. GOD DIDN'T SEND HIS SON INTO THE WORLD TO JUDGE THE WORLD, BUT THAT THE WORLD MIGHT BE SAVED THROUGH HIM. WHOEVER BELIEVES IN HIM ISN'T JUDGED; WHOEVER DOESN'T BELIEVE IN HIM IS ALREADY JUDGED, BECAUSE THEY DON'T BELIEVE IN THE NAME OF GOD'S ONLY SON.

"THIS IS THE BASIS FOR JUDGMENT: THE LIGHT CAME INTO THE WORLD, AND PEOPLE LOVED DARKNESS MORE THAN THE LIGHT, FOR THEIR ACTIONS ARE EVIL. ALL WHO DO WICKED THINGS HATE THE LIGHT AND DON'T COME TO THE LIGHT FOR FEAR THAT THEIR ACTIONS WILL BE EXPOSED TO THE LIGHT. WHOEVER DOES THE TRUTH COMES TO THE LIGHT SO THAT IT CAN BE SEEN THAT THEIR ACTIONS WERE DONE IN GOD." (JOHN 3:11-21)

Jesus is our Savior, our Friend, and our Redeemer. There is no question about these attributes of our Savior in keeping with His true nature as our Emmanuel. However, many do not consider Jesus' entire work in this earth as a mission. Jesus surrendered His place with the Father to come to earth and fulfill His ultimate mission of salvation. While here, Jesus Himself taught, engaged, and educated followers about relationship with God and the truth about what God wanted and needed us to know.

The purpose of Jesus' descent into this world was to show us and display for us the love of God. This was a concept that Israel experienced from time to time, but their understanding of the law changed the way that they viewed God's love. God's love became a prize, something merited and earned through obedience to the law. The Jews of Jesus' day, therefore, didn't see God as loving the entire world, but as loving only them. It didn't matter that they did not follow the law entirely or that they went through long periods of disobedience in God's sight – all that mattered to them is that they were the people who had received the law and were able to claim it.

Jesus proved to us that God loves everyone – the entire world – and that the salvation of the entire world has always been, is now, and always will be a part of God's eternal plan. Jesus opened the entire world to the first-century Jewish community who regarded itself as an isolated entity to maintain survival. Jesus' mission to proclaim and expound God's love in such a way that He literally lived it through His death. God's love became even more apparent through the resurrection, which proved to all of us that no matter how down and out someone is, no matter where they were, and no matter how long it might have been since someone died, they remain in the heart of God and in the end, death will not win.

At the heart of every mission, every work, every Gospel-oriented activity we undertake, Christ must be there, at the center of it all. We cannot preach Christ without adopting His nature in our lives that calls out to the entire world. Missionaries cannot be bigoted, angry, hostile people who use faith and religion to gain control over others or deem that a certain race or group of people is somehow inferior. God's ultimate statement to us through Christ was by love, and it is by love that all people, everywhere, may find the Father. Our purpose must be in Christ. Our calling must be in Christ. If we are to be missionaries and take on the call of going to a place that we are not from, working therein and becoming messengers of salvation, Christ must be within us and driving us from beginning to end.

Seventy sent on an early mission

AFTER THIS THE LORD APPOINTED SEVENTY OTHERS AND SENT THEM ON AHEAD OF HIM IN PAIRS TO EVERY TOWN AND PLACE WHERE HE HIMSELF INTENDED TO GO. HE SAID TO THEM, "THE HARVEST IS PLENTIFUL, BUT THE LABORERS ARE FEW; THEREFORE ASK THE LORD OF THE HARVEST TO SEND OUT LABORERS INTO HIS HARVEST. GO ON YOUR WAY. SEE, I AM SENDING YOU OUT LIKE LAMBS INTO THE MIDST OF WOLVES. CARRY NO PURSE, NO BAG, NO SANDALS; AND GREET NO ONE ON THE ROAD. WHATEVER HOUSE YOU ENTER, FIRST SAY, 'PEACE TO THIS HOUSE!' AND IF ANYONE IS THERE WHO SHARES IN PEACE, YOUR PEACE WILL REST ON THAT PERSON; BUT IF NOT, IT WILL RETURN TO YOU. REMAIN IN THE SAME HOUSE, EATING AND DRINKING WHATEVER THEY PROVIDE, FOR THE LABORER DESERVES TO BE PAID. DO NOT MOVE ABOUT FROM HOUSE TO HOUSE. WHENEVER YOU ENTER A TOWN AND ITS PEOPLE WELCOME YOU, EAT WHAT IS SET BEFORE YOU; CURE THE SICK WHO ARE THERE, AND SAY TO THEM, 'THE KINGDOM OF GOD HAS COME NEAR TO YOU.' BUT WHENEVER YOU ENTER A TOWN AND THEY DO NOT WELCOME YOU, GO OUT INTO ITS STREETS AND SAY, 'EVEN THE DUST OF YOUR TOWN THAT CLINGS TO OUR FEET, WE WIPE OFF IN PROTEST AGAINST YOU. YET KNOW THIS: THE KINGDOM OF GOD HAS COME NEAR.' I TELL YOU, ON THAT DAY IT WILL BE MORE TOLERABLE FOR SODOM THAN FOR THAT TOWN.

"WOE TO YOU, CHORAZIN! WOE TO YOU, BETHSAIDA! FOR IF THE DEEDS OF POWER DONE IN YOU HAD BEEN DONE IN TYRE AND SIDON, THEY WOULD HAVE REPENTED LONG AGO, SITTING IN SACKCLOTH AND ASHES. BUT AT THE JUDGMENT IT WILL BE MORE TOLERABLE FOR TYRE AND SIDON THAN FOR YOU. AND YOU, CAPERNAUM,

WILL YOU BE EXALTED TO HEAVEN?
NO, YOU WILL BE BROUGHT DOWN TO HADES.

"WHOEVER LISTENS TO YOU LISTENS TO ME, AND WHOEVER REJECTS YOU REJECTS ME, AND WHOEVER REJECTS ME REJECTS THE ONE WHO SENT ME."

THE SEVENTY RETURNED WITH JOY, SAYING, "LORD, IN YOUR NAME EVEN THE DEMONS SUBMIT TO US!" HE SAID TO THEM, "I WATCHED SATAN FALL FROM HEAVEN LIKE A FLASH OF LIGHTNING. SEE, I HAVE GIVEN YOU AUTHORITY TO TREAD ON SNAKES AND SCORPIONS, AND OVER ALL THE POWER OF THE ENEMY; AND NOTHING WILL HURT YOU. NEVERTHELESS, DO NOT REJOICE AT THIS, THAT THE SPIRITS SUBMIT TO YOU, BUT REJOICE THAT YOUR NAMES ARE WRITTEN IN HEAVEN." (LUKE 10:1-20, NRSV)

Jesus had a portion of the early disciples in training for leadership long before He ever died and rose again. Pentecost is the birthday of the church, but the hours of preparation prior to Pentecost provide foundation and insight into missions work for us.

In the Bible, we do see individuals sent by themselves for a task, but most of the time (especially in the New Testament) we see individuals working in teams. Luke 10 shows us this pattern clearly. The seventy were sent out in pairs, two by two, with specific instructions and purpose in their work:

- They were sent to towns and villages that He intended to visit (they did not go anywhere that was their idea, but everything was Christ's purpose and vision).

- The harvest (of souls) was plentiful, but there were only a few of them to do the job (they would feel like the work was greater than their ability to meet it, and they would feel inadequate considering the task).

- Pray for God to send able people to the harvest (prayer is an important component of missionary work; make the request that others might hear God's call and enter the work of missions).

- Go on your way (follow a specific course of movement and action, not the way that someone else thinks you should go but remaining diligent to the way you are appointed to go).

- You are sent out like lambs among wolves (people will be ready to attack and devour).

- Carry no purse, bag, or sandals (Bring only what you need, as carrying too many things leaves you susceptible to attack).

- Don't greet anyone on the road (remain focused on the task at hand; do not involve too many people in your business).

- Remain in the house that receives you (do your work where you are received; give yourself and your work some stability).

- The labor deserves his hire (when people want to give to you because they receive from your mission, receive it, whether hospitality or offering).

- Heal the sick wherever you are (work practical miracles that change the lives of those who are touched by the work, so they will be open to receiving teaching and instruction unto salvation).

- Proclaim the Kingdom of God (the Kingdom of God has come near to you, and salvation is open to all who will receive it)

- When you are not received, move on to the next place (not everyone is going to receive you).

This provides for us basic precepts of missions and ways to maximize finances, maintain our own balance and missionary function, and continue in missions for as long as possible. If a missionary is received, the individuals receive Christ; but if they reject the missionary, they reject Christ, because missionaries do not move and mobilize by their own function.

Once the Seventy returned, Jesus had further instructions for them. They were thrilled and excited by the miracles they were able to perform, but even Jesus instructed them to move away from such thinking. Why is this, and why is this important to missions?

The Seventy were not just told to go and do miracles; they were told to follow a certain pattern of instructions, perform miracles, proclaim the Kingdom, and only stay where they were received. It doesn't state the Seventy who went out were excited about anything aside from the realm of the miraculous they saw displayed among their work. In other words, they were excited about the results, but they were not as excited about the message of the Kingdom or proclaiming the Kingdom.

Today we see people I like to identify as "miracle chasers." They run from church service to church service, teaching to teaching, idea to idea, and message to message in search of that next miracle, spiritual high, or supernatural occurrence they will see. It's almost as if their belief is rooted in nothing but these experiences, and they cannot find a way to maintain or survive without seeing supernatural movements. It is fine to believe in the supernatural and to experience awe and amazement when God works the supernatural, even if it comes through us. There is no prohibition on such or on celebrating the things that God does. The problem comes in when it is all we chase after and when we hinge our entire faith on nothing but miracle chasing or seeking out supernatural manifestations. The Seventy were new at what they were doing, and it was new and exciting. They hadn't yet reached the "everyday" point where supernatural things didn't happen in their everyday life and they had to deal with the daily maintenance of church, ministry, and mission work. Jesus wanted them to be prepared for different experiences and expressions of faith. They needed to know God is with them, even if supernatural signs didn't always result.

When anyone starts out in missions, they start out with excitement. They want to do as much as possible, as quickly as possible. The temptation to handle things in a manner that brings about what are seen as immediate signs and results may quickly lead to disaster. Even in missions, God reminds us of the importance of order. He also reminds us of the importance of experience and proper training in missions activities, because to do so will lead to individuals who seek power without the proper form to establish a lasting ministry foundation in missions within a region.

Trials in missions

THEY WILL ARREST YOU, ABUSE YOU, AND THEY WILL KILL YOU. ALL NATIONS WILL HATE YOU ON ACCOUNT OF MY NAME. AT THAT TIME MANY WILL FALL AWAY. THEY WILL BETRAY EACH OTHER AND HATE EACH OTHER. MANY FALSE PROPHETS WILL APPEAR AND DECEIVE MANY PEOPLE. BECAUSE DISOBEDIENCE

WILL EXPAND, THE LOVE OF MANY WILL GROW COLD. BUT THE ONE WHO ENDURES TO THE END WILL BE DELIVERED. THIS GOSPEL OF THE KINGDOM WILL BE PROCLAIMED THROUGHOUT THE WORLD AS A TESTIMONY TO ALL THE NATIONS. THEN THE END WILL COME. (Matthew 24:9-14)

Nothing in the Bible ever gives the impression that missions work is an easy endeavor. If anything, the Bible is very clear in the fact that working in missions may very well be a difficult task that can cost someone their life, health, property, safety, or political freedom.

Matthew 24:9-14 isn't specifically about missions, but it certainly does apply to the rigors and complications of missions life. Family and friends don't always understand the call to missions, and a missionary may experience hostility before they even set foot on a foreign region or foreign soil. The Gospel is not an accepted part of every culture, and there are many nations and regions in this world that remain hostile to Gospel proclamation and missions activities. Not every missionary experiences the kind of persecution mentioned in this passage of Scripture, but at some point, every missionary will experience a certain degree of hostility as direct result of their missions activities.

Some have asked what is it about the Gospel that is so threatening. We are met with a variety of answers, but I believe the root of it lies at the fact that love is a revolutionary idea. No matter what era of history it may be, love is still threatening. It breaks down the traditional barriers put into place to defend a culture and preserve its identity. Everything unique and special about that culture has come about by its isolation, its separateness from every other nation in the world. People are afraid that opening their hearts to the Gospel is going to mean their entire worldview will change and with that will come a loss of their culture and their personal identity. The very thing that defines who they are may very well no longer be who they think they are.

Not everything about a culture is ungodly. In fact, there are many things about many cultures that are types of the relationship we should have with God and the church. God has never asked anyone to abandon every single sense of who they are and turn into other people, but that's what people automatically think happens when it is time for conversion. When we talk about being a new creature and made new, we automatically think undoing our entire identities is a part of that.

The history of missions is unfortunately dotted with people who have done just what I spoke of, making the experience of missions more difficult for subsequent missionaries. Christianity has often been associated with western society and along with the faith, the cultures and practices of missionaries a part of the teaching and indoctrination of diverse nations when coming forth with the Gospel.

Christianity did not begin in Europe or the United States. It began in the Middle East, in a culture and respective society far different from anything that we can imagine in western culture. It spread to nations in Africa, southern Europe, and India first, all of which are different than those customs that became associated with Christianity throughout the ages. Christianity is for anyone who becomes a "whosoever," anyone who is willing to transform from glory to glory and faith to faith, can do so wherever they are in the world, no matter their language, nation, or situation.

Going into the world

NOW THE ELEVEN DISCIPLES WENT TO GALILEE, TO THE MOUNTAIN WHERE JESUS TOLD THEM TO GO. WHEN THEY SAW HIM, THEY WORSHIPPED HIM, BUT SOME DOUBTED. JESUS CAME NEAR AND SPOKE TO THEM, "I'VE RECEIVED ALL AUTHORITY IN HEAVEN AND ON EARTH. THEREFORE, GO AND MAKE DISCIPLES OF ALL NATIONS, BAPTIZING THEM IN THE NAME OF THE FATHER AND OF THE SON AND OF THE HOLY SPIRIT, TEACHING THEM TO OBEY EVERYTHING THAT I'VE COMMANDED YOU. LOOK, I MYSELF WILL BE WITH YOU EVERY DAY UNTIL THE END OF THIS PRESENT AGE." (Matthew 28:18-20)

We discussed Matthew 28:16-20 and the spirituality of missions earlier, which means I am not going to spend a lot of time going over this passage again. I feel it's important to look at it briefly, considering Luke 10 and as a continuation and expansion of the commission given to the Seventy earlier in time. Instead of going to regional towns, the disciples who have remained with Jesus through to this point are given the command to go out into the world. The world is here, is there, in the immediate sense as they would have understood "the world" they believed it was the Roman Empire, for the harvest that Jesus has spoken long and hard about, and using the precepts outlined earlier in time, the disciples are ready to go out and proclaim the Gospel to the nations. Without the experiences and education of Luke 10, the disciples would not have been ready to take on the commands of Matthew 28:18-20.

Endowed with Power

THEOPHILUS, THE FIRST SCROLL I WROTE CONCERNED EVERYTHING JESUS DID AND TAUGHT FROM THE BEGINNING, RIGHT UP TO THE DAY WHEN HE WAS TAKEN UP INTO HEAVEN. BEFORE HE WAS TAKEN UP, WORKING IN THE POWER OF THE HOLY SPIRIT, JESUS INSTRUCTED THE APOSTLES HE HAD CHOSEN. AFTER HIS SUFFERING, HE SHOWED THEM THAT HE WAS ALIVE WITH MANY CONVINCING PROOFS. HE APPEARED TO THEM OVER A PERIOD OF FORTY DAYS, SPEAKING TO THEM ABOUT GOD'S KINGDOM. WHILE THEY WERE EATING TOGETHER, HE ORDERED THEM NOT TO LEAVE JERUSALEM BUT TO WAIT FOR WHAT THE FATHER HAD PROMISED. HE SAID, "THIS IS WHAT YOU HEARD FROM ME: JOHN BAPTIZED WITH WATER, BUT IN ONLY A FEW DAYS YOU WILL BE BAPTIZED WITH THE HOLY SPIRIT."

AS A RESULT, THOSE WHO HAD GATHERED TOGETHER ASKED JESUS, "LORD, ARE YOU GOING TO RESTORE THE KINGDOM TO ISRAEL NOW?"

JESUS REPLIED, "IT ISN'T FOR YOU TO KNOW THE TIMES OR SEASONS THAT THE FATHER HAS SET BY HIS OWN AUTHORITY. RATHER, YOU WILL RECEIVE POWER WHEN THE HOLY SPIRIT HAS COME UPON YOU, AND YOU WILL BE MY WITNESSES IN JERUSALEM, IN ALL JUDEA AND SAMARIA, AND TO THE END OF THE EARTH." (Acts 1:1-8)

Before the Pentecost experience, Jesus had a meeting with the eleven remaining apostles. These were not the only apostles in the Bible, but the first ones who followed Jesus throughout the duration of His earthly ministry. The fact that He was speaking exclusively to leaders who were going to be a foundational aspect of the church's work is most relevant, because it shows the nature of leadership in missions. Even though many think of missionary activity as a work that is for evangelists, the foundation of missions falls into the hands of apostles and prophets, as these two offices form the very foundation of the church (Ephesians 2:20-21).

Once again, Jesus appeared to those He'd taught from the beginning to give further instruction. He didn't just prove He was alive, but for forty days He met with them and taught them revelatory things about God's Kingdom. The first-century Christian leaders were not without training, nor were they without proper instruction. Jesus did not just hand them a Bible and hope they would understand its contents on their own. They were thoroughly equipped, purposed, and educated, and then He told them to wait.

The promise of the baptism of the Holy Spirit, which was poured out at Pentecost, is an intimate and essential aspect of proper missions understanding. Anyone can go with a textbook in hand to a community they've never been before and try to indoctrinate the people who live in that area. Without the Holy Spirit, true conversion cannot take place and all someone is doing is transfer information in a dead manner.

The Spirit and belief in the Spirit's activity is a must if anyone wants to work in missions, because without it, the guidance of God is missing. The direction to be led into all truth (John 16:13), hear from God about where to go and what to do when you are there, and the essence of our faith all stem from a proper and lasting move in the Holy Spirit, saturated unto the fire baptism that shall ignite our desire to do more and share the greatness of God with others.

A transient evangelist

THOSE WHO HAD BEEN SCATTERED MOVED ON, PREACHING THE GOOD NEWS ALONG THE WAY. PHILIP WENT DOWN TO A CITY IN SAMARIA AND BEGAN TO PREACH CHRIST TO THEM. THE CROWDS WERE UNITED BY WHAT THEY HEARD PHILIP SAY AND THE SIGNS THEY SAW HIM PERFORM, AND THEY GAVE HIM THEIR UNDIVIDED ATTENTION. WITH LOUD SHRIEKS, UNCLEAN SPIRITS CAME OUT OF MANY PEOPLE, AND MANY WHO WERE PARALYZED OR CRIPPLED WERE HEALED. THERE WAS GREAT REJOICING IN THAT CITY.

BEFORE PHILIP'S ARRIVAL, A CERTAIN MAN NAMED SIMON HAD PRACTICED SORCERY IN THAT CITY AND BAFFLED THE PEOPLE OF SAMARIA. HE CLAIMED TO BE A GREAT PERSON. EVERYONE, FROM THE LEAST TO THE GREATEST, GAVE HIM THEIR UNDIVIDED ATTENTION AND REFERRED TO HIM AS "THE POWER OF GOD CALLED GREAT." HE HAD THEIR ATTENTION BECAUSE HE HAD BAFFLED THEM WITH SORCERY FOR A LONG TIME. AFTER THEY CAME TO BELIEVE PHILIP, WHO PREACHED THE GOOD NEWS ABOUT GOD'S KINGDOM AND THE NAME OF JESUS CHRIST, BOTH MEN AND WOMEN WERE BAPTIZED. EVEN SIMON HIMSELF CAME TO BELIEVE AND WAS BAPTIZED. AFTERWARD, HE BECAME ONE OF PHILIP'S SUPPORTERS. AS HE SAW FIRSTHAND THE SIGNS AND GREAT MIRACLES THAT WERE HAPPENING, HE WAS ASTONISHED. (Acts 8:1-13)

Yes, it is true that the foundation of missions work is found in the apostles and prophets, but the evangelists are not without mention of their missions work. It is the zeal and enthusiasm of evangelists that inject life into any missions situation.

The Bible only mentions one evangelist by name, and that is Philip. Philip is the main figure in Acts 8, the second part of which we will discuss in the next chapter. What we see of the work of Philip is an intense desire to move forward, going varied places to preach Christ. He was so effective and persuasive in his method, the crowds listened to him with undivided attention.

The major aspect of missions work we should pay attention to in the work of Philip is the balance between signs and wonders and instruction. As was said earlier, we cannot do missions work properly without the Holy Spirit. We recognize the Spirit's activity through miracles and wonders that cannot be explained by means of this side of heaven, but we still are not to a place where we receive the work of the Holy Spirit through teaching. The Evangelist Philip displayed a balance in his workings; they were not all one way or the other. Such a balance proves life is found within the work and opens the door for hearts and minds to be changed as God does what only God can do best in a missionary setting.

The Gospel is for everyone

SPEAKING COURAGEOUSLY, PAUL AND BARNABAS SAID, "WE HAD TO SPEAK GOD'S WORD TO YOU FIRST. SINCE YOU REJECT IT AND SHOW THAT YOU ARE UNWORTHY TO RECEIVE ETERNAL LIFE, WE WILL TURN TO THE GENTILES. THIS IS WHAT THE LORD COMMANDED US:

I HAVE MADE YOU A LIGHT FOR THE GENTILES,
SO THAT YOU COULD BRING SALVATION TO THE END OF THE EARTH."

WHEN THE GENTILES HEARD THIS, THEY REJOICED AND HONORED THE LORD'S WORD. EVERYONE WHO WAS APPOINTED FOR ETERNAL LIFE BELIEVED, AND THE LORD'S WORD WAS BROADCAST THROUGHOUT THE ENTIRE REGION. HOWEVER, THE JEWS PROVOKED THE PROMINENT WOMEN AMONG THE GENTILE GOD-WORSHIPPERS, AS WELL AS THE CITY'S LEADERS. THEY INSTIGATED OTHERS TO HARASS PAUL AND BARNABAS, AND THREW THEM OUT OF THEIR DISTRICT. PAUL AND BARNABAS SHOOK THE DUST FROM THEIR FEET AND WENT TO ICONIUM. BECAUSE OF THE ABUNDANT PRESENCE OF THE HOLY

SPIRIT IN THEIR LIVES, THE DISCIPLES WERE OVERFLOWING WITH HAPPINESS.
(Acts 13:46-52)

The writings and work of the Apostle Paul are so well-known, we don't think much about what he did or how revolutionary it was. We take for granted that his writings are in the Bible, and we take for granted the way in which his ministry shaped the early church. The Apostle Paul's writings are among the earliest of Christian documents to circulate through the church, and much of what he wrote is older than the Gospel accounts themselves. His outlook, thoughts, ideas, leadership, and most of all, spiritual inspiration, were largely influential in the shape of the church and the way people viewed church, what it was, and how it functioned.

The reason so many people are drawn to the writings of the Apostle Paul is because of their inclusive nature. The Apostle Paul is a bit of an intrigue because we know so little about him and so much of his advice and words spark controversy and questions about his own life experiences and perspectives. What we do know about the Apostle Paul is that in his upbringing, he had a Jewish mother and a Roman father, meaning his own background most likely had integrated elements in it. He had been raised as a Jew but was exposed to paganism and diverse Gentile culture, thus poising him to be educated enough, open enough, and purposed enough to speak in such a manner that would interest Gentiles.

A tour through social media online sees numerous individuals with dotted, lofty claims of being "called to the nations." What this meant within a Biblical sense was doing the work of the Apostle Paul, being called to nations beyond Israel. Some of what we have already discussed expresses why this was such a radical idea: Israel was trying to maintain its identity, and it was shutting everyone else out in the process. Yet "being called to the nations" did not mean that one was a celebrity; it meant that one was a dedicated missionary, focused and dedicated on developing the church and strengthening churches already founded throughout the world. It signified not being exclusive to Judaism but being about nations beyond that of Israel.

The term "called to the nations" doesn't have an application for those who are not natively Jewish, because the immediate understanding was a separation of Jew and Gentile, not celebrity. It also is inappropriate to say one is "called to the nations" and use it to mean you are not called to minister to the church but to the unsaved, because the identity of being "called to the nations" had nothing to do with being born in church. The church was what those of the nations were called to belong, and to imply that there is something inherently wrong with church involvement or identity is counterproductive to the work of missions and the concept of being called.

This means every time someone claims to be "called to the nations" and they can't even name a nation other than their own or that they are using the term to indicate they are called to have a big ministry or think they will be visible to people all over the world...they have truly missed the point.

Last days missions

THEN I SAW ANOTHER ANGEL FLYING HIGH OVERHEAD WITH ETERNAL GOOD NEWS TO PROCLAIM TO THOSE WHO LIVE ON EARTH, AND TO EVERY NATION, TRIBE, LANGUAGE, AND PEOPLE. HE SAID IN A LOUD VOICE, "FEAR GOD AND GIVE HIM GLORY, FOR THE HOUR OF HIS JUDGMENT HAS COME. WORSHIP THE ONE WHO MADE HEAVEN AND EARTH, THE SEA AND SPRINGS OF WATER."

THEN I LOOKED, AND THERE WAS A WHITE CLOUD. ON THE CLOUD WAS SEATED SOMEONE WHO LOOKED LIKE THE HUMAN ONE. HE HAD A GOLD CROWN ON HIS HEAD AND A SHARP SICKLE IN HIS HAND. ANOTHER ANGEL CAME OUT OF THE TEMPLE, CALLING IN A LOUD VOICE TO THE ONE SEATED ON THE CLOUD: "USE YOUR SICKLE TO REAP THE HARVEST, FOR THE TIME TO HARVEST HAS COME, AND THE HARVEST OF THE EARTH IS RIPE." SO THE ONE SEATED ON THE CLOUD SWUNG HIS SICKLE OVER THE EARTH, AND THE EARTH WAS HARVESTED. (Revelation 14:6-7, 14-16)

The purpose of this book is not to drone on and on about various theories as pertain to the end times or the book of Revelation. There's enough available if one is interested in exploring that topic, so we won't be getting into those specifics in here. What we will look at is the missions-themed nature of Revelation, which is frequently overlooked in end times fervor.

The book of Revelation is not just a detailing of last days prophecy (although it does depend on what your definition of "last days" is and how that fits in with the experience of and revelation of the church. Revelation contains great insight into the nature and history of the church, showing it as the fulfillment of specific prophetic entity, unto itself, purposed and ready to do the work of God in a hostile world that is often unwilling to embrace it.

The term "angel" is often used to refer to a spiritual being that serves as a messenger of God, otherworldly in nature that can assume human form. This is not the only way that the term is used, however. Throughout the New Testament, "angel" was used to refer to apostles and church leaders (2 Corinthians 8:23, Revelation 1:20) because they were messengers of the Gospel. The parallels are obvious: those who are called to share the good news are sent as messengers, but before they are messengers themselves, they receive the message.

That's just what we see in Revelation 14: the angel coming with eternal good news to proclaim that news to everyone on earth. The underlying message is the glory of God, and the larger message is that the "harvest is ripe" and the time to harvest is now. We could literalize these events and see them through the lens of literal apocalypticism where a giant sickle comes down to harvest the world's largest crop, or we could see it in parallel with earlier Biblical passages that see the Gospel going forth to every nation, with God's workers eager and ready to collect the harvest that is now due.

Right up until the end of the church as we understand it, the Bible shows forth missionary activity and interest in spreading the Gospel. Until the time comes when Jesus returns, there will always be people God calls to do the work of missions and to take the Gospel to distant places so the Kingdom of God will continue to grow.

Chapter 5 Summary

- Jesus' entire work on this earth was a mission, from beginning to end. He proves that God loves everyone – the entire world – and that the salvation of the entire world has always been a part of God's eternal plan. At the heart of every mission we undertake, Christ must be there. We cannot preach Christ without adopting His nature in our lives that calls out to the entire world.

- By looking at Jesus' training of the Seventy, we can find a proper model for missions preparation and conduct for ministers, even today.

- Even in missions, God reminds us of the importance of order. He also reminds us of the importance of experience and proper training in missions activities.

- Nothing in the Bible gives the impression that missions work is easy. If anything, the Bible is very clear in the fact that working in missions may very well be a difficult task that can cost someone their life, health, property, safety, or political freedom. No matter what era of history it may be, love is still threatening. It breaks down the traditional barriers put into place to defend a culture and preserve its identity.

- Christianity has often been associated with western society and along with the faith, the cultures and practices of missionaries a part of the teaching and indoctrination of diverse nations when coming forth with the Gospel. Christianity began in the Middle East, in a culture and respective society far different from anything that we can imagine in western culture. It spread to nations in Africa, southern Europe, and India first, all of which are different than those customs that became associated with Christianity throughout the ages.

- Christianity is for anyone who becomes a "whosoever," no matter their language, nation, or situation. The world is here for the harvest; using the precepts outlined earlier, disciples are ready to go out and proclaim the Gospel to the nations.

- The foundation of missions falls into the hands of apostles and prophets, as these two offices form the very foundation of the church.

- The promise of the baptism of the Holy Spirit, which was poured out at Pentecost, is an intimate and essential aspect of proper missions understanding. Without the Holy Spirit, true conversion cannot take place.

- It is the zeal and enthusiasm of evangelists that inject life into any missions situation.

- The term "called to the nations" doesn't have an application for those who are not natively Jewish, because the immediate understanding was a separation of Jew and Gentile, not celebrity. It also is inappropriate to say one is "called to the nations" and use it to mean you are not called to minister to the church but to the unsaved, because the identity of being "called to the nations" had nothing to do with being born in church. The church was what those of the nations were called to belong, and to imply that there is something inherently wrong with church involvement or identity is counterproductive to the work of missions and the concept of being called.

- The term "angel" is often used to refer to a spiritual being that serves as a messenger of God, otherworldly in nature that can assume human form. This is not the only way that the term is used, however. Throughout the New Testament, "angel" was used to refer to apostles and church leaders (2 Corinthians 8:23, Revelation 1:20) because they were messengers of the Gospel. The parallels are obvious: those who are called to share the good news are sent as messengers, but before they are messengers themselves, they receive the message.

Chapter 5 Assignments

- Write an essay (5-8 sentences minimum) on the nature of Christ in light of missions. How was Christ's work a mission? How does Jesus Christ reveal to every missionary the heart of missions? How can you work to achieve a better sense of Christ's mission in your own missions?

- Write a summary report (3-5 sentences) on a nation that interests you. Looking at the church from their perspective, what would you say is their reception to the Gospel? Do you think they would be ready to receive the Gospel, or not? How would you, as a missionary, address this?

Image from Seven Years in Celon: Stories of Mission Life (1890)

CHAPTER SIX:
THE EPHESIANS 4:11 MINISTRY AND MISSIONS

———————————⌇⌇———————————

I believe that in each generation God has called enough men and women to evangelize
all the yet unreached tribes of the earth. It is not God who does not call.
It is man who will not respond!
(Isobel Kuhn[1])

THE evangelist is typically depicted as the worker of missions. We think about evangelists as the ones who go forth into the highways and byways, doing the work of conversion in the world. This is not an untrue concept of evangelist work, except for one fact: evangelists do not do their work alone. The work of missions requires teamwork from the entire Ephesians 4:11 ministry, all working together, all providing their necessary gifts and function to transform the work and fully equip each missions community or church that grows out of their establishments.

Contrary to popular belief, the church cannot survive with leadership that only consists of pastors and evangelists. We need the full Ephesians 4:11 ministry for the church to be all it is destined to be. This allows everyone's needs to be met. When we apply this to missions, it is most essential the Ephesians 4:11 ministries also steps up, ready and interested in the spread of the Gospel worldwide.

There's no question that ministry is expensive and it's easy to drown in the issues and problems that ministers face, especially if they deal with financial and membership complications. Doing the work of ministry is never easy. Dealing with the day-to-day ins and outs of it can mean we sometimes forget about missions and about the universal church.

If you are in leadership, at some point in time the Lord will, most likely, speak to your heart about missions. It might be to go on a mission, learn more about missions, or to support them, but God will open your vision to include missions as a part of your interest and purpose. If you are called, you are here for a destined work, and seeing your own work in missions insight will help you and those in your ministry care to develop a deeper sense of God and of the church universal, no matter where you are.

Why seeing the Ephesians 4:11 ministry in missions is important

HE GAVE SOME APOSTLES, SOME PROPHETS, SOME EVANGELISTS, AND SOME PASTORS AND TEACHERS. HIS PURPOSE WAS TO EQUIP GOD'S PEOPLE FOR THE WORK OF SERVING AND BUILDING UP THE BODY OF CHRIST UNTIL WE ALL REACH THE UNITY OF FAITH AND KNOWLEDGE OF GOD'S SON. GOD'S GOAL IS FOR US TO BECOME MATURE ADULTS—TO BE FULLY GROWN, MEASURED BY THE STANDARD OF THE FULLNESS OF CHRIST. AS A RESULT, WE AREN'T SUPPOSED TO BE INFANTS ANY LONGER WHO CAN BE TOSSED AND BLOWN AROUND BY EVERY WIND THAT COMES FROM TEACHING WITH DECEITFUL SCHEMING AND THE TRICKS PEOPLE PLAY TO DELIBERATELY MISLEAD OTHERS. INSTEAD, BY SPEAKING THE TRUTH WITH LOVE, LET'S GROW IN EVERY WAY INTO CHRIST, WHO IS THE HEAD. THE WHOLE BODY GROWS FROM HIM, AS IT IS JOINED AND HELD TOGETHER BY ALL THE SUPPORTING LIGAMENTS. THE BODY MAKES ITSELF GROW IN THAT IT BUILDS ITSELF UP WITH LOVE AS EACH ONE DOES ITS PART. (Ephesians 4:11-16)

Our understanding of the Ephesians 4:11 ministry and its relevance is directly related to the way in which we view leadership and the way that leadership interacts within the church. If we do not see the fullness of the Ephesians 4:11 ministry present in church, we do not have a teachable image of the work of Christ, living and active, in our church world today.

In Christ, we find the entire Ephesians 4:11 ministry. Jesus was an apostle, prophet, evangelist, pastor, and teacher (Matthew 10:41, Matthew 12:38, Matthew 13:57, Luke 4:14-21, John 10:11-14, Hebrews 3:1). None of us are all five ministry gifts in one at the same time, because that would mean we are Jesus. Instead, God created us to live interdependently: relying on Jesus and relying on the work of the Body to survive in connection with each project we undertake. It is a part of both being the Body of Christ, building up His nature and identity within all of us, and adopting His character within each one of us. This tells us a few important things about how God works:

- Yes, there are miracles, but most of the time, God works as we work together. It works in this way because God expects us all to grow in our likeness to become more like Him.

- God does not just work on His own, but He also works through each one of us.

- We must live in total obedience to God to see the results of God manifest.

- The church is held to a higher standard. That means as much as signs and wonders are part of our faith, as we grow, we may not see them in the same way we did at the beginning.

- Faith is an essential aspect of our trust in God, because we trust He will move on our behalf through someone else, as necessary.

It is the Ephesians 4:11 ministry that brings a sense of order and leadership to the church to oversee these different matters and make sure things function properly. Ephesians 4 outlines the following facets of five-fold work:

- **Reach the unity of the faith:** The unity of the faith meets the conditions found earlier in Ephesians 4, namely different doctrinal points that unite us together as a church. It is more than just saying we believe in certain things; it is understanding them to the point of walking them out in life and seeing the way that the basics of faith unite believers. They unite us because if we apply them properly, we can set ourselves aside and consider the good of the Body within the will of God rather than our own personal interests and desires.

- **Knowledge of the Son of God:** We can talk about Jesus as an historical figure, or even a concept, but true knowledge of the Son of God is knowing Him for ourselves, knowing Who He is, knowing what He is, and knowing how He has the power to change our lives. It is knowing Christ; living our lives with

Him and understanding Him in a way that we can live out, every day.

- **Grow to maturity:** Growing up is not a pleasant process in a natural sense. We must go through many uncomfortable and difficult stages that push us to our physical and mental limits. Growing in maturity as a church is no different. We bring a bunch of people together who, on the surface, have nothing in common. They come from different backgrounds, ethnicities, languages, countries, and circumstances. It's expected that their differences will bring about growth and change within them. It too, is a painful process. Not everyone gets along, not everyone likes each other, but something in this big jumble reveals to each of us what we need to change, who we are as people, what we need to do different, and how we need to develop more of who we are and claim to be in Christ. We are to grow up as part of being in church, not maintain comforts.

- **Protecting the church from false teaching:** False teaching camouflages as something we've always wanted, needed, or desired to hear. Satan gives us just enough of what we want to get us away from where we need to be. Through proper instruction, the Ephesians 4:11 ministry equips the church to avoid tempting pitfalls found in false teaching.

- **Speak the truth in love:** Speaking the truth in love is the difference between speaking a hard truth and just saying something in a hard manner. If we speak the truth in love, that means we stop trying to flatter and hurt others with our words. Before you automatically assume this is something you've never done, step back, be real with yourself, and think again. We've all flattered someone to get our way. We've all used the truth as a weapon to hurt someone else or win a "right fight." Every one of us has had the personal intention to make sure we feel superior as we get our point across to others. Using a concept of truth is the antithesis of truth. If truth exists to set us free, it does not exist to be used as a weapon to try and offend people. Truth is hard enough, which is why we are called to speak truth in love, and to word things in a manner that do not deliberately offend others. If leaders learn how to do this, then those who follow us will see more of Christ at work and will learn the proper way to interact and share the truth with others.

- **Growing every way into Christ:** This reiterates the principle of growing into maturity. We don't just grow up; we grow up in every way into Christ. When proper maturity is displayed among a leader, those who follow that leader can see Christ in that leader. The same is true of any member of the church. When people display proper maturity, they give those around them the chance to see Christ at work within them.

The work of the Ephesians 4:11 ministry is more than a commodity in missions; it is a necessity. For any church, anywhere in the world, to function as it should, we need to make sure the Ephesians 4:11 ministry has a presence in some way. To ignore the five-fold is to ignore the complete picture of Christ's leadership, a gift to the Body, and it is also to our own detriment. If the Ephesians 4:11 offices function fully, we will see far less conflict and issues among churches on the mission field because they will have the right teaching, leadership, and yes, even support to continue through the missions process, from start to finish, and beyond.

Apostle

I WAS APPOINTED A MESSENGER, APOSTLE, AND TEACHER OF THIS GOOD NEWS. THIS IS ALSO WHY I'M SUFFERING THE WAY I DO, BUT I'M NOT ASHAMED. I KNOW THE ONE IN WHOM I'VE PLACED MY TRUST. I'M CONVINCED THAT GOD IS POWERFUL ENOUGH TO PROTECT WHAT HE HAS PLACED IN MY TRUST UNTIL THAT DAY. (2 Timothy 1:11-12)

- **Spiritual call:** Reveal the mysteries of God

- **Spiritual purpose:** Establish the foundation of the church

- **Social call:** Reconciliation/diversity

Many talk about the role of the apostle in the modern church as one of "setting order." This is usually in the application of personal behavior, whereby apostles become gigantic pains in everyone's behind about what is right or wrong from a personal perspective. We have this concept of apostles today because they are often stepping in to church settings where churches are already established and functioning in some semblance but are not necessarily structured properly. The concept of an apostle in the modern church is almost of a big pastor, somewhat resembling bishopric oversight, in which they adopt a certain tone in each setting that harps on needed changes, sets leaders on a certain straightened course, and make general statements about the state of the church today.

There's one problem with this image, however, and it's that it isn't what apostles do if we examine Scripture. There is nothing wrong with apostles handling what needs to be handled, nor is there anything wrong with apostles working to set order when it is needed. This is not the primary work of the apostle, however. If we stick apostolic mindset into this narrow realm of thinking, apostles will never venture out to do much else. The way that apostles interact and they are called to function, the apostle's work is not established to go into pre-existing establishments and try to fix what is wrong with all of them. This is not to say apostles cannot do this, or that apostles should never do this, because we do see apostles working to maintain the church in the New Testament. They did deal with issues of order, and they did correct others. The center of what the apostle does, however, doesn't relate to personal issues; it relates to structure, and to the founding and needed structure to establish a functioning church. Apostles are not just here to fix messy churches; they are here to provide a foundation of the church, to work that foundation along with the prophet, and to put in place all that will build up a solid church structure.

The question remains: how is this accomplished? The word "apostle" literally means "one who is sent." According to the Scriptures, the apostle's work is twofold: reveal the mysteries of God (1 Corinthians 4:1-2) and establish the foundation of the church (Ephesians 2:20). The apostle's work is to implement structure in each church. Apostles teach, train, establish, and install leaders in every congregation; this is the apostle's specific work (Acts 2:42, 1 Corinthians 4:17, 1 Corinthians 12:28, Philippians 2:22, 1 Timothy 1:18). Apostles are a universal authority. They have been given authority in the universal church and have that authority wherever they go. They can handle matters as apply to the church, anywhere those issues may arise, whether or not they have founded that church themselves (Revelation 1:4). (A side note: This does not mean apostolic leaders go around, telling everyone where it's at and what everyone should do all the time. A part of spiritual maturity is learning when it is appropriate to do certain things and when it is not). The apostle serves as God's ambassador, or sorts, representing the cause of the Gospel wherever they go.

The original New Testament missionaries were all apostles. We do not see a single instance of an apostle who didn't do something, engage somewhere, or mobilize themselves for the spread of the church. The fact that the New Testament letters speak constantly of visits, correspondences in absence, and reminders of time spent together prove that apostles are called to be engaged in missions, active and involved in the world around them and with those people who become a part of the work of the church. Apostles are clearly the administrators of the church, as they ensure local and regional church leadership to be properly equipped for their work, and see to it that no church lacks substantial teaching or spiritual understanding (1 Timothy 4:1-9, 1 Timothy 5:22, 2 Timothy 1:6, Hebrews 6:2, 2 Peter 1:12-21, 2 Peter 2:1-22).

In their social call and purpose, the apostle's work relates to the spiritual call of reconciliation (2 Corinthians 5:11-21). This puts apostles at the forefront of social diversity, having the ability to work with diverse and different groups of people, adopting and understanding language, making the Gospel practical and applicable to a wide audience, having the ability to teach and interact with those who are not familiar to them, and embracing others because reconciliation is not just between us and God, it is also between all of us, one to another, makes the work of the apostle essential and purposed in missions (1 Corinthians 9:19-23).

Apostles must be on the forefront of missions activity because they are sent by God with an essential purpose for the founding of churches, especially in areas where churches have never existed or where churches do not seem able to sustain themselves. Establishing right leadership, proper structure, and right teaching goes a long way to ensure a long-term connectivity that will go beyond an initial trip or mission duration.

Some ways that apostles might work in missions with foundational authority include church founding and establishment; establishment and instruction through leadership institute, school, seminary, or training; cover of ministries, where leaders are mentored and developed; missions training organizations; doctrinal establishment and instruction; and media outreach.

Prophet

IN THE DAYS WHEN THE SEVENTH ANGEL BLOWS HIS TRUMPET, GOD'S MYSTERIOUS PURPOSE WILL BE ACCOMPLISHED, FULFILLING THE GOOD NEWS HE GAVE TO HIS SERVANTS THE PROPHETS. (Revelation 10:7)

- **Spiritual call:** Speak God's words in the earth

- **Spiritual purpose:** Establish the foundation of the church

- **Social call:** Repentance/justice

Our concept of a prophet today is someone who goes from church to church, speaking a word of knowledge or word of wisdom over people. Sometimes we might associate a prophet with someone who speaks great or grand social prophecies over a country, such as predicting a future president or a few general, sweeping, vague words that predict failure, grandeur, fortune, or destruction over a group of people or a nation. It doesn't seem to matter to us if the words of these so-called individuals happen, or they don't. People seem to throng to the modern idea of a prophet, hanging on to their words and defending them even if their prophecies are wrong.

This has led to a complete rush of disregard for prophets. People who are not a part of the false prophet groupies are critical, suspicious, and negative toward the concept of prophecy in the earth. This has convinced many that the gifts have ceased, and even if they believed them relevant at one time, so many false prophets have led them to believe prophecy is for another era.

The irony of the mess that the prophetic office has become comes down to one word: order. When people talk about needing "order" in the church, the office to set that order within the church, calling out needed repentance and addressing essential issues spoken from God's revelation is technically the prophet. This erosion of the prophet's authority has left true prophets with the complication of trying to operate true ministry, find places of refuge as well as acceptance, and driven them underground for fear of being associated with false prophets.

This is a terrible shame because prophecy is one of the most powerful aspects of church life and mission work, and trying to do church and missions without prophecy leads to undirected work that might lack true direction. At some point in every mission, a true prophet with a true vision and the true ability to hear from God should be a part of mission work.

Ephesians 2:20 tells us that both the apostle and the prophet create the foundation of the church. The apostle's work is more administrative, while the prophet's is more spiritual. The two offices present a powerful balance between losing sight of vision and maintaining spirituality as the church is structured and built. The basic work of a prophet is to deliver God's message to His people and can explain and discern all matters that relate to prophecy (Revelation 10:9-11). While being able to give a word of knowledge or a word of wisdom is most definitely a wonderful thing, both gifts are a part of the believer's gifts, and not specific to the work of a prophet. In other words, if you are relying on or hoping that someone's ability to give "word" makes them a prophet, you are mistaken. Prophets bring the voice of God to the structure and authority in the church, and that sets a certain level of order (Amos 3:7, 1 Corinthians 14:36-40, Ephesians 3:5). The work of the prophet brings a spiritual quality and purpose to all the church does, keeping it from becoming too much of an institution and maintaining its important spiritual nature (Ezekiel 2:1-10, Hosea 12:10). The prophet also discerns spirits present within people and the church, as a whole (1 Corinthians 14:31-32, 1 John 4:1-3).

In their leadership work, prophets train other prophets. They teach the necessary intimacy with God required to properly identify the voice of God as they go through different changes, seasons, and times in their lives (1 Samuel 19:18-24). Prophets have the unique challenge of maintaining their understanding of God's voice, developing a deeper sense of who He is and what He reveals. Like the apostle, prophets are also universal authorities, which must be operated and exercised with discernment (Ephesians 2:19-21).

In their social call and purpose, the prophet's work relates to the importance of justice, both in a spiritual and social sense (Psalm 17:2, Psalm 35:24, Jeremiah 5:5, Amos 5:24). Prophets should be deeply interested in the injustices that exist in the world, especially those perpetrated by individuals in the church. They have a keen sense of suffering and know that true Kingdom mindset and application are the only way to correct and fix the injustices in this world. Coupled with a sense of justice calls individuals to repentance. True prophets call out injustices when they see them and recognize that the root of such things is idolatry, selfishness, abandonment of faith, and demonic influence on the world.

The work of a prophet is necessary for missions because they speak on behalf of God. A prophet can assess spiritual need in a region, the spirits and strongholds present over a nation or regional group and can deliver the needed word to address the injustices and issues present therein. The prophet's unique spiritual voice can bring the vision of a group to fulfillment and fruition. It also goes without saying that the work of a prophet can provide insight and direction to a missions team and can also establish the foundation for prophetic work within a missions region, to equip those who live in that area to continue prophetic work after the prophet is gone.

Some ways that prophets might work in missions with foundational authority include prophetic interpretation and Biblical explanation; establishment and instruction through prophetic leadership institute, school of the prophets, seminary, or training; cover of ministries, where prophetic leaders are mentored and developed; media outreach; and doctrinal clarification.

Evangelist

THE LORD GOD'S SPIRIT IS UPON ME,
   BECAUSE THE LORD HAS ANOINTED ME.
HE HAS SENT ME
   TO BRING GOOD NEWS TO THE POOR,
   TO BIND UP THE BROKENHEARTED,
   TO PROCLAIM RELEASE FOR CAPTIVES,
     AND LIBERATION FOR PRISONERS,
   TO PROCLAIM THE YEAR OF THE LORD'S FAVOR
     AND A DAY OF VINDICATION FOR OUR GOD,
   TO COMFORT ALL WHO MOURN,
   TO PROVIDE FOR ZION'S MOURNERS,
   TO GIVE THEM A CROWN IN PLACE OF ASHES,
   OIL OF JOY IN PLACE OF MOURNING,
   A MANTLE OF PRAISE IN PLACE OF DISCOURAGEMENT. (Isaiah 61:1-3)

- **Spiritual call:** Make Christ known to all men

- **Spiritual purpose:** Preach Christ

- **Social call:** Redemption/mercy

I've already stated that when we think of missions, we automatically think of evangelists. Because evangelists are associated with preaching work (even though most individuals in the Ephesians 4:11 ministry also preach), we think preaching is what it takes to start a church and convince others who have never heard about God.

Even though the term "evangelist" is far from foreign in most church vernacular, it's a true shame that we don't really understand what evangelists do or the importance of the evangelist in the church. Many consider evangelists to be the first stop up the ladder of the Ephesians 4:11 ministry, only a starting point to ministry work. This is untrue, and it demeans the work of the evangelist in many ways. If people think the evangelist is nothing more than a starting point for ministry, they aren't going to treat it as a unique work among the five-fold that has a unique purpose.

Contrary to this popular belief, the work of an evangelist is not something everyone in the Ephesians 4:11 ministry can do, nor does it exist as a ministerial steppingstone. Evangelists are also not just people who go around to different churches to preach, although there is nothing wrong with an evangelist preaching at a church. Evangelists are different from apostles in level of authority, but they do preach and work beyond the borders of local churches.

The work of the Ephesians 4:11 offices proves that the evangelist cannot do their work alone. The "Christ bearer" of the Ephesians 4:11 ministry has the duty to carry the Gospel to the world, especially to the non-believer or an individual who lives separated from God (Acts 8:5-6, Acts 8:27-40). In doing their work, it is their goal to make Christ real through the power of preaching and to bring individuals to a place where they desire to join His Body, the church (Acts 8:10-12). The evangelist has a scope of universal authority, but they do not have formalized church authority. This means they are not superior to local or universal authorities but operate a parallel position to such that it helps the growth and management of the church (Isaiah 61:1-3). Evangelists can work independently, but they are still accountable to the church, to their own personal leadership and to those ministries they send individuals to belong or join, as those individuals are being equipped for their participation in a ministry (2 Timothy 4:5).

We could say that an evangelist oversees the souls of the unsaved or are otherwise lost, of those who need a pointing in the right direction, toward God and His Kingdom. This is an important part of missions, especially in areas where no church or formalized ministry exists. Evangelists need to go into these locations, along with others of the five-fold, and preach, reach out to, and minister to locals in that area, both as a group or one-on-one, expounding the way of truth and preparing hearts as they receive salvation and prepare for church participation.

In their social call and purpose, the evangelist's work relates to the importance of redemption in the practical application of mercy (Matthew 5:7, Matthew 9:13, Luke 1:50-58, Luke 10:37). Mercy is an important precept and an important part of salvation, and it's unfortunate that in the hardness of trying to preach against sin, many evangelists lose sight of their call to mercy and to walk with a heart of mercy. Through redemption, we find mercy, which is something we neither merit nor deserve, but find through our relationship with God. When it comes to working with non-believers and individuals who aren't right with God, mercy is a central tenant and feel they must have from those who convey the Gospel. Anyone can come with a hammer and use the Bible to make endless points about doing wrong, but it takes a true heart for the Gospel, a true spiritual insight, to make the mercy of God real and living through one's ministry.

The work of an evangelist is necessary for missions because Christ is the very center of missions, and He is the very heart of an evangelist's work. If we do not do missions for Christ, and to make Christ known, then we do them in vain. The evangelist reminds a mission's team about its purpose, why they are all there, and sits at the very center of the five-fold for that region. They can teach on Christ, preach about Him, make Him known, and make Him real to anyone who needs to hear of Him and receive Him. Their unique and special purpose keeps everyone focused and keeps people coming to the church ready to walk as part of its purpose.

Some ways that evangelists might work in missions include: preaching, expounding the nature of Christ, working with new believers, helping the church to stir belief about God and maintain a sense of Christ as the center of a church, expounding Christ in the Scriptures and Christ as the heart of the Scriptures, building up the church through new believers and converts, and media outreach.

Pastor

I WILL APPOINT SHEPHERDS WITH WHOM I'M PLEASED, AND THEY WILL LEAD YOU WITH KNOWLEDGE AND UNDERSTANDING. (Jeremiah 3:15)

- **Spiritual call:** Shepherd the people of God

- **Spiritual purpose:** Spiritual feeding

- **Social call:** Living the Gospel/practical need

The pastor is probably the most visible church minister in existence. Everywhere you go in the world, someone has heard of a pastor. In fact, the pastor is so notable, most people think of the Ephesians 4:11 ministry offices as extensions of the pastoral role in some way or another. The pastoral concept, with pastors overseeing a congregation and caring for the people therein, is a quaint, old-fashioned ideal that many still cling to as their identifying face of church and church life.

Church leadership is far more than just pastoral, but this does not mean pastors are irrelevant. Quite the contrary, in fact, which is disturbing as we see a popular rise in offices deemed more entertaining or glamorous, and a diminish of interest in true pastors who are interested in shepherding souls.

The word "pastor" literally means "shepherd." The pastoral office was prophesied by the Prophet Jeremiah (Jeremiah 3:15-16). This is the reason we don't have a ton of New Testament references for pastors: the first-century believers would have understood the pastoral office as a fulfillment of this prophecy. They also were very familiar with shepherds and drew inspiration on what pastors were to do from watching shepherds with their sheep. Literal shepherds feed, tend, and care for the flock entrusted to them, and ensure the flock remains together. Pastors do this on a spiritual level, for the congregations they lead (Jeremiah 12:10-17, Psalm 23:1-6).

Most people pastors work with are not leaders, nor are they called to leadership at the time they work with a pastor. This doesn't make pastoral work unimportant; on the contrary, it makes it very relevant. The consistency of a visible pastor, an individual who is willing to make that commitment and investment in their congregation, is an important connector between the spiritual and the everyday in people's lives. Lay members, or church individuals who are not leaders, need guidance and leadership, and it is the pastor who sees to that task. Pastors are a local authority, who have authority over the congregation assigned to them.

In their social call and purpose, pastors shepherd their people and their communities through practical application. A key of pastoral shepherding is everyday life, making the Gospel practical and livable. This may sound easy, but the truth is, it's a full-time job. Pastors might have experience with theology, but their purpose is not to serve as the theologians of the church. They are there to help people live life, making spirituality real and purposed, and making their witness known to others. This means a large part of their social call relates to everyday things people can do for others: loving their family, being good to others, feeding the hungry, drink to the thirsty, clothing the naked, visiting those in prison, caring for the sick, and taking in the stranger (hospitality) (Matthew 25:31-46). This gives congregations the opportunity to touch the lives of their communities, enact their faith, and see the practicality of the Gospel in all they do.

Pastors are needed for missions because we need good pastors to fill the pastoral role when churches are new. Training people who live in a missions region is optimal, but while the church is starting, established pastors are often needed so the other offices of the five-fold can do the work they are supposed to do as this new spiritual center births forth. It is possible for any member of the five-fold to do whatever they must by the grace of God, fulfilling duties temporarily in another office as a function, but it is much, much better if the work of missions embraces the entire fire-fold, with each member doing its job. We need the experience of pastors who are trained and ready to work with lay members as a church grows and develops into all God has for it to become.

Some ways that pastors might work in missions include pastoring new or young churches, teaching and preaching to their congregation, working stateside to support and prepare for the work of missions, working with lay members, community and church outreach, practical instruction, build up new believers and lay members, run Bible studies and classes, and use media outreach.

Teacher

MY BROTHERS AND SISTERS, NOT MANY OF YOU SHOULD BECOME TEACHERS, BECAUSE WE KNOW THAT WE TEACHERS WILL BE JUDGED MORE STRICTLY. WE ALL MAKE MISTAKES OFTEN, BUT THOSE WHO DON'T MAKE MISTAKES WITH THEIR WORDS HAVE REACHED FULL MATURITY. LIKE A BRIDLED HORSE, THEY CAN CONTROL THEMSELVES ENTIRELY. WHEN WE BRIDLE HORSES AND PUT BITS IN THEIR MOUTHS TO LEAD THEM WHEREVER WE WANT, WE CAN CONTROL THEIR WHOLE BODIES. (James 3:1-3)

- **Spiritual call:** Instruct the church through teaching

- **Spiritual purpose:** Spiritual discipline and spiritual literacy

- **Social call:** Education/information

It's not hard to put together the concept of what a teacher is according to the Scriptures, because we use the term in the same exact sense in secular culture. Teachers teach things to others, instructing and educating them on essential issues that are relevant to faith and life. When we think of teachers, we usually think of roles such as Sunday school instructors, but the role and work of the teacher goes far beyond just Sunday school. In the ancient church, teachers were among the most important figures, often working with new converts from conversion all the way through different education and rites of the church. They took a personal interest in those they taught, and in investing faith within those individuals.

Teachers and the role of the teacher are not as popular nor as heralded as they were in the early years of the church. This isn't the way God desires it to be, however. Teaching is seen as a lesser, or less important office, than universal offices deemed more glamorous and powerful. Teaching is not less important than any other office, and with the lack of solid instruction present in many church circles, it is more relevant than it's ever been.

Teachers, simply put, teach (Isaiah 30:20-21, James 3:13-14). The work of the teacher may range from the simple to the complex, handling everything from life matters, Christian education for a specific age group, to complicated theological topics. Teachers teach whomever God calls them to teach (Deuteronomy 4:1-10, 2 Timothy 2:22, Titus 2:4-7). A teacher may work with children, youth, adults, trainees, or in a school setting. They may work in a local church, in an institution designed to educate as pertains to church, or the universal church. Like evangelists, the teacher has a scope that might be universal in authority (beyond a local congregation) or without formalized church authority (meaning they are not superior to universal or local authorities but operate a parallel position that relates to growth and management of the church) (1 Corinthians 12:27-31). A teacher may also maintain a position of local authority, working exclusively in a local church under the authority of a local pastor.

In their social call and purpose, teachers are advocates of having an educated church. It is the job of the teacher to teach, to see that those who are a part of God's church are understanding of their faith, well-able to understand and present their beliefs, and to do so with poise, grace, and confidence. True teachers care about the overall education of the church, advocating balance and retaining information: they believe that we should obtain knowledge of the world around us and many fields of study because to know God's creation and all that He has done is to find Him as our Creator in a deeper sense. Teachers advocate education across the board; they believe in literacy and diverse studies; they advocate for educated clergy; and they stand as signposts of all that education – both natural and spiritual – can bring to a situation.

Teachers are needed in the missions field because dedicated attention to instruction is essential in regions where churches are new or where churches need to reorganize and structure properly. Without dedication to instruction, churches quickly fall apart. The work of a collective, small-group class and individualized instruction is not something other offices of the Ephesians 4:11 ministry can always offer. It's not an unwillingness that they don't want to, but that there are so many other roles they must fill, teaching in such a specific way is not always an option. It's also important to note that teaching is such an important facet of the Christian life, it takes more than just one office to complete the teaching picture that the church needs. The entire five-fold does teach, in different ways, but the work of the teacher is so essential and important, we need an entire office that dedicates itself to the work of instruction and ensure that those who receive the teaching understand it and receive clarification if it's needed.

Some ways that teachers might work in missions include teaching, teaching in young churches, working with experienced leaders to accomplish educational needs present within a church or mission, teaching on the local or regional level, instructing on missions, operating schools, and media outreach.

It is obvious from Bible study that the Ephesians 4:11 ministry is needed for missions work, because the Ephesians 4:11 offices exists to prepare the people of God for works of service. This is as true in a missions situation as it is in an established church. If we want the people of a church to build their Kingdom work up, we need to see the Ephesians 4:11 offices in action, active and dedicated to their spiritual purpose. The unity of the church is a core tenant of the Ephesians 4:11 ministry's operation, and seeing the offices in action is a powerful testament to the way the church can unify and work together, as one.

Chapter 6 Summary

- The church cannot survive with only pastors and evangelists. We need the full Ephesians 4:11 ministry for the church to be all it is destined to be, and to meet all needs. When we apply this to missions, it is essential the Ephesians 4:11 offices also step up, interested in the spread of the Gospel worldwide. For any church to function as it should, the Ephesians 4:11 ministry must be present.

- In Christ we find the entire Ephesians 4:11 ministry: Jesus was an apostle, prophet, evangelist, pastor, and teacher (Matthew 10:41, Matthew 12:38, Matthew 13:57, Luke 4:14-21, John 10:11-14, Hebrews 3:1). None of us are five in one. Instead, God has created us to live interdependently: relying on Jesus and relying on the work of the Body to survive in connection with every project we undertake.

- The essential facets of the Ephesians 4:11 ministry work are reach the unity of the faith, knowledge of the Son of God, grow to maturity, protecting the church from false teaching, speak the truth in love, and growing every way into Christ.

- The word "apostle" literally means "one who is sent." According to the Scriptures, the apostle's work is twofold: reveal the mysteries of God (1 Corinthians 4:1-2) and establish the foundation of the church (Ephesians 2:20). This means the apostle's work is to implement structure in each church. Apostles teach, train, establish, and install leaders in every congregation (Acts 2:42, 1 Corinthians 4:17, 1 Corinthians 12:28, Philippians 2:22, 1 Timothy 1:18). The original New Testament missionaries were all apostles. In their social call, the apostle ministers reconciliation, working to foster social diversity in the church (2 Corinthians 5:11-21, 1 Corinthians 9:19-23). They are sent by God with the purpose of founding of churches, especially in areas where churches have never existed or where churches do not seem able to sustain themselves.

- The basic work of a prophet is to deliver God's message to His people and also explain and discern matters that relate to prophecy (Revelation 10:9-11). Prophets bring the voice of God to the structure and authority in the church (Amos 3:7, 1 Corinthians 14:36-40, Ephesians 3:5). The work of the prophet brings spiritual quality to all the church does, keeping it from becoming too much of an institution and maintaining its important spiritual nature (Ezekiel 2:1-10, Hosea 12:10). Prophets train other prophets, working to teach the intimacy with God required for a prophet to properly identify the voice of God as they go through their different changes, seasons, and times in their own lives (1 Samuel 19:18-24). Like the apostle, prophets are also universal authorities, which must be exercised with discernment (Ephesians 2:19-21).

- In their social call and purpose, the prophet's work relates to the importance of justice, both in a spiritual and social sense (Psalm 17:2, Psalm 35:24, Jeremiah 5:5, Amos 5:24). Prophets should be deeply interested in the injustices that exist in the world, especially those perpetrated by individuals in the church. They have a keen sense of suffering and know that true Kingdom mindset and application are the only way to correct and fix the injustices in this world. Coupled with a sense of justice calls individuals to repentance. True prophets call out injustices when they see them and recognize that the root of such things is evil selfishness, abandonment of true spiritual practice, and demonic influence on the world. Prophets are necessary in missions because they speak on behalf of God.

- Ephesians 2:20 tells us that both the apostle and the prophet create the foundation of the church. The apostle's work is more administrative, while the prophet's is more spiritual. The two offices present a powerful balance between losing sight of vision and maintaining spirituality as the church is structured and built.

- The work of the Ephesians 4:11 ministry proves that the evangelist cannot do their work alone. The "Christ bearer" of the five-fold, has the duty to carry the Gospel to the world, especially to the non-believer or an individual who lives separated from God (Acts 8:5-6, Acts 8:27-40). In doing their work, it is their goal to make Christ real through the power of preaching and to bring individuals to a place where they desire to join His Body, the church (Acts 8:10-12). Evangelists oversee the souls of the unsaved or are otherwise lost, of those who need to be pointed in the right direction, toward God and His Kingdom. This is an important part of missions, especially in areas where no church or formalized ministry exists. Evangelists need to go into these locations, along with others of the Ephesians 4:11 offices, and preach, reach out to, and minister to locals in that area, both as a group or one-on-one, expounding the way of truth and preparing hearts as they receive salvation and prepare for church participation. In their social call and purpose, the evangelist's work relates to the importance of redemption in the practical application of mercy (Matthew 5:7, Matthew 9:13, Luke 1:50-58, Luke 10:37). The work of an evangelist is necessary for missions because Christ is the very center of both missions and evangelistic work. If we do not do missions for Christ, and to make Christ known, then we do them in vain.

- The word "pastor" literally means "shepherd." The work of the pastoral office was prophesied by the Prophet Jeremiah

(Jeremiah 3:15-16). Most pastors don't work with leaders, but laity. In their social call and purpose, pastors shepherd their people and their communities through practical application. A key of pastoral shepherding is everyday life, making the Gospel practical and livable. This means a large part of their social call relates to everyday things people can do for others: loving their family, being good to others, feeding the hungry, drink to the thirsty, clothing the naked, visiting those in prison, caring for the sick, and taking in the stranger (hospitality) (Matthew 25:31-46). In missions, we need good pastors to fill the pastoral role when churches are new. Training people who live in a missions region is optimal, but while the church is starting, established pastors are often needed so the other offices of Ephesians 4:11 can do the work they are supposed to do as this new spiritual center births forth.

- Teachers, simply put, teach (Isaiah 30:20-21, James 3:13-14). The work of the teacher may range from the simple to the complex, handling everything from life matters, Christian education for a specific age group, to complicated theological topics. Teachers teach whomever God calls them to teach (Deuteronomy 4:1-10, 2 Timothy 2:22, Titus 2:4-7). In their social call and purpose, teachers are advocates of having an educated church. It is the job of the teacher to teach, to see that those who are a part of God's church are understanding of their faith, well-able to understand and present their beliefs, and to do so with poise, grace, and confidence. In missions, teachers are sorely needed because dedicated attention to instruction is an essential in regions where churches are new or where churches need to reorganize and structure properly. Without dedication to instruction, churches quickly fall apart.

Chapter 6 Assignments

- Write a summary report (3-5 sentences) on a nation that interests you. Looking at the church from an Ephesians 4:11 perspective, what can each of the offices offer to the nation?

What offices are present there, and what change do they need in terms of understanding of the offices?

- Create a chart displaying the work of each office of the Ephesians 4:11 offices in missions.

The Punjab Indian Mission (1907-1969)

CHAPTER SEVEN:
REACHING OUT TO THE NATIONS

I thought it reasonable that I should seek the work where the work was the most abundant and the workers fewest."
(James Gilmour[1])

MISSIONS activity is difficult for many in church to fathom because church life has become increasingly isolated. The war between church and culture rages. Clever propaganda, news outlets and popular preachers give unsuspecting believers the impression that society wants to ruin them, people are against them, and the only way to maintain Christian identity is to stay unto oneself in a local church. This is viewed as a means of protection to the point of assuming it is the way we are supposed to be in Christianity; that such isolation is Christian and in accordance with Biblical principles.

This is not what the Bible teaches us at all, but there are many obstacles placed in the mindsets of believers about missions. As the world gets bigger, there are attempts to shrink it back down to a size seen as manageable and controllable. In this chapter, we are going to challenge these historical isolationist movements and the way they affect people considering missions, as well as giving a great look at the way the Bible is multicultural and reaches out to all humanity with the promise of salvation.

The question of the role of the church in the world

The fundamental question as to the church's purpose in the world has been an issue since the church first formed. Investigations into New Testament passages prove that everyone felt the way to go about things varied (1 Corinthians 1:10-17, 1 Corinthians 3:1-23). This was, perhaps, the most important reason for solid leadership. The church this side of heaven needs spiritual guidance. It is not sufficient to say each believer can figure everything out and still expect the church to function properly. The church is not an individual institution, but a collective Kingdom. Sorting out the right from the wrong goes to those leaders God appoints to do that job.

What the church is supposed to do seems obvious: the church's job is to represent Christ and to proclaim the Gospel, both through life and Gospel promotion. The way history has felt this should be done, however, has not always been the best approach. From conquests, to killings, to inquisitions, to squelching any voice except its own, to denominational fights, to competitive missions, to forced baptisms, to thinking politics will solve all our answers to missions, the approach we've taken to reach out to the world has certainly not always been effective. Christians have adopted disrespectful and offensive postures and tried via human means to try and reach the world by force. These various implementations throughout history have given others the message that Christianity, the church, and the Gospel are all exclusively western ideas, present and here to permeate foreign cultures for political and economic control.

JESUS REPLIED, "MY KINGDOM DOESN'T ORIGINATE FROM THIS WORLD. IF IT DID, MY GUARDS WOULD FIGHT SO THAT I WOULDN'T HAVE BEEN ARRESTED BY THE JEWISH LEADERS. MY KINGDOM ISN'T FROM HERE." (John 18:36)

The Bible clarifies for us that God's Kingdom is not of this world. That tells us while we can get a concept of Kingdom from looking at the world's Kingdom, God's Kingdom is not an entity of this world. When God talks about all nations worshiping Him and coming to know Him (Psalm 22:27, Psalm 117:1, Revelation 15:4) He is talking about something different from earthly concepts of worship.

To be a missionary, one must be multicultural in one's embrace. This means that no matter what culture or background someone comes from, you are willing to talk to them, right where they are, as they are. You're willing to try their food, if you are in their culture, adopt parts of their dress, and speak their language. You are willing to show respect to them, right where they are, as they are, even though they are different from you.

Missionaries have the unique task of overcoming themselves,

the ideas permeated in their cultural upbringing that their nation is superior to all others and that their culture is better than any other and surrender those things for the sake of Gospel proclamation. The missionary literally takes on the Gospel as their identity, recalling their citizenship is in heaven (Philippians 3:20). When we take on such powerful work and love, we are willing to shed ourselves of all that hinders our witness and love others, just as they are, wherever they are. To do this, we must recognize in full those things that hinder our witness.

Fundamentalism and modern Christianity

Most Christians worldwide would not classify themselves as Fundamentalists. Even most Evangelicals, who are notoriously identified as "conservative" in the Christian pool, do not meet the definition of being "fundamentalist" in its strictest definition. Nowadays, the term "fundamentalism" is applied to several different groups, including both Mormon and Muslim offshoots of their main religious denominations. The term "fundamentalist" actually applies to a Christian group that many attribute the founding thereof to the early twentieth century in direct opposition to a social issue: the teaching of evolution in schools.

The formation of fundamentalism isn't quite as simple as the Scopes Trial, although that is typically identified as the official root of the movement. The evangelical, holiness, and Pentecostal movements inspired a great rush of missions activity from western nations around the world. These ideas were not without their opposition, however, and their work spawned great missions activity as their ideologies opened the whole world to the watching church. In contrast with the traditional state churches, these churches placed their independence at the forefront of many different cultural statements of their day. Evangelical movements inspired worldwide revival, holiness movements inspired people to live their faith, and Pentecostalism inspired men and women everywhere to unite in prayer, regardless of color, and embrace the Holy Spirit's activity in our modern day.

Without explaining the long history of each of these movements, the thing that is most important to recognize is all three of them represented historical progress to their own point in history. Evangelicalism had its roots in the first and second Great

Awakenings, holiness was associated with Methodism, and Pentecostalism with the numerous groups and denominations that sprung from the informal Bible studies and disciple meetings that served as catalysts to allow the movement of the Spirit among them. This is not to say there were never splinter sects of these three main groups that sought to identify as more accurate or traditional (such as dispensationalism or Princeton Theology), but on the whole, as we will see momentarily, these were new, viable, traditionally-challenging, modern ideals in their original time frame and that in the process, their presence pushed the church into a multicultural state. With believers touched in different places worldwide, the church didn't look all one way or the other. There was room for some sense of diversity, at least on the surface in some movements, because of their internationally driven nature.

By the time Pentecostalism started to emerge as a viable force, much of the Evangelical community took issue with the integration and spiritual activity of Pentecostal meetings. Not all holiness movements embraced progress and change, and the evangelical community took on a staunch, more traditional tone in its nature. The more things changed, the more people wanted them to stay the same, and the wars and conflicts between the three prominent movements poised at the turn of the 1900s made their statement against each other, in more than one way. Media battles, newspaper debates, tracts, protest materials, and sermons all took pot shots at these three main independent movements, changing the world, expanding in missions, and, of course, competing with each other. It was obvious the world was changing, and new spiritual understandings were coming into vogue with those changes.

In mainline Protestantism, things were also changing, as the world grew to meet those differences. Rise of scientific advancements, evolution (Darwinism), and general Biblical examination and criticism were a general part of society and were also a part of the rush of advancements. Some denominations were quick to embrace modern ideas, coupled with general Biblical principles. Others also accepted newly available archaeological and historical data on Biblical understanding, which changed the way the Bible was understood and interpreted. This reflected changing attitudes and ideas, new information, and a broader sense of knowledge as available to the masses. Not everyone felt excited about the changes, however. The clash between an adaptation of change (known as modernism) and what is now known as fundamentalism displayed tensions in the church and society.

Fundamentalist Christianity stood for certain fundamentals that were opposed to their understanding of modernism, namely:

- The inerrancy of the Bible (not just its inspiration, but that each word in it is inerrant).

- Literal rendering and understanding of all Biblical accounts, especially miracles and creation (including details, such as given time frames).

- The virgin birth, bodily resurrection, and physical return of Christ.

- The atonement for humanity by Christ on the cross (substitutionary atonement).[2]

In contrast, modernism (Christian liberalism) was based on:

- Approaching Biblical scholarship without pre-conceived notions as apply to Biblical traditions (such as ones that may or may not have had Biblical origin), without emphasis of creeds, dogmas, or pre-conceived doctrinal understanding.

- Emphasis of God of love in the New Testament as supreme in nature to that of God presented in the Old Testament, sometimes creating a conflict therein, but often trying to reconcile what appears to be two extremes.

- Embrace of scientific information, even as apply to things which may be perceived to be miraculous in nature.

- Some of Jesus' miracles are perceived as metaphors to understand God's intervention within human events.

- Emphasis on the humanitarianism of Jesus and the need to make the Gospel living and practical through good works, in what is often called the "social Gospel."[3]

It's important to state that there are middle grounds in both perspectives, and not all fundamentalists or modernists take the extreme positions that many of their representatives have. Most Christians fall somewhere to the middle of the two extremes, favoring one side slightly more than another, and receiving some influence from both sides. The two, however, reflect how changing times resulted in changing attitudes, and some of these attitudes have filtered down to this present day.

In viewing the battle in this light, it is very clear that the battle between fundamentalists and modernists is one of tradition and understanding. Fundamentalism signifies far more than just these tenants of faith, however. A two-volume work, known as *The Fundamentals: A Testimony to the Truth*, was a series of 90 essays written by various authors and published between 1910 and 1915. What defined fundamentalism was what it was not, and what it was unwilling to become, as it saw the world and its ideas infiltrating the church.[4]

Fundamentalism was never a theological understanding that took the world by storm. It has only been embraced in its entirety by a limited number of believers, mostly in the United States. This does not mean it was without influence. Fundamentalist understanding gained ground through Bible colleges and conservative Christian seminaries, thus influencing the way individuals training for leadership would understand their work in ministry. Fundamentalists also did engage in some missions activity, but they did not have the impact they could have. There are many reasons for this. As an American born and bred religious group, they espoused American ideals about independence and authority which led to a lack of structure and confusion over ideals and concepts not specifically mentioned or of debate in the Scriptures. Without clear leadership and understanding of matters beyond the essentials, fundamentalism's perspective on itself was not enough to make it a solid world force on its own. Because Fundamentalism's perspective was that it was anti-modernism and anti-society, they were isolated to themselves. They staunchly believed they were not to have any part whatsoever in the world, and the world was not to influence them in any way, either. They didn't influence, and they were not influenced. Christianity was being lost to modern culture, and they would not allow their understanding or perspective to be altered, in any way. Its main key was identifiable separation, which leads to a lack of connection with others.

Fundamentalism wound up in denominations, including Baptist, Presbyterian, holiness groups, some smaller groups here and there, and of course, in some semblance most notably through Evangelicalism. Some fundamentalists identify as independent today, but for the most part, many of the ideas present in modern Evangelical Christianity found their home in Fundamentalist origins. Because the movement found its grounding in educational outlets, it's adapted into less extreme forms down to today.

Christian Reconstructionism

If we fast-forward now to the 1960s, we see another movement that stings of fundamentalism's identity, and it is known as the Christian Reconstructionist Movement. Its foundations are 1930s fundamentalism mixed with a sense of Dominionism and superiority to create a combination that could be deemed the political understanding of Fundamentalism.

Christian Reconstructionism was the idea of a man named Rousas J. (R.J.) Rushdoony (1916-2001), the son of Armenian immigrants. He grew up with Fundamentalist influences in his father's Presbyterian church and then matured to become a minister, proposing his own ideals in response to society's changes and his theological understandings.

Rushdoony believed Mosaic law should be the standard for American government, in a belief known as theonomy. Theonomy ascribes different realms or levels of authority: family, church, and state. Morality is designated to family and church, while civil government is responsible for criminal matters and national defenses. Even though this sounds clear cut, it's not, as definition for criminal matters are often defined by Christian Reconstructionists in moral terms, and the definition for crimes often fall into moral categories. This leaves civil authorities to enforce moral terms, often through the death penalty. The death penalty is , according to their understanding, issued for idolatry, homosexuality, witchcraft, adultery, blasphemy, and wayward teenagers.

There's no question that Rushdoony's system isn't practical in a secular society, especially given not everyone in the United States is Christian according to his beliefs of what one is, believes in upholding Mosaic law in modern times, adheres to Biblical identity, and that trying to define terms for things such as blasphemy or idolatry is subjective according to one's understanding.

Christian Reconstructionism, much like Fundamentalism, didn't work on its own. Very few people supported it, even in its heyday, and even fewer are interested in it today. Yet just like fundamentalism, Christian Reconstructionism and its ideas found a new home, dispersed in a new way, only this time, it was far more threatening. Instead of being a foreign entity that people found strange, now it was embraced as part of a culture that wanted to start an all-out war against the American government and the identity of church was to change as a whole. Now it finds its home in what we know as the "Religious Right."[5]

Apocalypticism

Apocalypticism is not a religion, but an ideology that has become a part of pop culture. It is not unique to our modern times or even to Christianity, but it has become very relevant to the isolationism, fear, and anti-multicultural stance that much of the evangelical church has generated from its fundamentalist ancestors.

The goal of apocalypticism is not to create fear and panic (at least on the surface), but that's exactly what it does. It is the belief of an imminent apocalypse, that the world will end within one's lifetime. The message of that imminent doom becomes the central nature of one's message. Because bad things are coming, people must be warned. The purpose of the warnings is for people to come to a knowledge of certain faith to avoid destruction.

Let me state that I think there's nothing wrong with studying the history of the church, the end times, examining cultural sociology considering Biblical understanding or prophecy, and that it's not wrong to be interested in Biblical prophecy. However, we need to understand the context of eschatological study and even prophetic study aren't grounds for evangelism. Nowhere in the Bible does it say that preaching the end of time is an appropriate message. Apocalypticism isn't about proclaiming the Kingdom of heaven at hand, but using assorted scare tactics, such as current event, news headlines, and government events to convince people that Christianity is being attacked and threatened in an invisible war against culture, things are going to continue to get worse, and that believers need to align themselves with these teachings so they know what is going to happen as it happens.

This extensive command to study the apocalypse doesn't seem to have any impact on false prophecy, however. No matter how many predictions seem to be made, people still seem to flock to dramatic end time preachers who convince them that new events are filling the void where their last falsely prophesied events leave off. This shows the ultimate reason why people not only employ apocalypticism, but why others follow it: it's dramatic and exciting, exemplifying the great final show-off between God and Satan.

It also creates an emotional panic, of sorts, which has led to severe miscommunication and conceptual understanding among Christians today. If the end is nigh in the way that apocalypticism promotes, then Christians are a tortured and persecuted group. This means any and every note of correction, secular address, civil law, or social implication that is somehow against what apocalypticism proclaims becomes fodder for persecution, causing those who believe its methods to feel mistreated or offended for their own misdeeds or their own lack of ability to live out their faith. This feeds their already paranoid mindsets, which has things getting worse all the time, clouding out the good that is being done and the advances of the Gospel that are made, everyday, by sincere believers.

There isn't one specific teacher of apocalypticism. It is an understanding that has resurfaced multiple times throughout history in many different forms. In modern times, apocalypticism gained notable interest through several authors and some television hosts popular in the 1970s and 1980s, such as Hal Lindsey (*The Late, Great Planet Earth*), Jack Van Impe (*Your Future: An A-Z Index to Prophecy*), and Edgar C. Whisenant (*88 Reasons Why the Rapture Will Be iIn 1988*). The concepts remain popular thanks to authors such as Pat Robertson (*The End of the Age*), John Hagee (*Earth's Final Moments*), Jonathan Cahn (*The Mystery of the Shemitah*), Tim LaHaye (the *Left Behind* series) and David Jeremiah (*Is This the End?*). The fact that many of these books have been bestsellers and that those who are on television regularly or make appearances are such a massive draw for audiences, shows us how dramatic and show-stopping of an idea that apocalypticism produces.

It's important for us to remember that concepts about the apocalypse and end times prophecies have been understood in different ways throughout history, and that some of those theories do not agree with modern ideals about eschatology. More than this, much of modern eschatology and interpretation has origins in the late 1800s through teaching known as dispensationalism. Dispensationalism divides up the history of salvation into different eras or ages, and along with dispensational theory comes much of what is known to be eschatological interpretation, which was a core tenant of fundamentalism. It does not support a historical understanding of eschatology, but it does make it clear that Christianity is, considering such understanding, attacked and threatened at any turn.

Apocalypticism has changed the way the evangelical community views preaching, because preaching becomes a herald of headlines rather than Gospel understanding. If the world is ending as they say it is, in as early as three to seven years, everyone is going to die or be judged, anyway. Those who are "left behind" are there because they deserve it. This gives people ammunition to stop evangelizing, stop witnessing, and yes, stop engaging in missions activity, because the whole world is deemed as evil and as persecuting true believers, anyhow. This is why you hear people talk about certain demographics of the population as unredeemable, not deserving of salvation, and viewed as individuals who are beyond help and who nobody can do a thing for, so just let them remain in their perceived sins. This is the opposite of evangelicalism, of the message that we should tell people the Gospel and all Jesus has done; it is, in fact, an outright refusal to expand the church and proclaim the Gospel.

The Religious Right

The Religious Right (also called the Christian right or New Christian Right) has a history that runs parallel to the apocalypticism of the 1970s, using the imagery and concepts therein to further its agenda that the world is ending, Christians are a persecuted minority, and the government is trying to destroy good Christians. The difference between the underlying message of apocalypticism and the religious right: the Religious Right believe in fighting back.

The origins of the Religious Right go back first to the 501(c)(3) tax codes, created in the 1960s, that established non-profit entities (such as churches, schools, and charities) as exempt from corporate income tax. Enacted laws because of the Civil Rights Movement moved for an end to public, organized discrimination, and non-profit agencies were no different than any other organization. A 1971 ruling gave the IRS the right to penalize non-profit organizations that openly practiced discrimination. In response, Bob Jones University (Greenville, South Carolina) challenged anti-discrimination under non-profit tax law because the evangelical, fundamentalist-founded school refused to admit black students, because they feared interracial dating on campus. Between 1971 and 1974, the school only admitted married black individuals. Between 1975 and 2000, the school had a policy that forbade interracial dating and marriage among its students. Despite a long fight, Bob Jones University lost the battle and were penalized by the IRS for enacting discriminatory policies on campus. Bob Jones University, however, felt this was against their First Amendment right and embarked in a long crusade to try and implement American governmental leadership that would allow them to govern their school as they desired, no matter how discriminatory its policies might be.

There were those fundamentalists and evangelicals who felt the government overstepped its bounds, along with Bob Jones University. Individuals such as Jerry Falwell (Thomas Road Baptist Church, Liberty University) and Paul Weyrich (political activist) jumped on the bandwagon to help with legal defense. In the process, those involved advocated Christians to get involved and change the tide of government by electing officials who shared their values.

By the 1980s, it was obvious the Religious Right had lost their war in favor of discrimination, but they also had to find new ways to use the finances donors had sent in and justify continued spending and cause. The challenging choice came up as to which new issues they should pursue as moral platforms. Prior to this point in history, the majority of Christians cross all denominations were politically involved as citizens, rather than as believers, and keep in mind that traditional fundamentalism was totally against involvement or activism with government. The Religious Right was the perfect outlet for combining fundamentalism and apocalypticism, and the result was instead of evangelizing or working in missions, people could vote the change they desired in office. In place of racism (which still largely remains through policy and social interaction) the Religious Right adopted anti-feminism, which was seen as the ultimate threat to the family, anti-abortion, which was seen as the ultimate murder in any and all situations, and anti-public schooling, pushing for parents to homeschool children or send them to private Christian schools. The mindset that everything outside of such thinking is evil caused individuals to isolate themselves further, avoiding multiculturalism (which was seen as a problem of the day) and to feel more persecuted than ever.[6]

Invisible enemies

If we look at our modern church outlook, the message we get in church is often negative, with overtones we should think positive and embrace a good outlook. The overall negativity is rooted in apocalypticism, which has, in many of its predictions, failed over the past 40 years. The headlines that warned of impending doom have been replaced by new ones, often accompanied with the same doom, only spoken of as being "much worse" or the promise of things "much worse" to come. Politics are failing. Laws are unjust. Christian values aren't upheld. There aren't a lot of answers as to just how much "worse" things can be in a non-abstract sense, but there's lots of emphasis on how bad things are right now. Even though life is much like it has always been for most believers, that's not the message we receive. We can't help ourselves. We can't stop what's coming. All we can do is try to shield ourselves from it.

Now the enemies we hear about are often nameless or abstract, based on concepts. We are told that we need to fight for our marriages, because they are being attacked. We need to fight for our children, because the world is vying for their attention. We need to fight terrorism. We need to fight Islam. We need to fight diverse enemies in different places as the ultimate diversion from what we should be doing.

Whether it's your family, your marriage, or something in your immediate realm, there is always going to be something therein that will keep you from proclaiming the Gospel, expanding your faith, or working in missions. There will forever be some reason why you shouldn't step out, some spiritual threat to your life, or something you need to handle right where you are. See, what they have done is convince every one of us that the immediate battle is so real, so personal, and so expedient, there is no time to fight or handle anything else. The world is coming to an end, everyone is out to get us, and we must sit, right here, on the defensive, all the time.

This should disturb every one of us because this is a clear spirit of fear at work in the church. It looks like a serious, dedicated believer who cares about their family and the world around them, but it's a diversion to keep us from spreading our faith and thinking about things, such as missions, church growth, and personal spiritual development. If we're always afraid, we're not going to grow, and we are not going to step out to do anything new.

This, at current, is the worldview of much of the church. Influenced by isolationist movements, our entire Christian worldview has been dictated by a few people who've constructed a message that we should not seek to influence our world in any way, shape, or form; we should just put our heads down, hope we vote someone in office who will espouse what we want, and fight invisible enemies rather than preaching the Gospel.

This is also completely opposite of what the Bible teaches us about our position as a church in this world.

Nations in the Bible

I WAS TOLD, "YOU MUST PROPHESY AGAIN ABOUT MANY PEOPLES, NATIONS, LANGUAGES, AND KINGS." (Revelation 10:11)

THEY SING THE SONG OF MOSES, GOD'S SERVANT, AND THE SONG OF THE LAMB, SAYING, "GREAT AND AWE-INSPIRING ARE YOUR WORKS, LORD GOD ALMIGHTY. JUST AND TRUE ARE YOUR WAYS, KING OF THE NATIONS. WHO WON'T FEAR YOU, LORD, AND GLORIFY YOUR NAME? YOU ALONE ARE HOLY. ALL NATIONS WILL COME AND FALL DOWN IN WORSHIP BEFORE YOU, FOR YOUR ACTS OF JUSTICE HAVE BEEN REVEALED." (Revelation 15:3-4)

THE NATIONS WILL WALK BY ITS LIGHT, AND THE KINGS OF THE EARTH WILL BRING THEIR GLORY INTO IT...THEY WILL BRING THE GLORY AND HONOR OF THE NATIONS INTO IT. (Revelation 21:24, 26)

ON EACH SIDE OF THE RIVER IS THE TREE OF LIFE, WHICH PRODUCES TWELVE CROPS OF FRUIT, BEARING ITS FRUIT EACH MONTH. THE TREE'S LEAVES ARE FOR THE HEALING OF THE NATIONS. (Revelation 22:2)

Eighteen different nations are mentioned in the Bible that we can recognize today, both in modern times and in history. There are numerous smaller nations that either no longer exist or are so ancient, we make our best guess as to what nations they would be part of if they still existed. Yes, the focus of much of the Old Testament is on Israel, but it is not exclusively on Israel. Before there was Israel, there was an entire history of people who lived in diverse nations and exhibited different cultural identities. In Israel, those called out of other nations came together to start a new one, that became the nation of Israel. Now, in church, God does the same thing, only instead of becoming Israel, we are a part of the Kingdom of God, noted for a certain sense of diversity that we do not see in other belief systems. We are one in our central tenets of faith, but we do not all speak the same language, look the same, speak the same, dress the same, eat the same, or do all the same things.

Nations are represented in different ways in the Bible: some are represented as sublime, some deceived, some good, and some bad. Ultimately, the promise of redemption is the same throughout the Bible, available to all nations as they see and recognize the promise of God and the hope of salvation. Just as there is promise for Israel, there is promise for all nations, for any individual person therein who chooses to become a part of the Kingdom of God.

To embrace missions is to embrace the nations: acknowledge what's different, praise what is good, recognize what is bad, and promote the Gospel in a way that those who are different can understand and adopt through ways familiar and understandable to them. It's not easy if we think everyone is out to get us and have convinced ourselves that everyone, everywhere is bad, but if we are able to see the promise of God, the heart and truth that everyone is God's child, but many are still unaware of that fact thus they do not embrace it, and that the Gospel can change and bring light into people's lives, we can see the grandeur of creation in each and every culture found throughout the world.

"The world" and the Roman Empire

In much of the New Testament, "the world" was representative (for those who heard the message, considered the message, or discussed it) of the Roman Empire. This was due, in part, to the fact that the Roman Empire dominated most of the Mediterranean, near Asian, some North African, and a large part of (what is now known as) European regions. The representation of the Roman Empire as such shows us the way that governmental and political powers can influence worldview, especially when it comes to world influence and dominance. As far as the people of New Testament times were concerned, the Roman Empire was, in fact, the entire world. Its expanse across many miles, national customs, languages, religious views, and ideas creates a "microcosm" for us in concept of a much larger "macrocosm." The Roman Empire serves as a first-century ideal of diversity and inclusivity; that the Gospel is, indeed for all, as the early workers of the church moved throughout the Roman Empire and into nations beyond within a few decades of the Resurrection.

THE FIELD IS THE WORLD. AND THE GOOD SEEDS ARE THE FOLLOWERS OF THE KINGDOM. BUT THE WEEDS ARE THE FOLLOWERS OF THE EVIL ONE. (Matthew 13:38)

WHY WOULD PEOPLE GAIN THE WHOLE WORLD BUT LOSE THEIR LIVES? WHAT WILL PEOPLE GIVE IN EXCHANGE FOR THEIR LIVES? (Matthew 16:26)

Understanding such helps us to recognize that missions, no matter how seemingly small, start where we are and expand out. We can have just as powerful a missions testimony and reach our "world" as if we jet off to a far-away nation. This is not to, in any way, minimize foreign missions. It is, however, to recognize that what we do to reach the world starts with what we understand and moves outward.

For God so loved the world...

We discussed the concept of the Incarnation of Jesus as a mission in an earlier chapter, so it is not a surprise that the work of Jesus was something unique, special, and life-changing in this world. The Incarnation of Jesus is also the complete antithesis of isolationism and separation, so prevalent and prevailing in the world today. In His Incarnation, we also see a prominent multicultural calling that is essential to missions work.

THERE WAS A PHARISEE NAMED NICODEMUS, A JEWISH LEADER. HE CAME TO JESUS AT NIGHT AND SAID TO HIM, "RABBI, WE KNOW THAT YOU ARE A TEACHER WHO HAS COME FROM GOD, FOR NO ONE COULD DO THESE MIRACULOUS SIGNS THAT YOU DO UNLESS GOD IS WITH HIM."

JESUS ANSWERED, "I ASSURE YOU, UNLESS SOMEONE IS BORN ANEW, IT'S NOT POSSIBLE TO SEE GOD'S KINGDOM."

NICODEMUS ASKED, "HOW IS IT POSSIBLE FOR AN ADULT TO BE BORN? IT'S IMPOSSIBLE TO ENTER THE MOTHER'S WOMB FOR A SECOND TIME AND BE BORN, ISN'T IT?"

JESUS ANSWERED, "I ASSURE YOU, UNLESS SOMEONE IS BORN OF WATER AND THE SPIRIT, IT'S NOT POSSIBLE TO ENTER GOD'S KINGDOM. WHATEVER IS BORN OF THE FLESH IS FLESH, AND WHATEVER IS BORN OF THE SPIRIT IS SPIRIT. DON'T BE SURPRISED THAT I SAID TO YOU, 'YOU MUST BE BORN ANEW.' GOD'S SPIRIT BLOWS WHEREVER IT WISHES. YOU HEAR ITS SOUND, BUT YOU DON'T KNOW WHERE IT COMES FROM OR WHERE IT IS GOING. IT'S THE SAME WITH EVERYONE WHO IS BORN OF THE SPIRIT."

NICODEMUS SAID, "HOW ARE THESE THINGS POSSIBLE?"

"JESUS ANSWERED, "YOU ARE A TEACHER OF ISRAEL AND YOU DON'T KNOW THESE THINGS? I ASSURE YOU THAT WE SPEAK ABOUT WHAT WE KNOW AND TESTIFY ABOUT WHAT WE HAVE SEEN, BUT YOU DON'T RECEIVE OUR TESTIMONY. IF I HAVE TOLD YOU ABOUT EARTHLY THINGS AND YOU DON'T BELIEVE, HOW WILL YOU BELIEVE IF I TELL YOU ABOUT HEAVENLY THINGS? NO ONE HAS GONE UP TO HEAVEN EXCEPT THE ONE WHO CAME DOWN FROM HEAVEN, THE HUMAN ONE. JUST AS MOSES LIFTED UP THE SNAKE IN THE WILDERNESS, SO MUST THE HUMAN ONE BE LIFTED UP SO THAT EVERYONE WHO BELIEVES IN HIM WILL HAVE ETERNAL LIFE. GOD SO LOVED THE WORLD THAT HE GAVE HIS ONLY SON, SO THAT EVERYONE WHO BELIEVES IN HIM WON'T PERISH BUT WILL HAVE ETERNAL LIFE. GOD DIDN'T SEND HIS SON INTO THE WORLD TO JUDGE THE WORLD, BUT THAT THE WORLD MIGHT BE SAVED THROUGH HIM. WHOEVER BELIEVES IN HIM ISN'T JUDGED; WHOEVER DOESN'T BELIEVE IN HIM IS ALREADY JUDGED, BECAUSE THEY DON'T BELIEVE IN THE NAME OF GOD'S ONLY SON.

"THIS IS THE BASIS FOR JUDGMENT: THE LIGHT CAME INTO THE WORLD, AND PEOPLE LOVED DARKNESS MORE THAN THE LIGHT, FOR THEIR ACTIONS ARE EVIL. ALL WHO DO WICKED THINGS HATE THE LIGHT AND DON'T COME TO THE LIGHT FOR FEAR THAT THEIR ACTIONS WILL BE EXPOSED TO THE LIGHT. WHOEVER DOES THE TRUTH COMES TO THE LIGHT SO THAT IT CAN BE SEEN THAT THEIR ACTIONS WERE DONE IN GOD." (John 3:1-21)

Jesus Christ came to earth from His position, His throne in heaven. He came in human flesh, as a Semite, walking among people who were far from heavenly beings. He ate what they ate, dressed as they dressed, spoke their languages (even had the distinguishable accent of where He lived and dwelt), and interacted with them, in their custom. Emmanuel, "God with us," came down and dwelt among men, reaching people right where they were, living as they lived. Jesus didn't put on airs, He didn't frighten people, and when He gave a prophecy, it wasn't clouded over with confusion from generation to generation. Jesus was Who He was, without losing Himself, available and interested in those that He walked with and among.

Perhaps the most important thing we need to realize is that Jesus never degraded anyone. He might have spoken against the self-righteousness that pervaded His time, He might have told people things that were true about themselves, but He never spoke to anyone with judgment. Jesus knew how to tell the truth without using that truth as a statement of argument or debate, which is something missionaries must learn how to do if they are to be effective. It is perfectly possible to do as Jesus did, and speak truth without condemning someone else, as hard as it might be for those of us in the flesh to do.

The woman at the well

JESUS HAD TO GO THROUGH SAMARIA. HE CAME TO A SAMARITAN CITY CALLED SYCHAR, WHICH WAS NEAR THE LAND JACOB HAD GIVEN TO HIS SON JOSEPH. JACOB'S WELL WAS THERE. JESUS WAS TIRED FROM HIS JOURNEY, SO HE SAT DOWN AT THE WELL. IT WAS ABOUT NOON.

A SAMARITAN WOMAN CAME TO THE WELL TO DRAW WATER. JESUS SAID TO HER, "GIVE ME SOME WATER TO DRINK." HIS DISCIPLES HAD GONE INTO THE CITY TO BUY HIM SOME FOOD.

THE SAMARITAN WOMAN ASKED, "WHY DO YOU, A JEWISH MAN, ASK FOR SOMETHING TO DRINK FROM ME, A SAMARITAN WOMAN?" (JEWS AND SAMARITANS DIDN'T ASSOCIATE WITH EACH OTHER.)

JESUS RESPONDED, "IF YOU RECOGNIZED GOD'S GIFT AND WHO IS SAYING TO YOU, 'GIVE ME SOME WATER TO DRINK,' YOU WOULD BE ASKING HIM AND HE WOULD GIVE YOU LIVING WATER."

THE WOMAN SAID TO HIM, "SIR, YOU DON'T HAVE A BUCKET AND THE WELL IS DEEP. WHERE WOULD YOU GET THIS LIVING WATER? YOU AREN'T GREATER THAN OUR FATHER JACOB, ARE YOU? HE GAVE THIS WELL TO US, AND HE DRANK FROM IT HIMSELF, AS DID HIS SONS AND HIS LIVESTOCK."

JESUS ANSWERED, "EVERYONE WHO DRINKS THIS WATER WILL BE THIRSTY AGAIN, BUT WHOEVER DRINKS FROM THE WATER THAT I WILL GIVE WILL NEVER BE THIRSTY AGAIN. THE WATER THAT I GIVE WILL BECOME IN THOSE WHO DRINK IT A SPRING OF WATER THAT BUBBLES UP INTO ETERNAL LIFE."

THE WOMAN SAID TO HIM, "SIR, GIVE ME THIS WATER, SO THAT I WILL NEVER BE THIRSTY AND WILL NEVER NEED TO COME HERE TO DRAW WATER!"

JESUS SAID TO HER, "GO, GET YOUR HUSBAND, AND COME BACK HERE."

THE WOMAN REPLIED, "I DON'T HAVE A HUSBAND."

"YOU ARE RIGHT TO SAY, 'I DON'T HAVE A HUSBAND,'" JESUS ANSWERED. "YOU'VE HAD FIVE HUSBANDS, AND THE MAN YOU ARE WITH NOW ISN'T YOUR HUSBAND. YOU'VE SPOKEN THE TRUTH."

THE WOMAN SAID, "SIR, I SEE THAT YOU ARE A PROPHET. OUR ANCESTORS WORSHIPPED ON THIS MOUNTAIN, BUT YOU AND YOUR PEOPLE SAY THAT IT IS NECESSARY TO WORSHIP IN JERUSALEM."

JESUS SAID TO HER, "BELIEVE ME, WOMAN, THE TIME IS COMING WHEN YOU AND YOUR PEOPLE WILL WORSHIP THE FATHER NEITHER ON THIS MOUNTAIN NOR IN JERUSALEM. YOU AND YOUR PEOPLE WORSHIP WHAT YOU DON'T KNOW; WE WORSHIP WHAT WE KNOW BECAUSE SALVATION IS FROM THE JEWS. BUT THE TIME IS COMING—AND IS HERE!—WHEN TRUE WORSHIPPERS WILL WORSHIP IN SPIRIT AND TRUTH. THE FATHER LOOKS FOR THOSE WHO WORSHIP HIM THIS WAY. GOD IS SPIRIT, AND IT IS NECESSARY TO WORSHIP GOD IN SPIRIT AND TRUTH."

THE WOMAN SAID, "I KNOW THAT THE MESSIAH IS COMING, THE ONE WHO IS CALLED THE CHRIST. WHEN HE COMES, HE WILL TEACH EVERYTHING TO US."

JESUS SAID TO HER, "I AM—THE ONE WHO SPEAKS WITH YOU."

JUST THEN, JESUS' DISCIPLES ARRIVED AND WERE SHOCKED THAT HE WAS TALKING WITH A WOMAN. BUT NO ONE ASKED, "WHAT DO YOU WANT?" OR "WHY ARE YOU TALKING WITH HER?" THE WOMAN PUT DOWN HER WATER JAR AND WENT INTO THE CITY. SHE SAID TO THE PEOPLE, "COME AND SEE A MAN WHO HAS TOLD ME EVERYTHING I'VE DONE! COULD THIS MAN BE THE CHRIST?" THEY LEFT THE CITY AND WERE ON THEIR WAY TO SEE JESUS.

IN THE MEANTIME THE DISCIPLES SPOKE TO JESUS, SAYING, "RABBI, EAT."

JESUS SAID TO THEM, "I HAVE FOOD TO EAT THAT YOU DON'T KNOW ABOUT."

THE DISCIPLES ASKED EACH OTHER, "HAS SOMEONE BROUGHT HIM FOOD?"

JESUS SAID TO THEM, "I AM FED BY DOING THE WILL OF THE ONE WHO SENT ME AND BY COMPLETING HIS WORK. DON'T YOU HAVE A SAYING, 'FOUR MORE MONTHS AND THEN IT'S TIME FOR HARVEST'? LOOK, I TELL YOU: OPEN YOUR EYES AND NOTICE THAT THE FIELDS ARE ALREADY RIPE FOR THE HARVEST. THOSE WHO HARVEST ARE RECEIVING THEIR PAY AND GATHERING FRUIT FOR ETERNAL LIFE SO THAT THOSE WHO SOW AND THOSE WHO HARVEST CAN CELEBRATE TOGETHER. THIS IS A TRUE SAYING, THAT ONE SOWS AND ANOTHER HARVESTS. I HAVE SENT YOU TO HARVEST WHAT YOU DIDN'T WORK HARD FOR; OTHERS WORKED HARD, AND YOU WILL SHARE IN THEIR HARD WORK."

MANY SAMARITANS IN THAT CITY BELIEVED IN JESUS BECAUSE OF THE WOMAN'S WORD WHEN SHE TESTIFIED, "HE TOLD ME EVERYTHING I'VE EVER DONE." SO WHEN THE SAMARITANS CAME TO JESUS, THEY ASKED HIM TO STAY WITH THEM, AND HE STAYED THERE TWO DAYS. MANY MORE BELIEVED BECAUSE OF HIS WORD, AND THEY SAID TO THE WOMAN, "WE NO LONGER BELIEVE BECAUSE OF WHAT YOU SAID, FOR WE HAVE HEARD FOR OURSELVES AND KNOW THAT THIS ONE IS TRULY THE SAVIOR OF THE WORLD." (John 4:4-42)

History hasn't been kind in its interpretation of the woman at the well. Most of us don't know that the early church assigned her a name, Photini (which means "light bearer"), and that she worked as an apostle for the rest of her life. Instead, we call her names: we've been told she's a harlot, a whore, a prostitute, a woman of sin, and degraded her into a state of near oblivion, where we give no relevance to who she was, at all. It doesn't seem to matter that Jesus never said any of that to her; He spoke the reality that she lived with a man she was not married to, but He didn't fill in the rest. It's possible he was a male relative, she was in a betrothal period, and He was advising her not to marry that man, that she was a caregiver, or other possibilities, as well. She was a woman who lived with a man to whom she was not married, after having five husbands. That's all Jesus said. He spoke her truth, her reality. He didn't say anything else that we impose upon her and her situation.

He also was speaking to a woman who was not a Jew. Thus, in His unique way, He was teaching all of us how to interact with those who are different from us, especially those who espouse part of our understanding rather than rejecting it all together.

The Samaritans were (and are) descendants of the land of Ephraim and Manasseh, with a capital city of Samaria. Earlier in this book, we read the basic account of their foundations: 2 Kings 17:24-41 is the history of how the Samaritan religion came to be. During the Assyrian captivity, the King of Assyria sent pagan neighbors to occupy Samaria. These people intermarried with the Israelite population in that area. Their religion was the result of the Levites' failed missionary attempts to educate those living therein. This population, known as "Samaritans," worshiped their own national gods at first, but started worshiping the God of the Hebrews. As henotheists (people who believe in a chief deity over their people but do not believe it is the only god), they attributed a lion invasion because they had not acknowledged the God of the Hebrews among them. They started to worship Him along with their own gods. The Levites educated the people in the law, but they retained their pagan customs. This mixture between the two resulted in the Samaritan religion, who call themselves "The Keepers." They also feel they are the true children of Israel, believing the Israelites perverted and lost the true faith. They believe only Moses was the true prophet and receive the first five books of the Old Testament but reject any additional Biblical revelation. Naturally, there was hostility between both groups.

The Samaritans show up in a few places in the Old Testament: They opposed the rebuilding of the temple after the Babylonian exile (Nehemiah 6:1-14), and they became a place of refuge for those outlaws of Judea, willingly receiving Israeli criminals (Joshua 20:6-7). Samaritans were considered the lowest of human races and Jews refused to have dealings with them. Thus, the fact that Jesus' longest dialogue with anyone in the Bible was with a Samaritan, a non-Jew, elevates the status of a culture regarded with disdain and dislike to that of equality with anyone else.[7]

Our major call for multiculturalism is to treat all people equally, with the same regard and respect we would treat anyone else. It's easy to say we are colorblind, we aren't racist, we aren't sexist, we don't discriminate against other cultures, and we don't consider those of other spiritual beliefs as inferior in their humanity to us, but the reality of our culture and much of our interactions with others speaks otherwise. From birth, we are trained to avoid multiculturalism. It is a part of the evolution of societies; to maintain the best survival rate, we are trained to think our identity is best and that others are inferior. Even though we may not be people given to overt attitudes of disdain for others who differ from us, there is some part of us that often thinks ourselves superior, more advanced, or more evolved than someone else. This becomes evident when we take on the work to evangelize, instruct, or interact with them in a spiritual setting because our tendency is to want to do things "our way," whether they are Biblical, or not.

Adopting a multicultural outlook starts when we can step back and accept that others don't see things the way we do. Jesus could have made the differences in their cultures apparent. He could have had a long-winded argument with her about all the differences between Jews and Samaritans and expounded on all the ways that the Samaritans were wrong in their beliefs. Notice that Jesus didn't do any of this, however. He received her as a person; He spoke truth to her without being demeaning or critical; and He reached her, right where she was, using customs, language, and understanding that would have been familiar to her.

The good Samaritan

When we read about the good Samaritan, we tend to read around its multiculturalism. We love what it says and think it sounds great for sermons, but the good Samaritan was about far more than just doing nice things for someone else: it was about breaking down the barriers that we've put in place as human beings.

A LEGAL EXPERT STOOD UP TO TEST JESUS. "TEACHER," HE SAID, "WHAT MUST I DO TO GAIN ETERNAL LIFE?"

JESUS REPLIED, "WHAT IS WRITTEN IN THE LAW? HOW DO YOU INTERPRET IT?"

HE RESPONDED, "YOU MUST LOVE THE LORD YOUR GOD WITH ALL YOUR HEART, WITH ALL YOUR BEING, WITH ALL YOUR STRENGTH, AND WITH ALL YOUR MIND, AND LOVE YOUR NEIGHBOR AS YOURSELF."

JESUS SAID TO HIM, "YOU HAVE ANSWERED CORRECTLY. DO THIS AND YOU WILL LIVE."

BUT THE LEGAL EXPERT WANTED TO PROVE THAT HE WAS RIGHT, SO HE SAID TO JESUS, "AND WHO IS MY NEIGHBOR?"

JESUS REPLIED, "A MAN WENT DOWN FROM JERUSALEM TO JERICHO. HE ENCOUNTERED THIEVES, WHO STRIPPED HIM NAKED, BEAT HIM UP, AND LEFT HIM NEAR DEATH. NOW IT JUST SO HAPPENED THAT A PRIEST WAS ALSO GOING DOWN THE SAME ROAD. WHEN HE SAW THE INJURED MAN, HE CROSSED OVER TO THE OTHER SIDE OF THE ROAD AND WENT ON HIS WAY. LIKEWISE, A LEVITE CAME BY THAT SPOT, SAW THE INJURED MAN, AND CROSSED OVER TO THE OTHER SIDE OF THE ROAD AND WENT ON HIS WAY. A SAMARITAN, WHO WAS ON A JOURNEY, CAME TO WHERE THE MAN WAS. BUT WHEN HE SAW HIM, HE WAS MOVED WITH COMPASSION. THE SAMARITAN WENT TO HIM AND BANDAGED HIS WOUNDS, TENDING THEM WITH OIL AND WINE. THEN HE PLACED THE WOUNDED MAN ON HIS OWN DONKEY, TOOK HIM TO AN INN, AND TOOK CARE OF HIM. THE NEXT DAY, HE TOOK TWO FULL DAYS' WORTH OF WAGES AND GAVE THEM TO THE INNKEEPER. HE SAID, 'TAKE CARE OF HIM, AND WHEN I RETURN, I WILL PAY YOU BACK FOR ANY ADDITIONAL COSTS.' WHAT DO YOU THINK? WHICH ONE OF THESE THREE WAS A NEIGHBOR TO THE MAN WHO ENCOUNTERED THIEVES?"

THEN THE LEGAL EXPERT SAID, "THE ONE WHO DEMONSTRATED MERCY TOWARD HIM."

JESUS TOLD HIM, "GO AND DO LIKEWISE." (LUKE 10:25-37)

Given what we spoke of about Samaritans in the last section, it's obvious the Jews viewed them as sub-human. They were not considered equal in any sense of the word. This attitude extended to other Gentile nations, as well. The Jews had the law, they felt that separated them from everyone else, but that separation wasn't in terms of responsibility or obligation. It became about being superior, which always leads to an attitude that disregards and mistreats others.

This isn't to say that the Samaritans were perfect; in fact, nobody is. The same attitude that the Jews displayed, many others display, as well. Humility doesn't make for good cultural survival, so there are many ways that bad interpersonal attitudes infiltrate our cultures. The good Samaritan, however, proves a few things to us and shows us some important things about our multicultural attitudes.

The first is that, whether saved or not, people can do good things and can do the right things. These are things we should be quick to point out, from the multicultural perspective, as steppingstones to instruction in Christian missions. The good that we do, the things that are right, the virtues that are expounded and important should be shown forth as God's message, a type of His interaction, with those who are first learning of Him or are learning more about Him.

The second is that in our fear of multiculturalism, our fear of doing things for others, we don't do the right thing ourselves. God commanded the Jews to treat foreigners in a certain way when they were among them in their land (Leviticus 19:33-34). He never said that the Jews should pick up their practices, but He did say they should be treated as anyone else in connection with the law, because the behavior of the Jew would be a witness to the foreigner. This tells us that the way God commands us to teach, interact with, and work with others who are different from us is often not about them; it's about our ability to live and interact for the sake of the Gospel. It's about whether we believe what we claim to believe and whether or not we really do believe it's God Who saves people, rather than us, ourselves, by trying to modify people's behaviors. The right thing is the right thing is the right thing, and we are not excused from doing the right thing because of our doctrinal beliefs.

The third is that our neighbor is everyone, even those who are different from us. It's easy to be nice, to reach out, to care about people who are just like us, and it's still amazing to note how few people are willing to do right by people when it's easy. Seeing "your neighbor" in people who are not like you is not easy for many. Our neighbors are everyone; they are as near to us as next door, as standing next to us, and we are responsible to be good to them, no matter who they are. This means your "neighbor" is:

- Christian
- Jewish
- Atheist
- Agnostic
- Gay
- Straight
- Bisexual
- Lesbian
- Queer
- Muslim
- Hindu
- Black
- Hispanic
- White
- Asian
- Native
- And anything else you can imagine among nations under heaven.

The good Samaritan proves to us all that there is a better way to be, and this is exactly the mindset we need to take into missions.

The Canaanite/Syrophoenician woman

Matthew calls her a Canaanite. Mark calls her a Syrophoenician. The truth is that the original Canaanites were displaced in history and lived in lands conquered by Phoenicians for generations. What exactly a "Syrophoenician" was is of some debate, because of the research I did for this section. It appears that the woman was from the province of Syria, of Phoenician origin, and was referred to as Syrophoenician as a distinction from the African Phoenicians (also called Carthaginians). Whatever the origin was, the Bible is clear that she wasn't a Jew and came from a background that was classified as antithetical to Israel.

In Biblical times, Jews often referred to Gentiles as "wild dogs" in the native Greek. They believed that the Gentiles were so unclean spiritually, they could make someone unclean according to the ceremonial traditions of the Old Testament. In reading the passage in English, many assume Jesus was referring to the woman in a derogatory manner. If we examine it closely, however, is this the case, or is Jesus making yet another case for multiculturalism?

FROM THERE, JESUS WENT TO THE REGIONS OF TYRE AND SIDON. A CANAANITE WOMAN FROM THOSE TERRITORIES CAME OUT AND SHOUTED, "SHOW ME MERCY, SON OF DAVID. MY DAUGHTER IS SUFFERING TERRIBLY FROM DEMON POSSESSION." BUT HE DIDN'T RESPOND TO HER AT ALL.

HIS DISCIPLES CAME AND URGED HIM, "SEND HER AWAY; SHE KEEPS SHOUTING OUT AFTER US."

JESUS REPLIED, "I'VE BEEN SENT ONLY TO THE LOST SHEEP, THE PEOPLE OF ISRAEL."

BUT SHE KNELT BEFORE HIM AND SAID, "LORD, HELP ME."

HE REPLIED, "IT IS NOT GOOD TO TAKE THE CHILDREN'S BREAD AND TOSS IT TO DOGS."

SHE SAID, "YES, LORD. BUT EVEN THE DOGS EAT THE CRUMBS THAT FALL OFF THEIR MASTERS' TABLE."

JESUS ANSWERED, "WOMAN, YOU HAVE GREAT FAITH. IT WILL BE JUST AS YOU WISH." AND RIGHT THEN HER DAUGHTER WAS HEALED. (Matthew 15:21-28)

JESUS LEFT THAT PLACE AND WENT INTO THE REGION OF TYRE. HE DIDN'T WANT ANYONE TO KNOW THAT HE HAD ENTERED A HOUSE, BUT HE COULDN'T HIDE. IN FACT, A WOMAN WHOSE YOUNG DAUGHTER WAS POSSESSED BY AN UNCLEAN SPIRIT HEARD ABOUT HIM RIGHT AWAY. SHE CAME AND FELL AT HIS FEET. THE WOMAN WAS GREEK, SYROPHOENICIAN BY BIRTH. SHE BEGGED JESUS TO THROW THE DEMON OUT OF HER DAUGHTER. HE RESPONDED, "THE CHILDREN HAVE TO BE FED FIRST. IT ISN'T RIGHT TO TAKE THE CHILDREN'S BREAD AND TOSS IT TO THE DOGS."

BUT SHE ANSWERED, "LORD, EVEN THE DOGS UNDER THE TABLE EAT THE CHILDREN'S CRUMBS."

"GOOD ANSWER!" HE SAID. "GO ON HOME. THE DEMON HAS ALREADY LEFT YOUR DAUGHTER." WHEN SHE RETURNED TO HER HOUSE, SHE FOUND THE CHILD LYING ON THE BED AND THE DEMON GONE. (Mark 7:24-30)

Jesus was about His mission, which at that point in time, was trying to minister to Israel. As we've already pointed out, Israel was lost. But because the Bible clarifies that salvation came first to the Jew, ministering to Jewish people was an integral part of His ministry. They needed to understand because the law was supposed to put them that far ahead in knowledge and understanding than the Gentile counterparts, and He needed to focus on the complete and total void present in Israel's reality when it came to spiritual matters. It would be like throwing food to the dogs, but not the dogs of derogatory Gentile slang. The word Jesus uses indicates a familiarity, of a small dog or pet, to say it would be like taking a portion of what He had been given and giving it somewhere other than it was destined to go or intended.

Jesus didn't abandon this woman, nor did He put her down. Instead, He tested her intentions, giving her the opportunity to voice her faith. In speaking to her as she did, she was able to prove she understood Who Jesus was and what He was saying to her.

Jesus' discussion with this woman and subsequent healing of her daughter shows us that Jesus was notable to all people, not just Jews. What He did was not just noticed by those He was specifically sent to work with at that time, but others took notice. This means whatever He was doing or teaching wasn't so specific to one group of people that others couldn't notice it and apply it to themselves. It was so notable, in fact, that others wanted what He had. In missions, this should teach us something powerful about our own work. What we have should be so notable that others take note of what we are doing, even if what we are doing is not specifically for them.

We should also be willing to take time to pay attention to the sincere, genuine requests of those who are in need, even if we aren't sent to work with that group at that time. There is nothing wrong with testing someone's sincerity through dialogue or discussion; in fact, I recommend this. Being multicultural means we are open to working with and assisting people from any race or culture, but it does not mean that we must entertain people who are trying to cause trouble or embody nonsense. Just as with all things, we need to properly discern where to spend our time and how we can best reach those who need what we have to offer without wasting energy on people who aren't serious.[8,9]

Becoming all things to all people

The focus of Biblical hermeneutics and exegesis as pertain to the miracles of Jesus is almost exclusively on Jesus. There is nothing wrong with studying the miracles that Jesus performed, but as we have seen throughout this chapter, the people who received those miracles are often just as important as the miracles performed. The healings, restorations, and miraculous workings of Jesus were not reserved to Israelites. They were something open to anyone who was willing to believe, and this paved the way for the work of the church and for an important principle that is found in the New Testament and defines the way I view my call to the apostolic: becoming all things to all people.

THOUGH I AM FREE AND BELONG TO NO MAN, I MAKE MYSELF A SLAVE TO EVERYONE, TO WIN AS MANY AS POSSIBLE. TO THE JEWS I BECAME LIKE A JEW, TO WIN THE JEWS. TO THOSE UNDER THE LAW I BECAME LIKE ONE UNDER THE LAW (THOUGH I MYSELF AM NOT UNDER THE LAW), SO AS TO WIN THOSE UNDER THE LAW. TO THOSE NOT HAVING THE LAW I BECAME LIKE ONE NOT HAVING THE LAW (THOUGH I AM NOT FREE FROM GOD'S LAW BUT AM UNDER CHRIST'S LAW), SO AS TO WIN THOSE NOT HAVING THE LAW. TO THE WEAK I BECAME WEAK, TO WIN THE WEAK. I HAVE BECOME ALL THINGS TO ALL MEN SO THAT BY ALL POSSIBLE MEANS I MIGHT SAVE SOME. I DO ALL THIS FOR THE SAKE OF THE GOSPEL, THAT I MAY SHARE IN ITS BLESSINGS. (1 Corinthians 9:19-23, NIV)

I've written on the passage of becoming all things to all people more than once, in more than one book and more than one context. It's a beautiful passage that we like to pass over in the Scriptures because its application is a lot harder than we might like to admit. We are fine with other people if we don't have to consider our call to change and become something they can identify with for the sake of the Gospel...but that's not what God calls us to do.

In missions, we will be in situations where people will be radically different than we are, and we will be the ones who are forced to adapt to others, rather than expect them to adapt to us. This is the opposite of what we are told in the west when it comes to matters of faith. We are told that if we give in, we are compromising our faith, and we will somehow lose our salvation. This is not what the Apostle Paul says, nor is it anywhere implied in the Bible. If we are not doing anything related to false worship, adapting by culture, dress, custom, language, diet, or understanding (especially understanding within cultural appropriation) is literally essential to the call.

We cannot operate in missions if we are so hung up on a hardened concept of faith that we can't reach out to everyone. Every one of us interested in missions needs to receive the instruction of God in how we can best reach out to the people we are called to work with so that they might become reconciled to God, wherever they may be on that issue in their lives. It means overcoming ourselves as the ultimate hindrance, making ourselves ready and willing vessels to do what is needed so people see salvation as an ultimate act of love. Loving people doesn't mean we believe everything they do is right. It doesn't change what God has called sin, nor does it minimize it. What it does do is help people see themselves and the things they do in a new light and introduce God to them in a context which is ordinary and everyday enough for them to understand. It also helps us to consider our own selves and what God has brought us from, causing us to be humble instead of arrogant, using holiness as an excuse to abuse others.

Revelation and multiculturalism

The last example of Biblical multiculturalism that we will examine comes to us from the book of Revelation. It might seem odd to look at Revelation in this light, especially because the book of Revelation is used to induce apocalypticism, which divides and drives people into states of fear regarding other cultures. In reality, Revelation is one of the most diverse books (if not the most diverse) in the Bible, because it brings the fullness of the church's international, multicultural purpose to the surface.

It's impossible to expound upon the full meaning of Revelation in one section of a book, thus I recommend my book, *All That is Seen and Unseen: A Journey Through the Book of Revelation* (Righteous Pen Publications, 2015) to any who might like to study Revelation more thoroughly. Here I will attempt to scratch the surface of the book, because understanding its purpose relates to its multicultural nature in its very core.

The purpose of the book of Revelation was to give prophetic power to the being of the church. In other words, Revelation is there to place the church in prophecy. We understand the prophecies as pertain to Israel, to the creation of a new people, and to Christ, but Revelation gives special focus on the church as Jesus' Bride, a part of prophetic history. It's our book, a revelation of the plan of God for the church, and that despite persecution, problems, discomforts, and attempts to annihilate it, it would, in fact, have the power to withstand until a new heavens and new earth come. Nowhere are the believers to retreat in the face of change and multicultural advance; instead, the church is to embrace believers from every walk of the planet and join in the eternal song of salvation.

Even though the world was still relatively small (in comparison to today) when Revelation was received, Revelation's contents reveal that the world was to become a much bigger and more complicated place. The symbols of Revelation represent many of those complications, written in language the first-century believers would be able to embrace and understand. For us, today, much of that leaves us scratching our heads and trying to decode things, piece by piece, without the foundational concepts believers back then would have had. By reducing Revelation to a giant codebook, we are missing the bigger point, and bigger picture that Revelation was trying to teach us. That bigger point is, was, and always will be, this: The church is important enough to be a central figure of history, and its nature as a multicultural center, as the answer to opposing world problems, fighting secular powers because it is the true Kingdom, is something we must fix our sights on to see the missionary multiculturalism present therein.

IT SAID, "WRITE DOWN ON A SCROLL WHATEVER YOU SEE, AND SEND IT TO THE SEVEN CHURCHES: TO EPHESUS, SMYRNA, PERGAMUM, THYATIRA, SARDIS, PHILADELPHIA, AND LAODICEA." (Revelation 1:11)

The seven churches of Revelation are one of the first indicators of the diversity present in the church. Within the seven churches, we see Greek, Jewish, Roman, Syrian, and Persian imagery, proving that the church of the first century was multicultural. It got that way because people were willing to proclaim the Gospel, throughout the world as they knew it, and incorporate as much education and faith as possible into diverse communities. The churches in Revelation 7 aren't just random, individual churches, they are the church. They are the very embodiment of every single one of us, working for the good with the bad, embracing things we shouldn't, walking away from things we need to run back toward, facing life, facing changes, facing hostile atmospheres and challenges. The seven churches of Revelation need to cause each of us to step back and examine our own selves and our own interactions with the church and also reflect to us that our church experience should not be all one way versus another. We should all express our willingness to interact with a diversity of believers, learning and growing together as we strive for perfection in Christ.

THEY TOOK UP A NEW SONG, SAYING,
"YOU ARE WORTHY TO TAKE THE SCROLL AND OPEN ITS SEALS,
   BECAUSE YOU WERE SLAIN,
   AND BY YOUR BLOOD YOU PURCHASED FOR GOD
      PERSONS FROM EVERY TRIBE, LANGUAGE, PEOPLE, AND NATION.
   (Revelation 5:9)

AFTER THIS I LOOKED, AND THERE WAS A GREAT CROWD THAT NO ONE COULD NUMBER. THEY WERE FROM EVERY NATION, TRIBE, PEOPLE, AND LANGUAGE. THEY WERE STANDING BEFORE THE THRONE AND BEFORE THE LAMB. THEY WORE WHITE ROBES AND HELD PALM BRANCHES IN THEIR HANDS. (Revelation 7:9)

THEN I SAW ANOTHER ANGEL FLYING HIGH OVERHEAD WITH ETERNAL GOOD NEWS TO PROCLAIM TO THOSE WHO LIVE ON EARTH, AND TO EVERY NATION, TRIBE, LANGUAGE, AND PEOPLE. (Revelation 14:6)

The ultimate multiculturalism of the Bible's contents is found here, in Revelation, proving its prophetic power that, indeed, all families of the earth were blessed because of Abram's lineage. All of us who believe are a part of it; all of us are needed. We are all a part of one Body, as we have called upon the Lord to be saved.

Now, as missionaries, we need to stand ready to reach the remaining peoples of the earth with the Gospel, so they can join this great, diverse, international number.

Chapter 7 Summary

- It is not sufficient to say each believer can figure everything out and we can expect the church to function properly. The church is not an individual institution, but a collective Kingdom. Sorting out the right from the wrong goes to those leaders God appoints to do that job.

- God's Kingdom is not an entity of this world. When God talks about all nations worshiping Him (Psalm 22:27, Psalm 117:1, Revelation 15:4) He is talking about something different from earthly concepts of worship.

- To be a missionary, one must be multicultural in embrace. This means that no matter what culture or background someone comes from, you are willing to respect them, right where they are, as they are.

- There are several modern issues that have changed interest in missions. These include Fundamentalist Christianity, modernism, and the battle that exists between the two. They present a clash between tradition and understanding. Fundamentalism caused isolation while modernism has presented theological conflict. Both theories gained ground through Bible colleges and seminaries.

- Christian reconstructionism was the idea of a man named Rousas J. (R.J.) Rushdoony (1916-2001). Rushdoony believed that Mosaic law should be the standard law for the American government, in an understanding known as theonomy. They ascribe different realms or levels of authority: family, church, and state. Morality is designated to family and church, while civil government is responsible for criminal matters and national defenses.

- Apocalypticism is the belief of an imminent apocalypse, that the world will end within one's lifetime. The central message is warning others of imminent doom. It uses assorted scare tactics, such as current event, news headlines, and government events to convince people that Christianity is being attacked and threatened in an invisible war against culture, things are going to continue to get worse, and that believers need to align themselves with these teachings, so they know what is going to happen as it happens. Concepts about the apocalypse and end times prophecies have been understood differently throughout history, and that some theories do not agree with modern ideals about eschatology.

- Dispensationalism divides the history of salvation into different eras or ages, and along with dispensational theory comes much of what is known to be eschatological interpretation, which was a core tenant of fundamentalism. It does not support a historical understanding of eschatology, but it does make it clear that Christianity is, considering such understanding, attacked and threatened at any turn.

- The origins of the Religious Right go back first to the 501(c)(3) tax codes, created in the 1960s, that established non-profit entities (such as churches, schools, and charities) as exempt from corporate income tax. Enacted laws because of the Civil Rights Movement moved for an end to public, organized discrimination, and non-profit agencies were no different than any other organization. A 1971 ruling gave the IRS the right to penalize non-profit organizations that openly practiced discrimination. In response, Bob Jones University (Greenville, South Carolina) challenged anti-discrimination under non-profit tax law because the evangelical, fundamentalist-founded school refused to admit black students, because they feared interracial dating on campus. There were those fundamentalists and evangelicals who felt the government overstepped its bounds along with Bob Jones University. Individuals such as Jerry Falwell (Thomas Road Baptist Church, Liberty University) and Paul Weyrich (political activist) jumped on the bandwagon to help with legal defense. In the process, those involved advocated Christians to get involved and change the tide of government by electing officials who shared their values.

- The Religious Right was the perfect outlet for combining fundamentalism and apocalypticism, and the result was instead of evangelizing or working in missions, people could vote the change they desired in office. In place of racism (which still largely remains through policy and social interaction) the Religious Right adopted anti-feminism, which was seen as the ultimate threat to the family, anti-abortion, which was seen as the ultimate murder in any and all situations, and anti-public schooling, pushing for parents to homeschool children or send them to private Christian schools.

- Now the enemies we hear about are often nameless or abstract, based on concepts. We are told that we need to fight for our marriages, because they are being attacked. We need to fight for our children, because the world is vying for their attention. We need to fight terrorism. We need to fight Islam. We need to fight diverse enemies in different places as the ultimate diversion from what we should be doing.

- Our Christian worldview has been dictated by a few people who've constructed a message that we should not seek to influence our world in any way, shape, or form; we should just put our heads down, hope we vote someone in office who will espouse what we want, and fight invisible enemies rather than preaching the Gospel.

- Eighteen different nations are mentioned in the Bible that we are able to recognize today, both in modern times and in history. There are numerous smaller nations that either no longer exist or are so ancient, we put forth our best guess as to what nations they would belong if they existed today.

- Nations are represented in different ways in the Bible, starting with the understanding that, in New Testament times, the immediate "world" (i.e., nations), was representative of the Roman Empire: some are represented as sublime, some deceived, some good, and some bad. Ultimately, however, the promise of redemption is the same throughout the Bible, available to all nations as they are able to see and recognize the promise of God and the hope of salvation. Just as there is promise for Israel, there is promise for all nations, for any individual person therein who chooses to become a part of the Kingdom of God.

- Jesus never degraded anyone.

- The Samaritans were (and are) a group descending from the land of Ephraim and Manasseh, with a capital city of Samaria. A mixture between paganism and Old Testament Judaism resulted in the Samaritan religion. Samaritans believe only Moses was the true prophet and receive the first five books of the Old Testament, but reject any additional Biblical revelation. There was and remains hostility between both groups.

- Our major call when it comes to multiculturalism is to treat all people equally, with the same regard and respect with which we would treat anyone else.

- The first is that, whether saved or not, people can do good things and can do the right things. These are things that we should be quick to point out, from the multicultural perspective, as steppingstones to instruction in Christian missions. The good that we do, the things that are right, the virtues that are expounded and important should be shown forth as God's message, a type of His interaction, with those who are first learning of Him or are learning more about Him.

- In our fear of multiculturalism, our fear of doing for others, we don't do the right thing ourselves.

- The third is that our neighbor is everyone, even those who are different from us.

- Jesus didn't abandon the Canaanite woman, nor did He put her down. Instead, He tested her intentions, giving her the opportunity to voice her faith.

- What we have should be so notable that others take note of what we are doing, even if what we are doing is not specifically for them.

- We should be willing to take time to pay attention to the sincere, genuine requests of those who are in need, even if we aren't sent to work with that particular group at that time.

- In missions, we will be in situations where people will be radically different than we are, and we will be the ones who are forced to adapt to others, rather than expect them to adapt to us.

- We cannot operate in missions if we are so hung up on a hardened concept of faith that we can't reach out to everyone.

- Revelation is one of the most diverse books (if not the most diverse) in the Bible, because it brings the fullness of the church's international, multicultural purpose to the surface. The purpose of the book of Revelation was to give prophetic power to the being of the church. Revelation is there to place the church in prophecy.

- Revelation's contents reveal that the world was to become a much bigger and more complicated place. The symbols of Revelation represent many of those complications, written in language the first-century believers would be able to embrace and understand.

- The seven churches of Revelation are one of the first indicators of the diversity present in the church. Within the seven churches, we see Greek, Jewish, Roman, Syrian, and Persian imagery, proving that the church of the first century was multicultural. It got that way because people were willing to proclaim the Gospel, throughout the world as they knew it, and incorporate as much education and faith as possible into diverse communities.

- The ultimate multiculturalism of the Bible's contents is found here, in Revelation, proving its prophetic power that, indeed, all families of the earth were blessed because of Abram's lineage. All of us who believe are a part of it; all of us are needed. We are all a part of one Body, as we have called upon the Lord to be saved.

Chapter 7 Assignments

- Visit a church that reflects the nation or culture you are interested in working with in missions. If no such church exists in your area, then watch such a church in a service online.

- Write a summary report (3-5 sentences) on the service you saw. What did you learn from that service?

- Write an essay (5-8 sentences) on the relevance of multiculturalism in missions. What stops you from embracing a multicultural view in your own life?

CHAPTER EIGHT:
MISSIONS ENVIRONMENT AND ATMOSPHERE

'Not called!' did you say?
'Not heard the call,' I think you should say.
Put your ear down to the Bible, and hear Him bid you go and pull sinners out
of the fire of sin. Put your ear down to the burdened, agonized heart of humanity,
and listen to its pitiful wail for help. Go stand by the gates of hell, and hear
the damned entreat you to go to their father's house and bid their brothers and sisters
and servants and masters not to come there. Then look Christ in the face —
whose mercy you have professed to obey — and tell Him whether you will join
heart and soul and body and circumstances in the march to publish His mercy
to the world.
(William Booth[1])

IT'S been said, "Wherever you go, there you are." If we think about this in terms of the demands of multiculturalism present in missions, there's something true and deep in this old expression. Wherever we are, that's where we are. We need to adjust ourselves to our atmosphere and consider what's around us, in kind. As we are called to be all things to all people (1 Corinthians 9:22), that call means we adapt to our surroundings rather than forcing ourselves on our surroundings. It is possible to do this without sinning against God or others, and the balance of how we take this monumental task on relates intimately to our level of faith and maturity.

How exactly we adjust to our surroundings is different in different places, and depending on the type of environment, we need to understand the basic situations we encounter and the things we will need to oversee and incorporate into our work.

A constant adjustment

The records we have of New Testament-era missions (both found in and outside of the Bible) depict the leaders of the church on long-term mission trips. The trips often had a primary destination along with several stops, side-trips, and visits to various cities, churches, and Christian communities along the way. The early apostles didn't just visit one city and done; over a period of years, they visited several communities, evangelizing and visiting areas unreached as well as those that were already in existence, to serve and encourage individuals everywhere they went.

THE CHURCH AT ANTIOCH INCLUDED PROPHETS AND TEACHERS: BARNABAS, SIMEON (NICKNAMED NIGER), LUCIUS FROM CYRENE, MANAEN (A CHILDHOOD FRIEND OF HEROD THE RULER), AND SAUL. AS THEY WERE WORSHIPPING THE LORD AND FASTING, THE HOLY SPIRIT SAID, "APPOINT BARNABAS AND SAUL TO THE WORK I HAVE CALLED THEM TO UNDERTAKE." AFTER THEY FASTED AND PRAYED, THEY LAID THEIR HANDS ON THESE TWO AND SENT THEM OFF. AFTER THE HOLY SPIRIT SENT THEM ON THEIR WAY, THEY WENT DOWN TO SELEUCIA. FROM THERE THEY SAILED TO CYPRUS. IN SALAMIS THEY PROCLAIMED GOD'S WORD IN THE JEWISH SYNAGOGUES. JOHN WAS WITH THEM AS THEIR ASSISTANT. THEY TRAVELED THROUGHOUT THE ISLAND UNTIL THEY ARRIVED AT PAPHOS... (Acts 13:1-4)

PAUL AND HIS COMPANIONS SAILED FROM PAPHOS TO PERGA IN PAMPHYLIA. JOHN DESERTED THEM THERE AND RETURNED TO JERUSALEM. THEY WENT ON FROM PERGA AND ARRIVED AT ANTIOCH IN PISIDIA. ON THE SABBATH, THEY ENTERED AND FOUND SEATS IN THE SYNAGOGUE THERE. AFTER THE READING OF THE LAW AND THE PROPHETS, THE SYNAGOGUE LEADERS INVITED THEM, "BROTHERS, IF ONE OF YOU HAS A SERMON FOR THE PEOPLE, PLEASE SPEAK." (Acts 13:13-15)

PAUL AND BARNABAS PROCLAIMED THE GOOD NEWS TO THE PEOPLE IN DERBE AND MADE MANY DISCIPLES. THEN THEY RETURNED TO LYSTRA, ICONIUM, AND ANTIOCH, WHERE THEY STRENGTHENED THE DISCIPLES AND URGED THEM TO REMAIN FIRM IN THE FAITH. THEY TOLD THEM, "IF WE ARE TO ENTER GOD'S KINGDOM, WE MUST PASS THROUGH MANY TROUBLES." THEY APPOINTED ELDERS FOR EACH CHURCH. WITH PRAYER AND FASTING, THEY COMMITTED THESE ELDERS TO THE LORD, IN WHOM THEY HAD PLACED THEIR TRUST.

AFTER PAUL AND BARNABAS TRAVELED THROUGH PISIDIA, THEY CAME TO PAMPHYLIA. THEY PROCLAIMED THE WORD IN PERGA, THEN WENT DOWN TO ATTALIA. FROM THERE THEY SAILED TO ANTIOCH, WHERE THEY HAD BEEN

ENTRUSTED BY GOD'S GRACE TO THE WORK THEY HAD NOW COMPLETED. ON THEIR ARRIVAL, THEY GATHERED THE CHURCH TOGETHER AND REPORTED EVERYTHING THAT GOD HAD ACCOMPLISHED THROUGH THEIR ACTIVITY, AND HOW GOD HAD OPENED A DOOR OF FAITH FOR THE GENTILES. THEY STAYED WITH THE DISCIPLES A LONG TIME. (Acts 14:21-28)

Our lesson from this fact: Missions environments aren't always about the destination or our ultimate goal, but often about the journey involved to get to wherever or whatever it is we desire to do long-term. Yes, we might have something in mind that God has placed on our hearts for missions, but that doesn't mean we will only do that one thing on a missions journey. There are plenty of places to visit, churches with which to fellowship, and people to meet along the way on a journey. Smaller projects, new ideas, and side-missions are very real things, all of which contribute to larger missions experience.

Here we learn the missions experience is not static. Each missions trip, encounter, and experience is about the journey as much as is about the end goal. Missions are a social project; something that causes us to interact with others in a different way. In it, we learn the world, our faith, and the message we proclaim is much bigger than us as individual people. As we go along, we adjust to the differences we find in each situation: different languages, cultures, styles, ideas, and experiences. In this, missions forces us to grow as much as they force us to reach out to others.

Let each be convinced in his own mind

Adapting to the environment starts by respecting the boundaries that are established in places we go. In every place in the world, there are certain established regulations, boundaries and observances. Sometimes we focus so much on change, we go into a place thinking we are going to change everything, all at once, and that to make our atmosphere more comfortable for ourselves, the change must be immediate. This is a wrong reason to do anything. Missions work is often uncomfortable. Missionaries take on the challenge of being in unknown territories with unexpected problems, having to always take the time and quick-thinking to problem-solve and proclaim the Gospel in creative ways, and engage as fast learners, adopting ourselves to whatever is around us.

WELCOME THE PERSON WHO IS WEAK IN FAITH—BUT NOT IN ORDER TO ARGUE ABOUT DIFFERENCES OF OPINION. ONE PERSON BELIEVES IN EATING EVERYTHING, WHILE THE WEAK PERSON EATS ONLY VEGETABLES. THOSE WHO EAT MUST NOT LOOK DOWN ON THE ONES WHO DON'T, AND THE ONES WHO DON'T EAT MUST NOT JUDGE THE ONES WHO DO, BECAUSE GOD HAS ACCEPTED THEM. WHO ARE YOU TO JUDGE SOMEONE ELSE'S SERVANTS? THEY STAND OR FALL BEFORE THEIR OWN LORD (AND THEY WILL STAND, BECAUSE THE LORD HAS THE POWER TO MAKE THEM STAND). ONE PERSON CONSIDERS SOME DAYS TO BE MORE SACRED THAN OTHERS, WHILE ANOTHER PERSON CONSIDERS ALL DAYS TO BE THE SAME. EACH PERSON MUST HAVE THEIR OWN CONVICTIONS. SOMEONE WHO THINKS THAT A DAY IS SACRED, THINKS THAT WAY FOR THE LORD. THOSE WHO EAT, EAT FOR THE LORD, BECAUSE THEY THANK GOD. AND THOSE WHO DON'T EAT, DON'T EAT FOR THE LORD, AND THEY THANK THE LORD TOO. WE DON'T LIVE FOR OURSELVES AND WE DON'T DIE FOR OURSELVES. IF WE LIVE, WE LIVE FOR THE LORD, AND IF WE DIE, WE DIE FOR THE LORD. THEREFORE, WHETHER WE LIVE OR DIE, WE BELONG TO GOD. THIS IS WHY CHRIST DIED AND LIVED: SO THAT HE MIGHT BE LORD OF BOTH THE DEAD AND THE LIVING. BUT WHY DO YOU JUDGE YOUR BROTHER OR SISTER? OR WHY DO YOU LOOK DOWN ON YOUR BROTHER OR SISTER? WE ALL WILL STAND IN FRONT OF THE JUDGMENT SEAT OF GOD. BECAUSE IT IS WRITTEN,

AS I LIVE, SAYS THE LORD, EVERY KNEE WILL BOW TO ME,
    AND EVERY TONGUE WILL GIVE PRAISE TO GOD.

SO THEN, EACH OF US WILL GIVE AN ACCOUNT OF OURSELVES TO GOD.

SO STOP JUDGING EACH OTHER. INSTEAD, THIS IS WHAT YOU SHOULD DECIDE: NEVER PUT A STUMBLING BLOCK OR OBSTACLE IN THE WAY OF YOUR BROTHER OR SISTER. I KNOW AND I'M CONVINCED IN THE LORD JESUS THAT NOTHING IS WRONG TO EAT IN ITSELF. BUT IF SOMEONE THINKS SOMETHING IS WRONG TO EAT, IT BECOMES WRONG FOR THAT PERSON. IF YOUR BROTHER OR SISTER IS UPSET BY YOUR FOOD, YOU ARE NO LONGER WALKING IN LOVE. DON'T LET YOUR FOOD DESTROY SOMEONE FOR WHOM CHRIST DIED. AND DON'T LET SOMETHING YOU CONSIDER TO BE GOOD BE CRITICIZED AS WRONG. GOD'S KINGDOM ISN'T ABOUT EATING FOOD AND DRINKING BUT ABOUT RIGHTEOUSNESS, PEACE, AND JOY IN THE HOLY SPIRIT. WHOEVER SERVES CHRIST THIS WAY PLEASES GOD AND GETS HUMAN APPROVAL.

SO LET'S STRIVE FOR THE THINGS THAT BRING PEACE AND THE THINGS THAT BUILD EACH OTHER UP. DON'T DESTROY WHAT GOD HAS DONE BECAUSE OF FOOD. ALL FOOD IS ACCEPTABLE, BUT IT'S A BAD THING IF IT TRIPS SOMEONE ELSE. IT'S A GOOD THING NOT TO EAT MEAT OR DRINK WINE OR TO DO ANYTHING THAT TRIPS YOUR BROTHER OR SISTER. KEEP THE BELIEF THAT YOU HAVE TO YOURSELF—IT'S BETWEEN YOU AND GOD. PEOPLE ARE BLESSED WHO DON'T CONVICT THEMSELVES BY THE THINGS THEY APPROVE. BUT THOSE WHO HAVE DOUBTS ARE CONVICTED IF THEY GO AHEAD AND EAT, BECAUSE THEY AREN'T ACTING ON THE BASIS OF FAITH. EVERYTHING THAT ISN'T BASED ON FAITH IS SIN. (Romans 14:1-23)

This passage of Scripture probably seems out of place, since it's not specifically about anything having to do with a missions environment. It is, however, a passage about adaptation. The longer I am a minister and the longer I am in missions, I hear the importance of adaptation in this passage and see its relevance in the church.

We like to generalize about people's placement and their faith levels by the way churches look. A rocking good worship band and a room full of matching T-shirts often makes people think it's a great church and everyone in there is on the same level. The truth about this, however, is that no local church and no person in the universal church is ever on the exact same level. The person who appears strongest in their faith can be the weakest one in the room. There is some truth to the accusation that the ones who try the hardest are also the ones who usually are lacking whatever's needed the most, and we tend to think people are something other than what they are. We like people who make the most spectacle, who draw the most attention to themselves, who influence others to follow after them. Unfortunately, we don't ask a lot of questions...we just follow in kind, after what might be the most popular.

This is because human nature likes its comforts in the familiar. We like to follow those people because they don't challenge us to grow in our faith. All of us want the assurance that we are good with God, as we are, and that we don't have to change in order to come to a place where we are more in alignment with His will. We want to think glory to glory and faith to faith is for someone else...or is some kind of abstract concept...rather than a reality that rolls with every one of us, every day. We want our beliefs to be solidly clear and unchanging...no matter what.

We fight adaptation because we don't want to be wrong, and adaptation is the "wiggle room" that we might not be right about everything we believe or understand in our faith. The way we understand the Bible largely comes from the influences around us, and those influences aren't always right. Romans 14 gives us great examples as pertain to influential issues: eating meat, vegetarianism, sacred day (holiday observances), regarding all days alike (not observing holidays) and regards of things as clean or unclean are largely subjective. They won't kill someone's faith or send them to hell, but they are things that people must step back and agree to disagree on. No one is forced to give anything up, but no one is forced to engage in such things, either. It is perfectly possible to be in a situation and refrain from things as much as it is to be in a situation and choose to engage.

Adaptation starts where we are, and our willingness to respect the boundaries and personal issues of others as well as people's personal perspectives when it comes to faith and issues of a faith nature. We aren't all in the same place and allowing someone to be in a different level of their faith than we are is not going to threaten our relationship with God. In missions, we are forced to adapt, or we will be unsuccessful in our task at hand. We must forsake our own personal desires to adapt to an environment alien to our own selves, leaving our comforts, experiencing life from a different perspective, different diets, different holidays and observances, different sanitation levels, different educational levels, and different cultural interactions for the sake of proclaiming and spreading the Gospel to a people who have never heard it and are not familiar with your customs, therein.

Successful missionaries know when to adapt and when to teach; how to teach within cultural appropriation; how to remain themselves while learning and growing from those around them who are radically different; and how to teach the essentials and embrace differences. By instructing, the best missionaries edify and encourage while teaching and orienting people to a new way that leads them to a greater sense of life.

Instructional aspects of missions

What we teach on a mission – and how we teach it – varies depending on where we are for a mission and the underlying purpose of that mission's work. This all relates to audience and to the level of exposure the audience has had to Christianity prior. Just because a church or ministry has had a presence somewhere doesn't mean its inhabitants have had the chance to learn about Christianity, and sometimes the presence of prior groups in an area can cause more harm than good. There are many instances of missions activity where the work itself winds up undoing anything and everything that had set its foot to that region prior.

Missions work should always revolve around an instructional component, whether that relates post-evangelism or to church building and establishment. The way this information is conveyed, however, changes among atmospheres and environments. For example, in a rural missions setting, you may deal with illiteracy, lack of resources and materials, long distances between locations, makeshift buildings, and heavy labor among those you work with, requiring them to work long hours. In urban missions, you may still deal with illiteracy, but for different reasons. You may see severe poverty, poor living conditions, financial struggles, multiple city ordinances, homelessness, government regulations, unemployment, hunger, and homelessness. Neither set of problems is more important than another but being prepared to instruct under such circumstances requires a preparedness within the missionary. There may be outstanding needs existing wherever you are that need to be met before you can ever preach the Gospel or speak a word to your desired demographic.

This is where social work heavily fits into missions work. While going somewhere and working on a project may not be the most spiritual endeavor, it's hard to preach the Gospel to someone, or teach someone to read or write, or even try to encourage church membership if the people you work with are so malnourished, they can't focus, walk long distances, or absorb what you try to tell them. If someone is sick due to their living conditions, it is going to be hard for them to pay attention to the learning or work at hand for them. It is, most likely, impossible for missionaries to solve all the problems that people have as a result of wherever it is they are, but the work of the social gospel must take its position among the call of mission work.

MY BROTHERS AND SISTERS, WHAT GOOD IS IT IF PEOPLE SAY THEY HAVE FAITH BUT DO NOTHING TO SHOW IT? CLAIMING TO HAVE FAITH CAN'T SAVE ANYONE,

CAN IT? IMAGINE A BROTHER OR SISTER WHO IS NAKED AND NEVER HAS ENOUGH FOOD TO EAT. WHAT IF ONE OF YOU SAID, "GO IN PEACE! STAY WARM! HAVE A NICE MEAL!"? WHAT GOOD IS IT IF YOU DON'T ACTUALLY GIVE THEM WHAT THEIR BODY NEEDS? IN THE SAME WAY, FAITH IS DEAD WHEN IT DOESN'T RESULT IN FAITHFUL ACTIVITY.

SOMEONE MIGHT CLAIM, "YOU HAVE FAITH AND I HAVE ACTION." BUT HOW CAN I SEE YOUR FAITH APART FROM YOUR ACTIONS? INSTEAD, I'LL SHOW YOU MY FAITH BY PUTTING IT INTO PRACTICE IN FAITHFUL ACTION. IT'S GOOD THAT YOU BELIEVE THAT GOD IS ONE. HA! EVEN THE DEMONS BELIEVE THIS, AND THEY TREMBLE WITH FEAR. ARE YOU SO SLOW? DO YOU NEED TO BE SHOWN THAT FAITH WITHOUT ACTIONS HAS NO VALUE AT ALL? WHAT ABOUT ABRAHAM, OUR FATHER? WASN'T HE SHOWN TO BE RIGHTEOUS THROUGH HIS ACTIONS WHEN HE OFFERED HIS SON ISAAC ON THE ALTAR? SEE, HIS FAITH WAS AT WORK ALONG WITH HIS ACTIONS. IN FACT, HIS FAITH WAS MADE COMPLETE BY HIS FAITHFUL ACTIONS. SO THE SCRIPTURE WAS FULFILLED THAT SAYS, ABRAHAM BELIEVED GOD, AND GOD REGARDED HIM AS RIGHTEOUS. WHAT IS MORE, ABRAHAM WAS CALLED GOD'S FRIEND. SO YOU SEE THAT A PERSON IS SHOWN TO BE RIGHTEOUS THROUGH FAITHFUL ACTIONS AND NOT THROUGH FAITH ALONE. IN THE SAME WAY, WASN'T RAHAB THE PROSTITUTE SHOWN TO BE RIGHTEOUS WHEN SHE RECEIVED THE MESSENGERS AS HER GUESTS AND THEN SENT THEM ON BY ANOTHER ROAD? AS THE LIFELESS BODY IS DEAD, SO FAITH WITHOUT ACTIONS IS DEAD. (James 2:14-26)

Once some of the more immediate needs are met, missionary instruction must match what is needed wherever it is. Urban areas may move at a faster pace; rural areas may move slower and start off with less information than an urban area. Matching one's mission to the flow, pace, and needs of a location cause the work to thrive and soar, even if it doesn't exactly match what might have been originally planned.

Urban missions

I KNOW YOUR HARDSHIP AND POVERTY (THOUGH YOU ARE ACTUALLY RICH). I ALSO KNOW THE HURTFUL THINGS THAT HAVE BEEN SPOKEN ABOUT YOU BY THOSE WHO SAY THEY ARE JEWS (THOUGH THEY ARE NOT, BUT ARE REALLY SATAN'S SYNAGOGUE). (Revelation 2:9)

I KNOW THAT YOU ARE LIVING RIGHT WHERE SATAN'S THRONE IS. YOU ARE

HOLDING ON TO MY NAME, AND YOU DIDN'T BREAK FAITH WITH ME EVEN AT THE TIME THAT ANTIPAS, MY FAITHFUL WITNESS, WAS KILLED AMONG YOU, WHERE SATAN LIVES. BUT I HAVE A FEW THINGS AGAINST YOU, BECAUSE YOU HAVE SOME THERE WHO FOLLOW BALAAM'S TEACHING. BALAAM HAD TAUGHT BALAK TO TRIP UP THE ISRAELITES SO THAT THEY WOULD EAT FOOD SACRIFICED TO IDOLS AND COMMIT SEXUAL IMMORALITY. IN THE SAME WAY, YOU HAVE SOME WHO FOLLOW THE NICOLAITANS' TEACHING. (Revelation 2:13-15)

TO THOSE WHO EMERGE VICTORIOUS, KEEPING MY PRACTICES UNTIL THE END, I WILL GIVE AUTHORITY OVER THE NATIONS— TO RULE THE NATIONS WITH AN IRON ROD AND SMASH THEM LIKE POTTERY— JUST AS I RECEIVED AUTHORITY FROM MY FATHER. I WILL ALSO GIVE THEM THE MORNING STAR. (Revelation 2:26-28)

BUT YOU DO HAVE A FEW PEOPLE IN SARDIS WHO HAVEN'T STAINED THEIR CLOTHING. THEY WILL WALK WITH ME CLOTHED IN WHITE BECAUSE THEY ARE WORTHY. (Revelation 3:4)

AS FOR THOSE WHO EMERGE VICTORIOUS, I WILL MAKE THEM PILLARS IN THE TEMPLE OF MY GOD, AND THEY WILL NEVER LEAVE IT. I WILL WRITE ON THEM THE NAME OF MY GOD AND THE NAME OF THE CITY OF MY GOD, THE NEW JERUSALEM THAT COMES DOWN OUT OF HEAVEN FROM MY GOD. I WILL ALSO WRITE ON THEM MY OWN NEW NAME. (Revelation 3:12)

AFTER ALL, YOU SAY, 'I'M RICH, AND I'VE GROWN WEALTHY, AND I DON'T NEED A THING.' YOU DON'T REALIZE THAT YOU ARE MISERABLE, PATHETIC, POOR, BLIND, AND NAKED. (Revelation 3:17)

In the last chapter, we looked at the multiculturalism present in the book of Revelation with specific mention for the seven churches found in the early chapters of Revelation's contents. They are relevant here because each of the seven churches of Revelation was located in an urban area. It also proves that the church, by its design, is here to exist as an urban entity. This is not to say churches cannot exist in rural or suburban areas, or that such churches are somehow sub-par in the eyes of God, because this is not true. It is true to say, however, that the suburban or rural church is often exalted as holier or more relevant to an urban counterpart, modeled as some sort of example for the entire church. Every church addressed in the New Testament falls into the category of an "urban church," located in cities that were trade routes, noted for travel, business, and social interaction. There are three main reasons why cities were noted for church activity: cities are where people are and that makes location relevant to dispersion of such a vital message, because urban areas host urban issues, including severe poverty, "throw away" people looking for a better life (orphans, widows, etc.), and there is also a diversity in spiritual belief present in urban areas, as people seek out hope and truth among the things they encounter and experience.

A brief examination of the churches of Revelation reveal to us spiritual issues that are common to urban areas:

- **Ephesus**: False leaders, perseverance through hardships, forsaking faith and priorities

- **Smyrna**: Suffering, poverty, slander, imprisonment

- **Pergamum**: False spiritualties, tests of faith, holding to false teaching

- **Thyatira**: Service, perseverance, false prophets,

- **Sardis**: Deceitful reputation, appearing to be one thing, but being something else, weakness, forgetting what was taught, a faithful few who remain true

- **Philadelphia**: Opportunity, little strength, deceptive factions, patient endurance, trial

- **Laodicea**: Spiritual indifference (lukewarmness), materialism, superficial prosperities, spiritual wretchedness, pitifulness, poverty, blindness, and nakedness

Because urban areas are so densely populated, they represent issues that are a part of everyone's spiritual life and spiritual experience. The issues faced by the seven churches of revelation are urban, but at the same time, they are also universal. The issues affect the entire church, and they also reach and represent the entirety of the Body. They also show us the mindset of individuals in urban areas, and the different things that influence the specific spiritual needs and challenges that exist therein.

Revelation's seven churches prove to us that the specific needs of urban churches have always existed. The struggle is real; it has always been there; and it always will be there. Some issues that we see among modern urban churches include:

- **Membership declines:** Churches everywhere have experienced membership decline. The rise of megachurches has caused smaller churches to lose members, and this hits urban churches in a few ways. The first is that the local church on the corner or in a storefront in the neighborhood was often the anchor of the community. It was a place people could go when they were in trouble, the neighborhood spiritual leader often knew everyone in that area by name or by family identity, and the church was involved in that community. As people flock to larger churches in suburban areas or other neighborhoods, local churches cannot sustain their overhead to keep the church operational. Even if they do keep their doors open, they often do not have enough money to maintain outreach or social programs.

- **High expenses:** Property in urban areas is expensive, even in lower income areas. Gentrification, urban sprawl, and forced relocation have raised rent even higher in neighborhoods that would not otherwise be so expensive. High expenses for church members mean they have less money to give to the church, and high overheads for the church mean that it takes that much more money to make a church functional or operational. High crime also makes insurance rates higher and makes theft that much more of a possibility for a church already struggling just to exist.

- **Lack of community unity:** It doesn't seem like anyone agrees with anyone today. This is nowhere seen more than in an urban area. The fact that people are more individualistic than ever and feel they are right, and others are always wrong has created communities without vision, often fighting over what is best, with some not caring at all.

- **Government abuses**: Police brutality. Biased court systems. Unfair laws. These things exist in rural areas as well as urban ones, but because there are more people in cities, these things become far more relevant among urban areas.

- **Poverty**: Only 15% of the world's poverty exists in urban areas.[2] Because urban poverty is compact rather than spread out, it leads to complications in living conditions: domestic violence, violence, unemployment, substance abuse, homelessness, alcoholism and crime all impact surrounding neighbors and neighborhoods, thus leading others to take note and address the results of poverty in any given circumstance. Even though none of these specified issues are unique to poverty situations, we often only take note of them when they exist among lower income populations.

- **Diversity**: The multiculturalism of the New Testament exists because the focus of New Testament work was in urban areas. Cities are host to a variety of races, citizenships, religions, nations, and identities, all of which come together (sometimes in peace, sometimes in hostility) to live and work in the pursuit of a better life.

- **Environment**: Pollution, overcrowding, noise, improper sanitation, building codes, needed sidewalk or sewer repairs, fights with the landlord over building conditions, and the like are all large aspects of city living and ministering.

Urban ministries require appropriate outreach to get to Gospel work: Homeless programs, feeding programs, shelter programs, clean water initiatives, literacy, higher education (GED and beyond), elementary schools, prison outreach, social justice, alternatives to violence, medical assistance, English as a Second Language, school uniform/supplies drive, job training, skill building, problem solving, drug and alcohol rehabilitation, domestic violence education, women's healthcare, and so on.

Seeing what exists in an area is the best way to "fill in the gaps." For example, in Raleigh, North Carolina, there are multiple programs for winter coats and jackets, held every year. There is no dental program for seniors. There are several homeless shelters, but there are few feeding programs. Matching what exists with what does not exist is the best way to make a statement for your mission work and gives unique opportunity to reach populations with the Gospel who otherwise would not hear of what was going on.

When it comes to Gospel proclamation, all the above factors impact how ready a community is to receive – or not receive – the work of the Gospel. When feasible needs are met, a community is more likely to take interest in reception and Gospel mobilization themselves. Urban environments are powerful for great, solid, thriving churches if they are approached correctly, which involves the following steps (which can apply to churches in any atmosphere):

- Identifying issues and needs that impact the reception of the Gospel.

- Meeting said needs, inasmuch as is possible.

- Mobilizing Gospel needs, parallel to practical needs, and reaching out as is necessary: either evangelization or leadership development.

- Training within the church for members to evangelize and bring people to church with them, communication exercises as well as Gospel and Biblical instructions.

- Focus on justice and community interest for a social Gospel approach for every church member, even after a mission is over.

Suburban missions

AND YE SHALL MEASURE FROM WITHOUT THE CITY ON THE EAST SIDE TWO THOUSAND CUBITS, AND ON THE SOUTH SIDE TWO THOUSAND CUBITS, AND ON THE WEST SIDE TWO THOUSAND CUBITS, AND ON THE NORTH SIDE TWO THOUSAND CUBITS; AND THE CITY SHALL BE IN THE MIDST: THIS SHALL BE TO THEM THE SUBURBS OF THE CITIES. (Numbers 35:5, KJV)

AND HE TOOK AWAY THE HORSES THAT THE KINGS OF JUDAH HAD GIVEN TO THE SUN, AT THE ENTERING IN OF THE HOUSE OF THE LORD, BY THE CHAMBER

OF NATHANMELECH THE CHAMBERLAIN, WHICH WAS IN THE SUBURBS, AND BURNED THE CHARIOTS OF THE SUN WITH FIRE. (2 Kings 23:11, KJV)

AND THE FIVE THOUSAND, THAT ARE LEFT IN THE BREADTH OVER AGAINST THE FIVE AND TWENTY THOUSAND, SHALL BE A PROFANE PLACE FOR THE CITY, FOR DWELLING, AND FOR SUBURBS: AND THE CITY SHALL BE IN THE MIDST THEREOF. (Ezekiel 48:15, KJV)

Some in Missiology might question if suburban mission work is a legitimate undertaking. It is my argument that it is, because people who live in the suburbs need Jesus just as much as anyone in an urban or rural setting does. It is unfortunate because most suburban areas are not considered for mission settings, as due to what they represent. As a result, a large mission field is often ignored, and missed, for missions purposes.

I think that Missiology dislikes the suburbs for missions activity because suburban dwellers are seen as churchgoers who participate in missions by contributing to them financially. As a demographic, suburban dwellers may visit a mission or may go on a trip, but they are not typically a group thought of as needing Jesus or needing missions intervention. In truth, suburban missions are quite different from the extremes of urban or rural mission work. They are not as physically intensive but often take a great toll on a missionary from a mental and emotional perspective.

Not all suburbs are bustling with profits, but suburbs are often associated with upper middle-class individuals who don't desire to live with the complications and issues of city life. There are many reasons why someone may decide to live in the suburbs, including fear of harm or danger, high cost of living, traffic, or perceived bad neighborhoods. Suburbs are attractive to many who don't mind daily commutes and different expenses to foot the bill for a quieter lifestyle.

Suburban living isn't typically much cheaper than city living, especially in suburbs that are close to an urban area. The further out one goes, the cheaper costs become. Rural living is usually the most inexpensive, while suburban living can sometimes be equivalent or more than city living. This isn't a problem for many in the suburbs, however, because suburb living goes with a city income. This means people in the suburbs often have lifestyles to match their incomes, complete with the identities of what we now classify as "family values": yearly family vacations, large holiday celebrations, children who are shuffled to and from school and social events, and other marks of social prosperity among different cultures.

One thing that is often cheaper in the suburbs is commercial property. Commercial land is also cheaper, because suburbs aren't typically regarded as business centers. There is more land to be had at a lower rate. This has driven an entire spiritual movement to the suburbs, one that no one ever considered. This entity is the megachurch, a reflection of suburban ideas, living, attitudes, and interests. While they do not all exist outside of cities, many do – and they flourish in these areas due to lower costs and lots of people who crave certain comforts of spirituality.

When we discussed urban missions, we examined the fact that the church's basic design is as an urban entity. One of the deeper spiritual reasons for this is because the church exists to address issues that make people feel uncomfortable. True spirituality hits at the very fabric of our being and challenges us to make changes that we might not otherwise consider. While in the natural our concerns manifest in material forms (we won't have enough money or something else to survive), God proves that our spiritual concerns should be a much higher priority. If we are lousy people, if we don't care about others, if we don't care about our world, all the materialism in the world won't save us. It won't amount to much of anything when all is said and done, and earthly pursuits aren't going to matter in the scope of eternity.

That's the catch with suburban life: it's about right now, about materialistic pursuit, rather than eternal ones. That's just what the megachurch focuses on and emphasizes: comfort rather than spiritual discomfort. The churches emphasize comfort: comfortable clothes, comfortable atmospheres, comfortable beverages, comfortable messages. No one is forced to look at the materialism of their lives and realize it doesn't matter if they aren't right with God. The people in the suburbs can be educated, they can be prosperous, they can even seem to "have it all," but having it all doesn't matter if the Lord is not in it.

Some interests of suburban missions include:

- **Complacency**: Suburban living is about comfort and maintaining a certain level of comfortable living. Complacent people are not as apt to seek God as someone who experiences discomfort, and this means many in the suburbs aren't concerned about eternity or their eternal fate.

- **Intellectualism:** Faith for many in suburban areas is more of an intellectual pursuit rather than a genuine spiritual seeking or need. With more money, someone in the suburbs might pursue numerous spiritual interests and hobbies at once. For example, someone might take an interest in yoga or seek out a self-help seminar that costs more than a mortgage payment or take a trip to Tibet to seek out spiritual enlightenment. Someone in a poorer area might not have the money or the interest to invest in something like this but would rather seek what is immediate and accessible to meet their basic needs.

- **Pursuit of a lifestyle:** Everyone wants to "keep up with the Joneses," but when you just don't have the money to do it, it becomes less of a focus. If money is there to have the latest phone or gadget, trade in a car every three years, go on vacation, or have whatever your neighbors have or do, the temptation exists to always live competition with others.

- **Debt:** While people in suburban areas do have more money than those in poverty areas, debt is a reality for many of them. With a competitive nature to look like everyone else, overspending is a reality.

- **Hidden family secrets:** We're quick to think teenage pregnancy, drunken brawls, domestic violence, drug abuse, and alcoholism only happen in poor urban areas. The suburbs are full of the same problems seen in poor, urban areas, but they are kept under tight wraps for fear someone might discover them. Suburban lifestyles maintain secrecy for years that often come out at a most inopportune time.

- **Classism:** Suburban living equates to living within a certain class, thus those of other classes are sometimes seen as substandard, lazy, ignorant, or unfortunate.

Therefore, suburban ministries require appropriate outreach to get to Gospel work: Globalization, missions interest, grade schools, drug and alcohol rehabilitation, doctrinal instruction, domestic violence education, and so on...

Suburban areas are often in great need of spiritual education. Megachurches often lack the needed structure, accountability, and teaching to make an impact on someone's life and help them discover Christianity in a way that will bless their everyday lives. Suburban believers need to see salvation and faith beyond their own experiences, realizing that materialism isn't the answer to everything and that they should give to others out of their abundance. With a stronger spiritual understanding, suburban missions should help believers to mobilize the Gospel, engaging in evangelism, being able to share and understand the basics of their faith with others, and focus on establishing solid, committed churches that can bring change and life to their suburban communities.

Rural missions

BUT HOUSES IN SETTLEMENTS THAT ARE UNWALLED WILL BE CONSIDERED AS IF THEY WERE COUNTRY FIELDS. THEY CAN BE BOUGHT BACK, AND THEY MUST BE RELEASED AT THE JUBILEE. (Leviticus 25:31)

IF I GO INTO THE FIELDS,
*   I SEE ONLY THE SLAIN IN BATTLE.*
IF I ENTER THE CITY,
*   I SEE ONLY THOSE SUFFERING FROM FAMINE.*
EVEN BOTH PROPHET AND PRIEST
*   WANDER ABOUT AIMLESSLY IN IGNORANCE.* (Jeremiah 14:18)

AFTER THAT HE APPEARED IN A DIFFERENT FORM TO TWO OF THEM WHO WERE WALKING ALONG IN THE COUNTRYSIDE. (Mark 16:12)

The work of the Gospel isn't a competition versus urban, suburban, or rural lifestyles. It is true that information spreads faster in cities than it does in rural areas, and that the original work of the church was seen in cities rather than rural areas. This doesn't mean we can't have rural churches, or that rural churches are less important or less relevant. It simply means that the origin of the church itself is found in urban areas, and that church life in rural areas may be a little different than in urban ones.

Rural churches are at the heart of many communities. There are many people living in rural areas all over the world, in diverse places, with unique challenges. Rural areas may not be the flashiest places to live, but they provide important agricultural and natural needs for the entire human population. With the lowest populations, government infrastructures don't always allow for the needs of rural areas, thus making many of them low on levels of social and economic development. Without needed funds, people in rural areas do without many things those in urban or suburban areas take for granted. Lack of transportation, accessible roads, and lack of technology leaves people in rural communities without the things they need...and some, without the Gospel.

Some issues that we see among modern rural churches include:

- **Lack of diversity**: Rural areas aren't very diverse. They usually consist of groups of families that have lived in the area for generations or of migrant workers who come through due to land or crop availability. There aren't many people who are different from those who've always been there, and this leads to isolation in thinking and attitude. Without exposure to other cultures and types of people, it's easy to think a group is superior or the way that things are done among that group is always right, without question.

- **Prejudice**: Prejudice exists everywhere, but the way it takes form is often different. Prejudice is prejudice, however, no matter how it is packaged. Rural areas often resent outsiders in any form and are more apt to develop prejudicial attitudes about people who have differences from what is classified as the "norm." Note: this is not to say every person in a rural area is prejudiced, not by a long shot, but to simply observe that such attitudes are very common in rural areas.

- **Poverty**: 85% of the world's poverty is found in rural areas.[3] Whereas urban poverty might include housing (however poor quality it might be), rural poverty might have a basic exterior shelter, such as a shack, a makeshift shanty, with a dirt floor and no running water or indoor bathroom facilities. In the west, people associate poverty with laziness (which is certainly not the case), but in other nations, poverty is associated with the hardest of work, with agricultural work in the fields for long hours while people struggle to sell a few assorted goods to feed their families one day at a time. The issues associated with poverty in the west still exist elsewhere, such as domestic violence, drug and alcohol abuse, lack of education and training, lack of jobs, hunger, homelessness, and lack of medical care, on top of high infant and often adult mortality rates.

- **Unemployment:** Corporations and businesses go where the skilled workforce goes; thus, unemployment tends to lag in rural areas.

- **Sanitation:** Akin to poverty is poor sanitation. In many parts of the world, hygiene is a commodity. Lack of access to clean water, cleaning supplies, proper toilet and bathing facilities, and the ability to cook and clean dishware, clothes, and other household items may not exist.

- **Government corruption:** Corrupt governments exist everywhere, but they are more frequently discovered in urban areas. Once the news comes out, there are enough people to mobilize, protest, and work activism projects against corruption. In rural areas, it takes longer to receive information and there aren't enough people to mobilize and bring about change. Corrupt governments mean those in rural areas often suffer the most as forgotten citizens.

- **Lack of education:** Individuals living in rural areas are typically not as well educated as those who live in urban areas, because there aren't as many opportunities for schooling. When opportunities do exist, they either come at a high financial cost or are not the same quality as an urban education.

- **Slower pace:** Rural areas don't move as fast as urban ones. Information tends to take longer to reach rural areas. As a result, church work is different in rural areas; it follows a slower pace, doctrinal reflections tend to be older, and beliefs are more conservative and fundamental in approach. This means individuals in rural areas may be more apt to do things the way they have always done them or may be highly resistant to change.

- **Lack of technology:** There are still parts of the world without regular electricity, computers, internet access, cell phone towers, sanitation, and other essential means that can equate to education, business, and learning.

Therefore, rural ministries require appropriate outreach to get to Gospel work: Feeding programs, shelter programs, clean water initiatives, sanitation initiatives, literacy, higher education (GED and beyond), elementary schools, globalization, social justice, alternatives to violence, medical assistance, school uniform/supplies drive, scholarship funds, job training, skill building, problem solving, drug and alcohol rehabilitation, domestic violence education, women's healthcare, Fair Trade initiatives, and so on...

Much like in urban areas, seeing what exists in an area is the best way to "fill in the gaps." There may very well be feeding programs in rural areas, but there may not be a program for educational opportunities. When it comes to Gospel proclamation, all the above factors impact how ready a rural community is to receive – or not receive – the work of the Gospel. Rural missions need to see the practicality of working together, of the way that the Gospel can change and impact their lives and can create new hope and life in areas that might otherwise die without spiritual intervention.

Chapter 8 Summary

- No local church and no person in the universal church is ever on the exact same level. The person who appears strongest in their faith can be the weakest one in the room.

- We fight adaptation because we don't want to be wrong, and adaptation is the "wiggle room" that we might not be right about everything we believe or understand in our faith.

- Adaptation starts where we are. Successful missionaries know when to adapt and when to teach; how to teach within cultural appropriation; how to remain themselves while learning and growing from those around them who are radically different; and how to teach the essentials and embrace differences.

- Missions should always have an instructional component, whether that's post-evangelism or church building and establishment. What we teach on a mission – and how we teach it – varies depending on where we are for a mission and the purpose of that mission's work.

- The church, by its design, is here to exist as an urban entity. This is not to say churches cannot exist in rural or suburban areas, or that such churches are somehow sub-par in the eyes of God. There are three main reasons why cities were noted for church activity: cities are where people are and that makes location relevant to dispersion of such a vital message, because urban areas host urban issues, including severe poverty, "throw away" people looking for a better life (orphans, widows, etc.), and there is also a diversity in spiritual belief present in urban areas, as people seek out hope and truth among the things they encounter and experience. Seeing what exists in an area is the best way to "fill in the gaps."

- Revelation's seven churches proves the specific needs of urban churches have always existed. The struggle is real; it has always been there; and it always will be there. Urban environments are powerful for great, solid, thriving churches if they are approached correctly, which involves the following steps (which can apply to churches in any atmosphere): Identifying issues and needs that impact the reception of the Gospel, meeting said needs, inasmuch as is possible, training within the church for members to evangelize and bring people to church with them and communication exercises as well as Gospel and Biblical instructions.

- People who live in the suburbs need Jesus just as much as anyone in an urban or rural setting does. True spirituality hits at the very fabric of our being and challenges us to make changes that we might not otherwise consider. While in the natural our concerns manifest in material forms (we won't have enough money or something else to survive), God proves that our spiritual concerns should be a much higher priority.

- Suburban areas are often in great need of spiritual education. Megachurches often lack the needed structure, accountability, and teaching to make an impact on someone's life and help them discover Christianity in a way that will bless their everyday lives. Such believers need to see salvation and faith beyond their own experiences, realizing that materialism isn't the answer to everything and that they should give to others out of their abundance.

- Rural churches are at the heart of many communities worldwide, as there are many people living in rural areas all over the world, in diverse places, with unique challenges. Rural missions need to see the practicality of working together, of the way that the Gospel can change and impact their lives, and can create new hope and life in areas that might otherwise die without spiritual intervention.

Chapter 8 Assignments

- Write a summary report (3-5 sentences) on an area or region that you feel called to in missions. Is that area urban, rural, or suburban? Applying what you read in the text, how can you summarize some of the needs they have?

- Connect with a minister somewhere who is in an area where you are interested in operating missions or who has experience in that nation. Conduct an interview with them about what it is like to minister in that area and what they see because of their missions work. Provide a report on that interview (at least one page in length).

CHAPTER NINE:
PRACTICAL PREPARATION FOR MISSIONS

If God's love is for anybody anywhere, it's for everybody everywhere.
(Edward Lawlor[1])

AS you prepare for a missions trip, you'll probably experience a rush of different perceptions and emotions about the experience. There will be people who want to pray for you and who are excited to see you off on your journey. Some might offer to help fund part of your trip, and others might be quick to offer items or assorted advice about where you are going and what you'll do when you get there. Some people might ask for souvenirs or for pictures in front of famous landmarks. You might start to feel overwhelmed, question your work, or wonder what you are about to do.

This is perfectly normal, as missions work is a big undertaking. It is normal to have some questions and even doubts. It is also perfectly fine to recognize the practical aspects of missions that aren't real deep and spiritual, which may become overwhelming at points in the process. In this chapter we are going to offer the big deep breath every missionary needs to take as they move along and take some practical steps to ensure a missions trip comes forth as productively and hassle-free as possible.

Knowing the work to which you have been called

I cannot stress this point enough: you need to know the work to which you have been called. This might sound like a spiritual endeavor, and in some sense, it is, but it is also a practical aspect. If you have any question as to whether God is sending you on that mission trip and it is more than a little self-doubt, you need to reassess the trip and spend some time with God, making sure that God has called you to take on the task you are about to do.

It is completely normal to have some questions about the work of missions in your own life, especially if you are going on a mission trip for the first time or to a place that is far removed from what you know. Missions work is a great honor of service for the Lord, no doubt, but it is also a big undertaking. Acknowledging this does not, in any way, diminish the calling, nor does it put it down. The work of missions can be intimidating and there can be questions that we all have as we start to break down the planning of a mission into doable steps and are aware of all that we must do, and leave behind, in the process.

THEREFORE, AS A PRISONER FOR THE LORD, I ENCOURAGE YOU TO LIVE AS PEOPLE WORTHY OF THE CALL YOU RECEIVED FROM GOD. (Ephesians 4:1)

THEREFORE, BROTHERS AND SISTERS, BE EAGER TO CONFIRM YOUR CALL AND ELECTION. DO THIS AND YOU WILL NEVER EVER BE LOST. (2 Peter 1:10)

It may very well be that God is at the heart of what you are doing and you are indeed called to do it, but others have clouded over the vision with their own suggestions, methods, and doubts. There is also the possibility of taking on something that isn't wise for you to do, perhaps at this point in time. If you are going on a mission, you need to know exactly why you are going, what you will do while you are there, leave a little wiggle room for things to not go as perfectly as planned, and to be overall prepared (as much is as possible) for anything and everything to take place.

Prior to a missions trip, every missionary needs to take some time with God and sit in His presence, relaxing and allowing the stress factors of the upcoming trip to dissipate. As missionaries, we are called to hear from God on behalf of people we do not know well and plan a trip that will meet the needs of a people different from us in more ways than one. This requires a missionary to have the good sense of spiritual direction, able to hear the inward witness of the Spirit at work within them and guiding them to what they need to do in each situation that will arise. Having good help, such as solid five-fold leaders of differing offices along with them, makes the trip that much better and makes it that much easier to hear from God and know the necessary direction to take in every situation.

Self-awareness and proper self-assessment

One thing I talk about frequently when it comes to matters of church, identity, and placement is the issue of being properly self-aware. When I speak of being self-aware, I am talking about an individual's ability to esteem themselves properly, knowing what they are good at, what they are not good at, what they are suited for, and being humble enough to accept the fact that they are not suited for, nor good at everything. This comes about as an individual steps back from the things they do in their lives and admits they do not do everything well, nor are they as efficient with some things as they are with others. It's what some refer to as "being real" with oneself. It's also vitally important for successful missions (and successful ministry, at that). As ministers, we can waste so much time trying to prove something about ourselves through the work that we do, the things that we say, and the way we appear to other people. We do this to gain some sense of ourselves, some sense of our own confidence and bolstering through ministry and doing this is so detrimental to ministry vision and purpose.

THE PRECIOUS SONS OF ZION, COMPARABLE TO FINE GOLD, HOW ARE THEY ESTEEMED AS EARTHEN PITCHERS, THE WORK OF THE HANDS OF THE POTTER! (Lamentations 4:2, KJV)

LET NOTHING BE DONE THROUGH STRIFE OR VAINGLORY; BUT IN LOWLINESS OF MIND LET EACH ESTEEM OTHER BETTER THAN THEMSELVES. (Philippians 2:3, KJV)

Nobody goes into ministry as a perfect person, and nobody remains in ministry through perfection. This is a myth and lie we tell ourselves to make it look like we are better than we really are. Every one of us hopes ministry will provide us with something, with a sense of ourselves that we can't get somewhere else. Preachers love big offerings, the applause they get when they say something the congregation really likes, and we know how to tailor our messages to perfectly suit the reaction we desire. It's a dirty secret, but it's a true one. This is why self-assessment and awareness are so essential to ministry: we can easily start believing we are the person who knows how to rally a crowd rather than truly listening to the Spirit and think all our human efforts are really God at work.

Self-assessment means we stop pursuing things that are just not God, no matter how we spin them, in our lives. You do not have to be the minister that writes a ton of books, has a ton of DVDs available, or who thinks they have so many spiritual gifts, there isn't room for another one in your life. You can be a minister who does whatever it is that God instructs you to do, no matter how different it might be.

The missions field is not the place for trying to use human methods to get personal adoration and praise from others. Not only is a language barrier possibly present, but odds are also good that all the things you typically do to rally a crowd won't work wherever you are. With different cultures come different expectations for speakers, ministers, and preachers, and all those things you do over here that everyone thinks are so cute and funny won't translate properly wherever you're going. In fact, they may cause offense or be perceived to be done in bad taste.

The missions field is a place where ministers have to see what they are made of and deal with themselves in a way they do not have to encounter while running a church circuit. A natural talent or aptitude for public entertainment does not work in missions. People want to see and experience the power of God, not someone who can make a public spectacle of themselves. Thus, being self-aware is essential to a successful mission. Do what you know you are called to do, what you are seasoned and appointed to do, and don't go adding a lot of details to that calling or to that work while you are on missions.

Learning to be peaceful within oneself

While writing this book, I saw a meme online that said: "Maturity is realizing how many things don't require your opinion." This should stop and make us all examine our own behavior, especially when it comes to missions work. As leaders, we are supposed to be adults, grown-ups who know when to be silent and when to speak, as the Bible instructs. If we watch social media, or pulpit preaching, or general conversations, however, we aren't seeing a lot of this maturity, this essential self-control, within a leader's walk.

This is because leaders today feel the intense competition to try and prove they are something. We tell ourselves we must speak to make a teachable moment out of something and instruct everyone else, but the truth is that we like to have people see our side or agree that we are right. If we're the first to point something out, we like that even better. Yes, sometimes we have teachable moments, but if we always just must get our input in and can't stand an admonition to be quiet or to refrain from speaking, there's something in that for us to look at within ourselves. There's a difference between trying to instruct and just not being able to withhold an opinion, and successful ministry requires learning the difference.

AND TO ESTEEM THEM VERY HIGHLY IN LOVE FOR THEIR WORK'S SAKE. AND BE AT PEACE AMONG YOURSELVES. (1 Thessalonians 5:13, KJV)

THOSE WHO MAKE PEACE SOW THE SEEDS OF JUSTICE BY THEIR PEACEFUL ACTS. (James 3:18)

THEREFORE, DEAR FRIENDS, WHILE YOU ARE WAITING FOR THESE THINGS TO HAPPEN, MAKE EVERY EFFORT TO BE FOUND BY HIM IN PEACE—PURE AND FAULTLESS. (2 Peter 3:14)

MAY YOU HAVE MORE AND MORE MERCY, PEACE, AND LOVE. (Jude 1:2)

The term "peace" doesn't just mean having the absence of strife or difficulty. Peace is about wholeness and completion and reaching a place where we don't need to do anything specific or special in order to feel content and strengthened within ourselves. Even if we don't speak, even if we don't get our way, even if we deal with strife, difficulty, or disappointment, we are not disturbed because it doesn't change who we are or what we are about.

Learning to be peaceful within ourselves changes our outlook on life and ministry and makes it less relevant to voice and do so many of the things we waste time doing to try and get attention or prove something about ourselves. This ties in with missions because missions challenge who we are and what we are about. If we aren't at peace within ourselves, we will find a missions trip to be a confusing journey. The distractions that naturally come along on a missions trip will be successful, and the experience will be spent jumping from thing to thing, leaving the missionary confused and empty. Once again, we are also dealing with the questions about adapting to other cultures and the reality that being so opinionated is often considered rude, disagreeable, and not met with many cheers like Americans fascinated with homegrown entertainment often do. Other cultures may find such behavior as completely off-putting, placing a missionary in an awkward position throughout the remainder of their work. Missionaries must be reasonably confident in their calling and knowledgeable about how to do what they need to do, with an inner quietness that doesn't prompt them to try and draw needless or empty attention to get others to follow them.

Handling anxiety

ANXIETY LEADS TO DEPRESSION, BUT A GOOD WORD ENCOURAGES. (Proverbs 12:25)

THROW ALL YOUR ANXIETY ONTO HIM, BECAUSE HE CARES ABOUT YOU. (1 Peter 5:7)

Each person has their own level of anxiety over situations and circumstances. Through our lives, we learn how to handle those moments of discomfort the best way we can. On missions, don't be surprised if your own personal anxieties surface or if you experience anxieties you have never experienced before. The best thing to do in such situations is take a step back, a deep breath, and forge ahead to do whatever it is that you are there to do. It may very well not be easy, but doing so with confidence and poise is something that translates well everywhere.

Traveling

YOU STUDY MY TRAVELING AND RESTING. YOU ARE THOROUGHLY FAMILIAR WITH ALL MY WAYS. (Psalm 139:3)

If you aren't very experienced at traveling, you will be in for many new experiences and excitements. If you are more seasoned at travel, you will still be in for some surprises, especially if you have never been out of the country before. Most of us know that travel is an involved thing, but when we are going somewhere for missions, the way we handle ourselves in travel is more relevant than ever. Travel is exciting, but it becomes an immense hassle if one isn't properly prepared with a mindset of travel.

This means a missionary needs to put on their travel hat and be prepared for the various forms of travel they will encounter on a missionary trip. It is customary to fly to an overseas destination, but that is, most likely, not the only form of transit you will encounter on a trip. Depending on where you go, the trip itself might prove to be quite diverse in travel accommodation. Here are a few things to keep in mind:

- Most nations require an individual to acquire a passport to leave national borders. Many additional nations require a visa if an individual is planning to remain in their nation for any substantial length of time. This is not the case for every country or every trip, so a missionary should aware themselves of where they are going and what is required to visit or stay in that country for the length of time they will be there.

- International airline accommodations vary between nations. Sometimes it is better to fly business or first class if you are going to parts of the Middle East, Africa, or Asia.

- Many nations have only a few major airports that receive international flights. If you are flying into a regional airport, you will probably fly into a major airport and then take a much smaller plane to a regional one.

- Much of the world still relies on train transportation between nations, especially in Canada and Europe. It is usually inexpensive and reasonably comfortable.

- Land transportation in less developed nations is often uncomfortable and unlike transport within the United States or parts of Europe. Roads are often poorly constructed, and vehicles are smaller. Trips via car, bus, or sometimes cab may be long, bumpy, and highly congested.

- Most airlines allow for at least one free checked bag weighing somewhere between 25 and 50 pounds, depending on the distance of the trip. If a bag is over the designated weight, it can cost anywhere from $25 to $150 per bag, each way. It is advisable to travel as lightly as is feasible, as travel with many items can get cumbersome as luggage is dragged around different airports, in and out of vehicles, and is always a possibility of being stolen or lost.

- Security clearances are required to board an airplane to any nation. This requires passing through a metal detector, scanning of any carry-on luggage brought on board, removal of shoes and outerwear, and passport clearance. When one returns to the United States, they have to go through customs, a process by which they are required to pay tax on any items they bought out of the nation and are now bringing back with them. Customs also clears passengers to ensure they do not have any illegal or hazardous items with them that they smuggle into the country.

- Changing time zones (especially many at once) can be an exhausting experience. Rest and adjustment periods should be considered for extreme changes.

Communication

THEY WERE TALKING TO EACH OTHER ABOUT EVERYTHING THAT HAD HAPPENED. (Luke 24:14)

When you get to wherever you are going, how do you intend to let everyone you know that you're safe and you are getting ready to settle in as a missionary. Are you going to call? Are you going to send a Facebook message? Maybe an email?

Whenever you cross international waters, telephone plans that do not include proper international plans will not work. This means if you don't have an expensive international phone plan, you won't be able to make cellular phone calls until you return to the United States. If you don't stay with a host who lets you use their phone (if they even have a phone that makes international calls), you'll have to make sure that your tablet, laptop computer, or smartphone with internet access can communicate for you.

That having been said, Wi-Fi is not available everywhere in the world. It is available in most places, but not everyone has it in a church or private residence, and it is not always free. It's also worth proceeding with caution when using public Wi-Fi, as hackers typically steal information over public Wi-Fi units. Depending on where you are in the world, this may range from a sublime concern to a serious matter of personal security.

Therefore, when it comes to using Wi-Fi overseas, especially if it is unsecured, limit your usage to communication with family, friends, and church members back home. Don't use the time to buy some outfit you must get on Ebay or a bunch of items on Amazon. It's unwise to try and access banking information, as well. Make sure you can communicate and keep emergency contact information on hand while traveling, but don't expect to do a whole lot of buying and selling online while overseas with an American-based bank account.

Medical

A JOYFUL HEART HELPS HEALING, BUT A BROKEN SPIRIT DRIES UP THE BONES. (Proverbs 17:22)

Depending on where one goes, a missionary may or may not be required to receive certain medical care and attention prior to entering another country. It is best to discuss any travel plans with a doctor or a travel medicine clinic at least four weeks prior to an international trip. There may or may not be requirements for proving you do not have certain diseases to enter certain countries, certain courses or rounds of medication prescribed to prevent certain diseases, and in some instances, vaccines are required or recommended. The standard setup for care often divides vaccinations into those classified as required, recommended, or routine. At current, the only required vaccination for travel is yellow fever when an individual is going to sub-Saharan Africa or parts of South America. Recommended vaccines are those recommended to travelers based on diseases prevalent or existing wherever they plan to go. These include vaccines for rabies, typhoid fever, or certain types of encephalitis. Routine vaccines are ones that most in developed nations received in childhood but may be brought up to date (such as diphtheria, tetanus, measles, hepatitis A and B, or rotavirus). If you are going somewhere and you receive courses of antibiotics or a vaccine, make sure you are prepared for any side effects or possible reactions to whatever is administered, giving yourself plenty of time to heal before the trip begins.

If you have health insurance, it is wise to investigate if your insurance will cover any accidents, illnesses, or issues you may encounter overseas. Most government-funded insurances do not cover accidents or medical issues that occur outside of the United States. While many nations do have free health coverage for citizens, it does not extend to visitors in their nation. Health care availability and services may also not be as readily available in developing nations as they are in more developed nations. In such instances, the quality of care, cleanliness or sterilization, and evolution of medical practice may be diminished.

Language

FROM THESE THE ISLAND-NATIONS WERE DIVIDED INTO THEIR OWN COUNTRIES, EACH ACCORDING TO THEIR LANGUAGES AND THEIR CLANS WITHIN THEIR NATIONS. (Genesis 10:5)

THEREFORE, IT IS NAMED BABEL, BECAUSE THERE THE LORD MIXED UP THE LANGUAGE OF ALL THE EARTH; AND FROM THERE THE LORD DISPERSED THEM OVER ALL THE EARTH. (Genesis 11:9)

It probably doesn't need to be said, but the entire world does not speak English. While it is a commonly spoken language in business and is considered a standard language in many parts of the world, this is not true everywhere. In some countries, as many as thirty or more languages may be spoken, some of which do or do not overlap with other languages in that region. If you are planning to do mission work for more than a few days in any particular area, you need to have mastery of at least one major language spoken in that particular location.

Worldwide, the most spoken languages are[2]:

- **Mandarin Chinese** (China, Taiwan, Singapore)

- **English** (United Kingdom, Ireland, Africa, the Americas and Caribbean, India, Pakistan, Singapore, Sri Lanka, Australia, Pacific Islands)

- **Spanish** (Spain, Central America, Latin America, the United States)

- **Hindi** (India, Nepal, Fiji, Pakistan)

- **Arabic** (Middle East, northern Africa, parts of Asia)

- **Malay/Indonesian** (Indonesia, Brunei, Malaysia, Thailand, Singapore)

- **French** (France, Belgium, Luxembourg, Monaca, Switzerland, twenty nations in Africa, Canada, French Guiana, Haiti, Martinique, Guadeloupe, and in three Pacific Islands)

- **Bengali** (India and Bangladesh)

- **Portuguese** (Brazil, Portugal, Mozambique, Cape Verde, Angola, Guinea-Bissau and Sao Tome)

- **Russian** (Russia, Armenia, Azerbaijan, Byelorussia, Estonia, Georgia, Kazakhstan, Kyrgyzstan, Latvia, Lithuania, Moldova, Tajikistan, Turkmenistan, Uzbekistan, Ukraine)

- **German** (Germany, Switzerland, Austria, Belgium, Luxembourg, parts of Canada)

- **Japanese** (Japan)

- **Punjabi** (Pakistan and India)

- **Javanese** (Indonesia and Suriname)

- **Telegu** (India)

- **Korean** (Korea)

Depending on where you feel called to go, the general advice is to learn a general language that can serve you in more than one place in the world. There are many free apps (such as Duolingo) available today to help you learn a foreign language. Even if you do not become fluent in the language (and such would require a translator for preaching or church work), it is advisable to speak enough of a language to get by, read signs, complete commerce and transactions, and understand the basics of general discussion when interacting with citizens of a nation.

Financial

TELL PEOPLE WHO ARE RICH AT THIS TIME NOT TO BECOME EGOTISTICAL AND NOT TO PLACE THEIR HOPE ON THEIR FINANCES, WHICH ARE UNCERTAIN. INSTEAD, THEY NEED TO HOPE IN GOD, WHO RICHLY PROVIDES EVERYTHING FOR OUR ENJOYMENT. (1 Timothy 6:17)

The finances of missions are always a tricky game, from start to finish. As a rule, missions trips are financed by the missionaries who feel the push and the call to go on them, usually without any financial support from the area or region where they are going to work. This means a missionary needs to appropriately budget a plan to live and finance their stay, within reason, for the duration of a mission. There are ways to reduce costs, such as living with hosts, in connection with families or a church property, and to live, as the Bible speaks, within the hospitality of a culture or group. This is not always possible in new regions, however, and this means a missionary must do their research to recognize what is going on, and when, so they can be financially prepared.

A missions trip costs anywhere between a few hundred dollars to several thousand dollars, depending on the location of the mission, the cost of travel to the nation, and the overhead expense for living and operating a mission work. This does not count the expense of church operation, which at some point in time should fall into the hands of those there who attend and work in the church community. It's clear that hosting a mission can cost money, and even with exchange rates, it can still be an expensive endeavor.

It is customary for missionaries to create a basic proposal and petition for finances from churches (often through presentations), sponsors, denominations, churches, and regular individuals who are willing to finance a mission trip. Often, they require a regular report, newsletter, or presentation upon return to the United States in exchange for sponsoring the mission trip for a time.

Whenever you make a trip out of the United States, you must notify your bank and credit card companies within seven to ten days to avoid having your accounts frozen while overseas if you use them for any purpose. It should also be mentioned that some credit and debit cards charge transaction fees on any foreign purchases, and some cards are not set up for usage in international settings. The major companies that are set up for international usage include:

- Discover/Diner Rewards
- American Express
- Capital One Venture
- Chase Sapphire Preferred
- BankAmericard Travel Rewards

In some countries, American debit or credit cards are not received and accounts cannot be accessed from ATMs. The most recent reason this may happen is the switch from traditional magnetic stripe cards to chip cards, with other nations far ahead in the process than American retailers. Some places simply don't take American credit or debit cards, some only take debit cards, and some only take the currency of a country or checks from locals.

Currency also changes from country to country. Whenever you arrive in one country, you will need to convert your currency into the current exchange rate of that nation at an airport shop, an ATM, or currency exchange store in a tourist area. Don't be surprised if exchange rates aren't equivalent, and in some instances, you may receive a lot of local currency or little currency.

Economics

FRAUD AND LIES—
    KEEP FAR FROM ME!
DON'T GIVE ME EITHER POVERTY OR WEALTH;
    GIVE ME JUST THE FOOD I NEED. (Proverbs 30:8)

Economics is the system by which we rate our markets (buying, selling, production). Most of us probably took economics in school, but a lot of the way it was described flew in one ear and out the other. As adults, we are far more interested in economics than we were back then, for one simple reason: we live the results and impacts of economics, every day, up close and personal. The world of international economy changes minute by minute. It also deeply impacts the state of a nation or region. Over the past ten years, we've watched the economy rise and fall in different regions and seen its impact on job markets worldwide, as nations have had their entire economies collapse, sometimes overnight.

The economics of a region dictate how they produce, buy, and sell therein. Before going to a nation, it is wise to learn about the economic system in place and how that system works (or sometimes does not work) for the people therein. Things that relate to economics include:

- Agriculture
- Business
- Finance
- Health Care
- Education
- Family life
- Law
- Politics
- Religion
- National customs
- Social structures
- War
- Science
- Environmental impact[3]

The way these things interact together to create an entire economic reality and structure is complicated. Education impacts job force, health care impacts a worker's ability to perform their job, family life, law, politics, and religion effect what people think they are able to do and what they are able to achieve or try, and national custom, social structure, scientific achievement, war, and terrain all relate to what people find themselves feasibly able to do, within the confines of their cultural understanding.

It's wise to understand all the different aspects that touch the world of economics wherever you are going. There are, most likely, social customs, attitudes, politics and concepts that are extremely foreign to you and may impact on your mission or interaction with locals at some point. It is also wise to learn about whatever is present in a country because the economy and politics present there impact your life, what you are or are not able to do, and govern your stay while working in that nation.

Chapter 9 Summary

- You must know the work to which you have been called. If you are going on a mission, you need to know why you are going, what you will do while there, leave a little wiggle room for things to go imperfectly, and to be prepared (as much is as possible) for anything and everything to take place.

- Every missionary needs to take some time with God and sit in His presence, relaxing and allowing the stress factors of the upcoming trip to dissipate. As missionaries, we are called to hear from God on behalf of people we do not know well and plan a trip that will meet the needs of a people different from us in more ways than one. This requires a missionary to have the good sense of spiritual direction, able to hear the inward witness of the Spirit at work within them and guiding them to what they need to do in each situation that will arise.

- Nobody goes into ministry as a perfect person, and nobody remains in ministry through perfection.

- Self-assessment means we stop pursuing things that are just not God, no matter how we spin them, in our lives. The missions field is a place where ministers see what they are made of and deal with themselves in a way they do not have to encounter while running a church circuit. A natural talent or aptitude for public entertainment does not work in missions.

- Learning to be peaceful within ourselves changes our outlook on life and ministry and makes it less relevant to voice and do so many of the things we waste time doing to try and get attention or prove something about ourselves. This ties in with missions because missions challenge who we are and what we are about. If we aren't at peace within ourselves, we will find a missions trip to be a confusing journey.

- A missionary needs to be prepared for the various forms of travel they will encounter on a missionary trip.

- Missionaries need to have a communications plan. The most spoken languages are: Mandarin Chinese, English, Spanish, Hindi, Arabic, Malay/Indonesian, French, Bengali, Portuguese, Russian, German, Japanese, Punjabi, Javanese, Telegu, Korean.

- It is best to discuss any travel plans with a doctor or a travel medicine clinic at least four weeks prior to an international trip. There may be requirements for disease testing, rounds of medication, vaccines, or health issues to address.

- Missions trips are financed by the missionaries who feel the push and the call to go, usually without any financial support from the region where they go to work. This means a missionary needs a budget to live and finance their stay, within reason, for the duration of a mission. It is customary for missionaries to create a basic proposal and petition for finances from churches (often through presentations), sponsors, denominations, churches, and regular individuals who are willing to finance a mission trip.

- Whenever you make a trip out of the United States, you must notify your bank and credit card companies within seven to ten days. Some credit and debit cards charge transaction fees on any foreign purchases, and some cards are not set up for usage in international settings. In some countries, American debit or credit cards are not received and accounts inaccessible at ATMs. Currency also changes from country to country, and whenever you arrive in one country, you will need to convert your currency into the current exchange rate of that nation at an airport shop, an ATM, or currency exchange store in a tourist area.

- Economics is the system by which we rate our markets (buying, selling, production). Most of us probably took economics at some point in school, but a lot of the way it was described flew in one ear and out the other. The economics of a region dictate how they produce, buy, and sell therein.

Chapter 9 Assignments

- Gain an understanding of the news and current events beyond that which is often filtered through American television. Watch a news broadcast through an "alternative" source, such as:

  - Free Speech TV
  - Democracy Now!
  - Al Jazeera
  - Asianet News
  - BBC
  - CCTV
  - DW-TV
  - Euronews
  - Africa 24
  - Channels TV

  Watch a program online or on television and create a report on the differences you note in reporting (at least one page in length). What did you find that you miss with standard programming? What insight did this program give you into the circumstances and situations going on in the world?

- Look up a video on Youtube that displays how English sounds to a non-English speaker. Write a brief 3-5 sentence statement on the insight you gained in listening to this program.

- Learn the language and economic situation of a nation that interests you for missions activity and write 3-5 sentences about the situation therein. Include an app or program you can use to learn the language of that nation.

Missionary Jennie V. Hughes and Shi Meiyu, from the front of their book,
Chinese Heart-Throbs (1920)

CHAPTER TEN:
DETECTING SPIRITUAL STRONGHOLDS
AND SPIRITUAL PITFALLS IN MISSIONS

—————————⌒⌒⌒⟋——————————

If God calls you to be a missionary, don't stoop to be a king.
(Jordan Grooms[1])

WHENEVER you transfer from one area to another, it is important to recognize that different spiritual strongholds and pitfalls exist in different places. You might be very familiar with whatever impacts where you live or typically minister, but going to a new region means you will encounter new things that you may have never considered before. It's easy to think that doing the work of missions is easy to prepare for and it sounds easy enough to go into an area and think that all you must do is preach to have an impact, but missions work is more complicated than that. Sometimes we must tear down before we can build up, and the work of missions can be frustrating for a missionary who isn't properly trained in spiritual identification and warfare.

A note: I am not going to get into the specifics of spirits and the history of demonology and issues related to that in a large way in this chapter. That is a separate course, book, and instructional platform all together. What we are going to talk about here are some identifying techniques and general information that can help a missionary with a background in spiritual discernment and identification to do the work of ministry at hand, rather than growing swallowed up by spiritual issues that distract or damage the missions work.

A personal testimony

When I went to the Netherlands on mission in 2013, I didn't consider any of the things we will discuss in this chapter. The truth is that my trip to the Netherlands was not specifically for missions when I first discussed making the trip, but it became obvious the trip would become a mission, one where I was sent to go and assist a ministry over there with existing issues and leadership problems. I had some missions experience prior, especially within regional work in the United States, but I didn't think much about spiritual strongholds or spirits that might hinder the work. I was somewhat familiar with the ministry hosting me, and I did know they had some issues. I just didn't realize how many they had and what an impact it would make on the trip itself and my ability to minister to those who were there.

I will fully admit I thought I knew what I was getting into. I knew the history of the Netherlands and its role in the Protestant Reformation. I knew vaguely that there were some issues within the European church, but I didn't think that I would have to encounter massive and intense spiritual warfare when I went to Europe. I figured the experience would be much like working in leadership missions training in the United States, so I did not do a lot of background research into where I was going or what I might find.

I did see things I see in the United States while in the Netherlands, but I also saw an intensity of spiritual warfare I was simply not prepared to address. I came against power and control, but the way it manifested was not in a form I was used to handling. The spirits behind these different behavioral manifestations were unfamiliar to me, and I spent the entire mission trip trying to address them with methods and mannerisms I was more accustomed to using. In the end, things did seem to get better. Once I returned to the United States, the spirits surfaced again, this time in form against me and my own work. Not only did these people come against and attack me and my ministry, the spirits that controlled their lives started impacting my own. I had trouble focusing and concentrating after I returned, and their spiritual squabbles filtered down to hit every member of my own ministry.

I tell this story because the truth is that I was not prepared. I expected my missions experience to be much like the others I'd had prior, and I didn't consider that this trip was going to turn into a deliverance run that was unlike anything I'd seen before. I have done deliverance and worked in deliverance ministry, but it never occurred to me that this particular trip had its own strongholds and spiritual pitfalls, and that despite my best efforts, I simply was not prepared for what I was to encounter while there. What happened to me can happen to anyone in missions. As ministers, we miss things, we overlook things, we don't always address things as serious as they may be, and we all have hits and misses in this work because we don't pay attention to signs and signals that God sends us along the way to alert us.

As missionaries, we need to recognize spirit manifestations in those we deal with and those specific spirits that are invited into regions due to beliefs, traditions, or culture. This is not, in any way, to put down anyone's culture, traditions, or beliefs, but an acknowledgement that the history and culture of a region play heavily into the spirits that may manifest there. It also doesn't necessarily mean that everyone is "possessed" or "evil," but that people's influences can have spiritual origins and that it's not enough to just tell someone not to do something.

A word of caution as we proceed: While in missions and as individuals, we need to make sure that a spirit of pride does not overcome us, because pride causes us to fall. As missionaries, we need to be careful about taking on things we are simply not prepared to handle, and we need to be honest with ourselves about our gifts and abilities. If deliverance ministry is not an area of expertise for your work, it's probably better you address methods of deliverance with individuals in areas of behavior modification and monitoring. It is my own recommendation that every missions trip involves a properly called and qualified, proven deliverance minister who understands the nature of deliverance on missions and can prepare and discern spirits surrounding a region, present in individuals, and in situations as arise through missions work.

Avoiding the temptation to identify everything as a "spirit"

Whenever you start talking about "spirits," everyone has an opinion about what qualifies as a "spirit." You might hear them talk about the spirit of Jezebel or the spirit of Leviathan, but odds are good they don't know what they are talking about. Truth be told, there are only a few things mentioned as "spirits" in the Bible, and most of them are never mentioned when people start trying to identify spirits, of sorts. Biblical mention of spirits is also not all negative, or improper. The Bible talks about spirit in a good context in more than one place, including the Spirit of truth (1 John 4:6), an excellent spirit (Proverbs 17:27), and a humble spirit (Proverbs 16:19), among many others. This tells us it is possible to have a good spirit about us; spiritual identification is not always bad. It is essential to recognize spirits at work in people and to acknowledge them, when they are good and edifying, and when they are difficult or need address.

Other spirits mentioned in the Bible aren't always so positive or life-affirming. They include[2]:

- **Heaviness** (Isaiah 61:3 and Proverbs 16:2)

- **Infirmity** (Luke 13:11)

- **Fear** (2 Timothy 1:7)

- **Wounded/crushed** (Proverbs 18:14)

- **Evil** (1 Samuel 16:14)

- **Unclean** (Matthew 12:43, Zechariah 13:2, Mark 5:2-20)

- **Stupor** (Romans 11:8)

- **Anti-Christ** (1 John 4:3)

- **Error** (1 John 4:6)

- **Brokenness** (Proverbs 17:22)

- **Disobedience** (Ephesians 2:2)

- **Lying** (1 Kings 22:21-23)

- **Prostitution** (Hosea 4:12)

- **Divination** (Acts 16:16)

- **Deceiving** (1 Timothy 4:1)

- **Perversity:** (Isaiah. 19:14)

- **Jealousy:** (Numbers 5:14)

- **Haughtiness** (Proverbs 16:18)

We aren't going to get into the specifics of what these spirits are or what they do, beyond recognizing that much of what we classify as a "spirit" in church today has no Biblical foundation. The spirits that we see here relate very much to people's states of mind and character rather than generalizations against a person's nature. More than anything, what we see here is clear evidence that the way people may interact, behave, and feel may have a spiritual connection or a connection to their spiritual state. None of this means we should run around in judgment or screaming at everyone for these different issues. It also doesn't mean that deliverance, as we understand it in connection with casting out or exorcism, is appropriate for every "spirit" mentioned here. What it means is that we need to be uniquely aware of the way people interact and the spirits behind those actions. If we properly recognize what is present, then we know how to pray and how to interact with individuals who display these characteristics.

We need to avoid the temptation to label people as this, that, or something else. The Bible mentions only a few demons by name, a handful of spirits (as we have seen here), and only a few key identifying factors when it comes to matters of spiritual possession or identity. Spirits are a part of all our lives, they are a part of the cultures we have grown up in, and whether we like to admit it or not, indignancy and bullying are a large part of the haughty spirits that infiltrate western societies. Just as much as we stand back and discern what is present elsewhere, we also need to stand up and recognize what is present within us.

Familiar spirits

One aspect of spirit identification that is seldom, if ever, discussed pertains to a classification of spirit known as "familiar spirits." They are mentioned in ten different Old Testament passages: Leviticus

19:31, Leviticus 20:6, Deuteronomy 18:11, 1 Samuel 28:3, 1 Samuel 28:9, 2 Kings 21:6, 2 Kings 23:24, 2 Chronicles 33:6, Isaiah 8:19, and Isaiah 19:3. They are always associated with magic, spellcasting, and engaging with witchcraft, which echoes its prohibition. The question remains, however: what are they, and how do we identify them?

Every single human being has spirits of one form or another "around" them. We would call these "familiar spirits," beings that seek to cause confusion and trouble in our lives. They are spiritually conjured through witchcraft or controlling behaviors and come to us in the form of deception, as deceased relatives, ideals, hopes, dreams, or maybe even everything we want. We can either allow these spirits to have sway over the little things we do and the ways in which we treat others, or we can choose to follow God and do things the way He would have us do them. It doesn't begin and end with that declaration, however. Familiar spirits are called such for a reason - they know about us, what makes us tick, the hurts and pains that we have incurred in our lives, and the different ways in which we are easily tempted, scorned, hurt, or offended. These spirits work in various ways to get our attention and influence our behavior as they play upon our emotions, temptations, and states of thought and feeling to get us to behave in a carnal, or "fleshly" manner. Familiar spirits operate to get sway over us and introduce us to spirits that are more difficult to overcome and break in our lives. Every single one of us has them and identifying them helps us to be more honest about ourselves. They also help us to see what is present in a situation, what can work against the advance of a mission, and how we can best help and assist others as we go about our missionary work in each situation.

Spiritual history in a region

WE AREN'T FIGHTING AGAINST HUMAN ENEMIES BUT AGAINST RULERS, AUTHORITIES, FORCES OF COSMIC DARKNESS, AND SPIRITUAL POWERS OF EVIL IN THE HEAVENS. (Ephesians 6:12)

Mission work exists to bring the Gospel to a region, area, or nation either for the first time or more fully in its execution. Spirits, conditioning, culture, familiar spirits, and ways that people interact with one another can all relate to a group's resistance or interest in the Gospel. One of the best ways to understand what is coming and what a missionary will find is to study the spiritual history in the specific region where you will serve.

Studying spiritual history is about more than just saying a certain religious group is dominant somewhere or even learning about the specific mechanics of a region. When we study the spiritual history of a region, we make the effort to study the entire history of that area, starting at the beginning and moving all the way to the present day. This includes:

- The original indigenous religions found in an area

- The first organized religious systems and the methods by which they came into that area

- Historically organized religious systems present in a region and the way they maintained their status in that region

- Current organized religious systems present in that region and the way in which they maintain their status and position in that region

- Ways that traditional and organized religious systems overlap, intersect, and have co-mingled

- Nature of deities worshiped throughout the different changes and adjustments to spiritual systems over time

- Ritual, rite, and social custom associated with different spiritualties present in that area

- Holiday observances

These are all essential to understanding spirits, spirituality, and yes, even economic factors in a certain location. We've all heard about the way that sharia law changes the climate of a nation, but sharia law is not the only thing a missionary should concern themselves with if they go into another nation. No nation has one singular worship structure that, in its origin, is completely pure of influence or infiltration of culture. All of us, no matter what we believe, are influenced and impacted by our culture and the traditions that have gone before us, no matter what they might have been. The mixing of different religious and spiritual systems is known as syncretism, and syncretism is something present, to a certain extent, everywhere. Things were mixed, re-mixed, and mixed again throughout the ages to create what we see before us, today. That is part of why our salvation is a process; something we work out by fear and trembling, as we see the needed changes in our lives. Sometimes the traditions and cultures overlap and intermix so well, we don't know where what we believe comes from. In salvation's process, we get the revelation as is needed, right where we are, so we can see and grow in a greater way toward all God calls us to be and understand.

As missionaries, we are here to start or guide through this spiritual process. It's not always easy; it is frustrating at times and can be quite stressful. People don't always readily understand or receive what we are trying to teach them. Some things are just not as obvious to others or as readily understood at the time we present it. Knowing things behind the scenes and seeing spiritually how it all has come together helps us to know what we will encounter and what needs doing each step of the way in all things.

Spirits over regions

JESUS ASKED HIM, "WHAT IS YOUR NAME?"

HE RESPONDED, "LEGION IS MY NAME, BECAUSE WE ARE MANY."

THEY PLEADED WITH JESUS NOT TO SEND THEM OUT OF THAT REGION. (Mark 5:9-10)

Along with spiritual history comes the specific nature of spirits and the mannerisms and character we often see in people present in an area or region. It's not to say that it is always a negative thing, nor is it meant in a sense of judgment. It's an awareness, as is everything else we are touching upon in this chapter, to recognize and perceive what is present and what we will have to encounter or deal with in the process.

For example, I have dealt with people from nations that are, very clearly, out of touch with the fact that they lie. It's not one person, or two, or a few, but every interaction I have had with an individual in those particular countries consist of lies. When confronted, the individuals who lie don't see it as lying. They see it as their unique interaction, their way of communication.

When I took the time to research the different history of their countries, I was able to see how the lying spirit took root in their people. Thus, to see spirits present over regions, you need to acquaint yourself with their spiritual history, as well as their secular history, different governments involved in the interactions with that nation, occupations, slavery, politics, and social customs.

Religious systems

ISN'T YOUR RELIGION THE SOURCE OF YOUR CONFIDENCE; THE INTEGRITY OF YOUR CONDUCT, THE SOURCE OF YOUR HOPE? (Job 4:6)

Most nations have a dominant religious system at the helm of their cultural system. It may or may not be the original religious group in that area, but for whatever reason, it has taken the central spot within their nation's history of devotion.

In the west, religion is almost treated as a commodity of sorts, something we fulfill or take interest in after we've met our regular obligations for living. This has not been the case throughout history, nor is it the case in other countries. In many parts of the world, religion takes the central focus and meaning for how people live, work, and consider their identities as individuals. Knowing the religious systems present in a region, what people believe and how that impacts their lives makes a very big difference in a successful or unsuccessful mission.

Respecting authorities

In modern times, missionary activity has taken on a bit of a controversial quality that varies from years past. We will speak more about this in the last chapter of this book. One of the most controversial ways it has changed is the way that missionaries approach respect of local authorities in their work. There are missionaries who go into a region with the deliberate intent of undermining and disrespecting laws and regulations in place and do so with full defiance of intent because they feel it is their right to preach the Gospel in that land or area.

Missionaries who do this prove they do not have a heart for

their people, nor a heart for the work they are doing. We cannot do what we do to try and appease our own egos, because this represents a counterfeit spirituality. We also can't work in a region through missionary activity out of defiance or hate. Showing clear disregard for the laws or regulations of a nation is contradictory to the message of hope and love that we try to spread around the world. If we don't respect the kingdoms in place, we cannot impress respect for the eternal Kingdom through our work.

EVERY PERSON SHOULD PLACE THEMSELVES UNDER THE AUTHORITY OF THE GOVERNMENT. THERE ISN'T ANY AUTHORITY UNLESS IT COMES FROM GOD, AND THE AUTHORITIES THAT ARE THERE HAVE BEEN PUT IN PLACE BY GOD. SO ANYONE WHO OPPOSES THE AUTHORITY IS STANDING AGAINST WHAT GOD HAS ESTABLISHED. PEOPLE WHO TAKE THIS KIND OF STAND WILL GET PUNISHED. THE AUTHORITIES DON'T FRIGHTEN PEOPLE WHO ARE DOING THE RIGHT THING. RATHER, THEY FRIGHTEN PEOPLE WHO ARE DOING WRONG. WOULD YOU RATHER NOT BE AFRAID OF AUTHORITY? DO WHAT'S RIGHT, AND YOU WILL RECEIVE ITS APPROVAL. IT IS GOD'S SERVANT GIVEN FOR YOUR BENEFIT. BUT IF YOU DO WHAT'S WRONG, BE AFRAID BECAUSE IT DOESN'T HAVE WEAPONS TO ENFORCE THE LAW FOR NOTHING. IT IS GOD'S SERVANT PUT IN PLACE TO CARRY OUT HIS PUNISHMENT ON THOSE WHO DO WHAT IS WRONG. THAT IS WHY IT IS NECESSARY TO PLACE YOURSELF UNDER THE GOVERNMENT'S AUTHORITY, NOT ONLY TO AVOID GOD'S PUNISHMENT BUT ALSO FOR THE SAKE OF YOUR CONSCIENCE. YOU SHOULD ALSO PAY TAXES FOR THE SAME REASON, BECAUSE THE AUTHORITIES ARE GOD'S ASSISTANTS, CONCERNED WITH THIS VERY THING. SO PAY EVERYONE WHAT YOU OWE THEM. PAY THE TAXES YOU OWE, PAY THE DUTIES YOU ARE CHARGED, GIVE RESPECT TO THOSE YOU SHOULD RESPECT, AND HONOR THOSE YOU SHOULD HONOR. (Romans 13:1-7)

Spirits or not, the rules that are established in a nation or region are there, and we must show proper respect to the authorities and individuals in place, no matter how we may feel about them personally. If you are called as a missionary to work in an area that has restrictions on missionary activity, following the rules is the best way to go. It shows honor and respect to the authorities, and it also shows that as Christians, we honor that which exists, even if we do not agree with it and do not follow the custom ourselves. When it comes to missions in hostile or difficult regions, missionaries must put on their thinking caps, develop deep spirituality, and find ways to do things that are not direct defiance of laws or regulations.

Chapter 10 Summary

- As missionaries, we need to recognize spirit manifestations in those we deal with and specific spirits invited into regions due to beliefs, traditions, or culture. This is not to put down anyone's culture, traditions, or beliefs, but to acknowledge the history and culture of a region play heavily into the spirits that may manifest.

- While in missions, we need to make sure a spirit of pride does not overcome us, because pride causes us to fall. We must be honest with ourselves about our gifts and abilities.

- Biblical mention of spirits are also not all negative, or improper. The Bible talks about spirit in a good context in more than one place, including the Spirit of truth (1 John 4:6), an excellent spirit (Proverbs 17:27), and a humble spirit (Proverbs 16:19), among many others. Some other spirits mentioned include the spirit of heaviness, infirmity, fear, wounded/crushed, evil, unclean, stupor, anti-Christ, error, brokenness, disobedience, lying, prostitution, divination, deception, perverse, jealousy, and haughtiness.

- What we see here is clear evidence that the way people may interact, behave, and feel may have a spiritual connection or a connection to their spiritual state

- We need to avoid the temptation to label people. The Bible mentions only a few demons by name, a handful of spirits, and only a few factors when it comes spiritual possession or identity. Spirits are a part of all our lives.

- Every single human being has spirits of one form or another "around" them. We would call these "familiar spirits," beings that seek to cause confusion and trouble in our lives. They are spiritually conjured through witchcraft or controlling behaviors and come to us in the form of deception, as deceased relatives, ideals, hopes, dreams, or maybe even everything we want.

- Studying spiritual history is about more than just saying a certain religious group is dominant somewhere or even learning about the specific mechanics of a region. When we study the spiritual history of a region, we make the effort to study the entire history of that area, starting at the beginning and moving all the way to the present day. This includes: The original indigenous religions, the first organized religious systems, historical organized religious systems present in a region and the way they maintained their status, current organized religious systems present in that region and the way they maintain their status, ways that traditional and organized religious systems overlap, nature of deities worshiped over time, ritual, rite, and social custom associated with different spritualties present in that area, and holiday observances.

- As missionaries, we are here to start or guide through this spiritual process. It's not always easy; it is frustrating at times and can be quite stressful. People don't always readily understand or receive what we are trying to teach them.

- Spirits or not, the rules that are established in a nation or region are there, and we have to show proper respect to the authorities and individuals in place, no matter how we may feel about them personally.

Chapter 10 Assignments

- Research the dominant religion of the area where you desire to work as a missionary. Create a PowerPoint slideshow on the religion, including major theology, beliefs, and practices.

- Given what you discovered, write a short summary report (3-5 sentences) about what possible spirits you may encounter in your missionary experience.

CHAPTER ELEVEN:
THE HEART OF MISSIONS FROM THE VIEW OF THE MISSIONARY

No one has the right to hear the Gospel twice, while there remains someone who has not heard it once."
(Oswald J. Smith[1])

NO book on missions is complete without a look at missionaries throughout the ages. We won't be getting into a history of missions here, but looking at the experiences of missionaries down through the ages helps to inspire our own call and see the historical lineage that we become a part of as we work within the realm of missions work.

The work of hagiography, or the biographies of the saints of the church, has provided us with important details of the legacies of missionaries the world over. Not every documented individual in a hagiography is a missionary, but many of them are. Even though the purpose of the hagiography is to extol the best values and principles of those who have been Christians throughout history, hagiography provides us many wonderful stories, especially about early missionaries, who impacted the world for Christ.

The original 12 Apostles (First Century)

The first 12 apostles: Peter, Andrew, James (son of Zebedee), John, Philip, Bartholomew, Matthew, James (son of Alpheus), Thomas, Simon, Jude Thaddeus, and Matthias (selected to replace Judas) all worked as missionaries: Peter (d. 64-68; worked in Samaria, Antioch, Rome)[2]; Andrew (d. mid-late 1st century; worked in Scythia, Thrace,

Georgia, Cyprus, Romania, Ukraine)[3]; James (son of Zebedee, d. 44; worked in Jerusalem, Spain, Iberia)[4]; John (6-100; worked in Judea, Patmos, Ephesus, Rome)[5]; Philip (d. 80; worked in Greece, Phrygia, Syria)[6]; Bartholomew (1st century; worked in Armenia, Ethiopia, Mesopotamia, Parthia, Lycaonia, India)[7]; Matthew (1st century; worked in Ethiopia, Phrygia)[8]; James (son of Alpheus, d. 62; worked in Egypt)[9]; Thomas (d. 72; worked in India)[10]; Simon (d. 65 or 107; worked in Egypt, Persia, Armenia, Lebanon, Samaria, Iberia, Britain)[11]; Jude Thaddeus (1st century; Judea, Samaria, Idumaea, Syria, Mesopotamia, Libya, Lebanon, Persia, Armenia)[12], and Matthias (d. 80; Cappadocia, Judea, Georgia)[13].

Thecla (30-?)

Thecla was a female Christian convert moved by the Apostle Paul's teaching on virtue. As she desired to be baptized, she wound up baptizing herself! Her experiences with the Apostle Paul caused her to discover her own apostolic call, and she pursued the apostolic ministry. Having been taught by the Apostle Paul, she displayed much of his influence in her ministerial work. Her own family did not support her and ministry was difficult, but she continued in the work she was there to do. Her experiences and ministry are documented in an apocryphal book known as *The Acts of Paul and Thecla*, which was well-circulated and cited by the apostolic church. Thecla has been cited as a role model for women and has been hailed as "the apostle and protomartyr among women." Church traditions have also considered her an "equal to the apostles," thus recognizing her important role as an early church leader.[14]

Pantaenus (d. 200)

Pantaenus was a stoic Greek philosopher who converted to Christianity within the first two hundred years of the church. He's best known for working in education and catechism, attempting to make Christian ideas understandable to those interested in schools of Greek philosophy. He was also an early missionary to India (possibly South Arabia or Ethiopia) where he met Christians who claimed to have copies of Matthew's Gospel in Hebrew, obtained from the Apostle Bartholomew.[15, 16]

Nina of Georgia (296-335)

Nina of Georgia (a European nation near Russia) was a missionary to the nation of Georgia through much of her life. She was born in Cappadocia, in what is now modern-day Turkey. From a young age, Nina was raised by her aunt, who was a nun. When she heard stories about those who had never known God, Nina was deeply moved and grieved for unbelievers. After experiencing a vision calling her to Iberia (now the modern-day area of Georgia), Nina went forth with her companions to proclaim the Gospel. From her work, almost single-handedly, the entire nation of Georgia came to Christian belief. Her Impact even reached those in places of power, including the Tsar and his family, the Tsarina and her family, and most of the government officials. She was a powerful preacher of the Word, a woman of influence, and a worker of miracles. Nina is now known as "equal to the Apostle Andrew," "reed-pipe of the Holy Spirit," and "enlightener of Iberia."[17]

Patrick (387-461)

The legendary "St. Patrick" is a controversial figure. There's a question as to how much recorded of his life is reality and how much of it is legend. Though dates for his life are provided, it's possible they are not accurate. For example, Ireland never had snakes for Patrick to drive out. Some believe much of Patrick's lore relates to Palladius, who was bishop of Ireland before Patrick. There's also question as to the ethics involved in Patrick's work, including forced conversions and violence in evangelism. From what we do know, Patrick was born in Britain under the governance of the Roman Empire. His father was a deacon and his grandfather a priest. Patrick himself was not into faith, and did not identify as a Christian. When he was 16, Patrick was kidnapped by Irish pirates and brought him to Ireland, where he was a slave for six years. During his enslavement, Patrick converted to Christianity. He escaped his captor and returned home, studying his faith more clearly. After a vision, Patrick returned to Ireland to work and serve the people there as a missionary. Legend has it that Patrick was not received and had to move further north. He baptized, ordained priests, converted wealthy, interested women to the faith, and dealt with government officials. His experience as a missionary was not always positive, and he also dealt with government opposition, imprisonment, and robbery.[18, 19]

Matrona, Abbess of Constantinople (5th Century)

Matrona, Abbess of Constantinople was from Perge Pamphylia, in what is now Asia Minor. She was married to a wealthy man named Dometian, and had a daughter named Theodota. After moving to Constantinople, she spent her days praying in church and repenting for sin. One day while in prayer, Matrona met two Eldresses named Eugenia and Susanna. She desired to follow their example and began living an ascetic life, dedicated to fasting and prayer. Her husband was opposed to her spiritual development, and they grew apart. Matrona left her family in pursuit of God's work. She resolved to follow God wherever He led. Her daughter was left in the care and educational trust of Eldress Susanna, and she disguised herself as a man after a dream which showed her surrounded by monks. Her husband pursued her at this time, and so the dream spoke to her as a voice of protection. When she was discovered in a male monastery, she was sent to the women's monastery. She then became the abbess of the monastery at Emesa.

Matrona's work spread far and wide and included healing as well as evangelism. When she was warned her husband discovered her fame, she retreated to Jerusalem, Mt. Sinai, and then Beirut, where she lived in an abandoned pagan temple. When young women desired her instruction, a new monastery started in Beirut. Later, she left there and started another convent in Constantinople, traveling and working to spread the Gospel wherever she went.[20]

Fourteen Apostles of Ireland (470-600)

Ireland has a rich history of apostles post New Testament times, and the 14 Apostles of Ireland are no different. They came out of the monastic movement present in that era, having studied under Finnian's monastic school. Although these men were regarded as "monastics," the Apostles of Ireland worked as the apostles did. They traveled, preached the Gospel, established churches, and trained leaders. They were Finnian of Clonard (470-549; founder, Clonard Abbey, with an average of 3,000 scholars); Ciaran of Saighir (d. 530; first saint born in Ireland, Bishop of Ossory); Ciaran of

Clonmacnoise (d. 546; teacher and church founder); Brendan of Birr (d. 573; student, monk, and abbot); Brendan of Clonfert (484-577; known as "the Navigator," "the Voyager," "the Bold," set out with sixty other monks in a leather boat, crossing the Atlantic all the way to the North American continent, evangelizing all the way and then back to evangelize Wales, Scotland, and Iona); Columba of Terryglass (d. 522; took over as instructor once Finnian became ill); Columba of Iona (521-597; known as "Dove of the Church" and "Black Bear," worked in evangelism in Scotland and trained missionaries); Mobhi of Glasnevin (unknown; founder of the city of Glasnevin, which was originally a monastery); Ruadhain of Lorrha (d. 584; founder and first abbot at Lorrha, operated embassy to King Diamait); Senan of Iniscathay (b. 488; founder of Inis Cathaig monastery and five churches); Ninnidh the Saintly of Lough Erne (Unknown; known as "Ninnidh of Inismacsaint" and "Ninnidh the Pious," known for medical eye treatments and work in healing); Laisren mac Nad From (d. 564; founder of a monastery in Devenish); Canice of Aghaboe (515-16-600; traveled to many lands in spread of the Gospel and led an army to overcome Druidic rule); and Finnian of Moville (495-589; missionary and teacher of Druim Fionn and teacher of Columba).[21]

Alopen (Seventh Century)

Alopen was a missionary from the Church of the East (also known as the Nestorian Church), most likely a Syrian. He was the first recorded missionary to reach China. He worked during the Tang Dynasty, arriving in 635 from the Silk Road. He brought Scripture, sacred books, and images along with him, and was widely accepted due to a decree of tolerance in place in China at that time. Writings, known as *The Jesus Sutras*, were translated and disseminated thanks to Alopen's connection to Taizong. In 638, the first church was built in China, with recognized leadership. Alopen was then recognized as bishop.[22]

Boniface (675-754)

Boniface (born as Winfrid, Wynfrith or Wynfryth) was the first to organize Christian churches in what we now know as central and northern Europe (Netherlands, Switzerland, Germany, eastern

France, and Celtic nations, such as Ireland). In many ways, Boniface helped establish Western Christianity throughout Europe. Little is known of his early life, although it is believed he came from a wealthy family. As a child, he was educated at a monastery in Exeter, England. He studied as a priest for religious life and set out in 716 on missionary work throughout the continent of Europe. He worked in Frisia, Utrecht, Nursling, Rome (was established as the missionary bishop of Germania), and Fritzlar, where he built a chapel. Later, a monastery and church were built on the same site. He also became the main overseer of churches in Salzburg, Regensburg, Freising, and Passau. The work of Boniface was particularly notable in those of his students and those he led, who also went on to found and oversee churches and abbeys.

In 754, Boniface returned to Frisia and baptized many there. This would prove to be his final act, as he was attacked by a group of robbers near Dokkum during what was supposed to be a church meeting. To the very end, he encouraged those he worked with to remain peaceable and lay down their weapons.[23]

Anna Nitschmann (1715-1760)

Anna Nitschmann was a Moravian Brethren missionary, poet, and hymnist. From the time she was 14, she served as the Chief Eldress of the Renewed Moravian Church, working as a spiritual mentor, counselor, and teacher to the church's female members. She did her itinerant missions work in Southeast Pennsylvania, going to Europe to work in what was then a colony of Britain. When she completed her work, she returned to work in the congregations of Moravia.[24]

William Carey (1761-1834)

William Carey was founder of the English Baptist Missionary Society. He worked as a missionary to India for most of his life, and his method of missionary activity became the pattern by which mission work is structured. Prior to missions, William was a pastor whose heart for those who'd never heard the Gospel was strong. In 1793, he and a doctor went to Calcutta, then a year later, William moved to Mudnabati, Bengal to preach, teach, and translate the Bible. His work extended to Frederiksnagar (near Calcutta) in 1800, and he and two other men founded a powerful mission at that location. He translated the Bible into Bengali, Oriya, Marathi, Hindi, Assamese, and Sanskrit, as well as into almost thirty other languages and dialects. He taught language and grammar in six different languages and established a printing press at Serampore. His work included education, advocacy against infanticide and suttee, founded the Agricultural Society of India, and encouraged Indian citizens to become missionaries.[25]

Charlotte "Lottie" Moon (1840-1912)

Charlotte "Lottie" Digges Moon came from a wealthy Virginia family that valued education and desired her to receive the best education possible. AS a person, Lottie was uninterested in religion until she was in college, where she underwent a spiritual awakening. After college, she worked as a teacher and helped poor families in the southern United States. When she was 33, Lottie heard the call to join her younger sister in missions. She spent over forty years in missions, teaching and evangelizing in China. She was one of the first to embrace cultural adaptation, as she wore Chinese clothes and embraced Chinese culture. In missions, Lottie faced plague, famine, and war, but nothing stopped her. She remained faithful to her work, to the very end.[26]

Anne Luther Bagby (1859-1942)

Anne Luther Bagby was the first woman from the Texas Baptists to become a foreign missionary, working in the nation of Brazil. For sixty-one-years, she pioneered in the mission field, inspiring six of her nine children to follow in her footsteps and also become missionaries.

Anne was born in Kentucky and came with her family, as her father was to be the president of Baylor Female College (now known as the University of Mary Hardin-Baylor). She was baptized in the Mississippi as her family traveled to Texas when she was eleven years old. At age 19, Anne felt the call to become a missionary, but she first became a teacher after graduating from college in 1879. She married in 1880 and organized the first Woman's Missionary Union in Texas. In 1881, she and her husband went to Brazil as missionaries. In partnership with Zachery and Kate Taylor, Anne and her husband created the first Baptist church for Brazilians in the Salvador Bahia region of Brazil. They started with five members, including a converted priest. Both Anne and her husband were arrested for baptizing members and were then later released. In 1891, the work moved to Rio de Janerio and Sao Paulo City, where Anne created a school for girls. It grew to become twice the size of any other Protestant school in Brazil at that time.[27]

Amy Beatrice Wilson Carmichael (1867-1951)

Irish-born Amy Beatrice Wilson Carmichael had a life-changing experience when she was seventeen years old: she and her brothers helped an old, poor woman with a heavy bundle. Such work and assisting such a woman was regarded as disrespectable, and Amy was notably embarrassed. As she completed the task, she heard the words of God to her in her life: "Gold, silver, precious stones, wood, hay stubble — every man's work will be made manifest; and the fire shall try every man's work of what sort it is. If any man's work abide..." These words inspired Amy to spend her life helping the poorest of the poor worldwide, and began her life-long pursuit of missions, knowing she had been called by God without question.

Amy was the founder of Welcome Evangelical Church in Belfast, Ireland, starting a Sunday class for women, working until they had five hundred people in attendance, weekly. She went on to spend more than half a century in mission work, and later more than fifty-five years as a missionary in India, despite the fact that the work was hard for her and she spent long periods of time in physical weakness and discomfort. She worked specifically with orphans and young girls who were forced into prostitution by temple priests. Her work in India is known as the Donhavur Fellowship and has become a sanctuary for thousands of children over the years. She was author of over 35 books, including her best-known, *God's Missionary*.[28]

Susanna Carson Rijnhart (1868-1908)

Susanna Carson Rinjart, also known as "Doctor Susie," was a Canadian missionary and medical doctor in Tibet. She was the second woman from the west to visit, explore, and work in Tibet. After marrying Petrus Rinjhart (a Dutch former missionary), they left for China while in their first year of marriage. They worked independently, from independently raised funds, despite criticism that working without a denomination would cause them trouble. In 1895, they arrived in Kumbum, Tibet, home to about 3,600 monks. They set out to learn Tibetan, work among the people, and eventually arrive in Lhasa, the capital of Tibet. By the time they arrived, no westerner had visited Lhasa in fifty years. After a Muslim revolt, Susie and her husband were invited to the monastery to assist in medical care. They became close with the abbot, and well-respected. In 1896 the Rijnharts moved to Tankar to open and operate a medical dispensary. They were known for their good relations with the Chinese government, accepted by the people for their adaptation of custom and dress, and lived with only small sums of money received from the dispensary work.

The team never made it to Lhasa. While in transit, extensive disaster struck. Susie's baby died. They were attacked by bandits, their guides wounded, horses stolen, and goods lost. Susie never saw her husband again after he tried to find some support or assistance for their trip to a remote area. She was left alone to find her way, avoid rape and robbery, crossing mountain ranges, to Kangding, where she finally arrived on November 26, 1898. She was able to meet up with the China Inland Mission, which helped her to return home about two years later. In 1902 she returned to China with the Foreign Christian Missionary Society, and in 1905 she married James Moyes, a man she met while in Kangding a few years earlier. Her health failed, she returned to Canada in 1907 and after having a baby son in January 1908, died in February of that year.[29, 30]

Philip James "Jim" Elliot (1927-1956)

Philip James "Jim" Elliot was a missionary of the Plymouth Brethren born in Portland, Oregon. He was pious and serious in his faith, and even delayed marriage (which he did eventually do in 1953) so both he and his wife could be properly prepared for missions work. He worked among the Quichua Indians of Ecuador for his entire missionary life. Along with his wife and four other missionaries, they began work with the Huaoroni tribe, an unreached Indian group, in 1955. It took several months to establish contact, and on January 8, 1956, a meeting was arranged. All five of the missionaries, except for Jim's wife, were speared to death.[31]

Chronicles of missionaries worth reading

- *Foxe's Book of Martyrs* (note: not all were missionaries, and some question the accuracy of some of the history presented; however, overall, an important and inspiring read)

- *God's Missionary* (Amy Carmichael)

- *Gladys Aylward: The Little Woman* (Gladys Aylward, Christine Hunter)

- *Christianity Rediscovered* (Vincent J. Donovan)

- *A Passion for the Impossible*: The Life of Lilias Trotter (Miriam Huffman Rockness)

- *Declaration* (sometimes called *Confession*) and *Letter to the Soldiers of Coroticus* (Patrick of Ireland)

- *The Brendan Voyage: Sailing to America in a Leather Boat to Prove the Legend of the Irish Sailor Saints* (Tim Severin)

Chapter 11 Summary

- The work of hagiography, or the biographies of the saints of the church, has provided us with important details of the legacies of missionaries the world over. Not every documented individual in a hagiography is a missionary, but many of them are.

- The original 12 Apostles were all missionaries.

- Thecla was an apostle who studied under the Apostle Paul and worked as a missionary, hailed as "the apostle and protomartyr among women."

- Pantaenus was an early missionary to India (possibly south Arabia or Ethiopia) where he met Christians who claimed to have copies of Matthew's Gospel in Hebrew, obtained from the Apostle Bartholomew.

- Nina of Georgia (a European nation near Russia) was a missionary to the nation of Georgia through much of her life. She is now known as "equal to the Apostle Andrew," "reed-pipe of the Holy Spirit," and "enlightener of Iberia.

- Patrick became a Christian when he was a slave, kidnapped by Irish pirates. After a vision, Patrick returned to Ireland to work and serve the people there as a missionary. Legend has it that Patrick was not received, and had to move further north. He baptized, ordained priests, converted wealthy, interested women to the faith, and dealt with government officials.

- Matrona, Abbess of Constantinople's work included healing as well as evangelism and founding monasteries in different locations across the Middle East and Asia Minor.

- The fourteen Apostles of Ireland worked as the apostles did. They were: Finnian of Clonard, Ciaran of Saighir, Ciaran of Clonmacnoise, Brendan of Birr, Brendan of Clonfert, Columba of Terryglass, Columba of Iona, Mobhi of Glasnevin, Ruadhain of Lorrha, Senan of Iniscathay, Ninnidh the Saintly of Lough Erne, Laisren mac Nad From, Canice of Aghaboe, and Finnian of Moville.

- Alopen was a Syrian missionary from the Church of the East. He was the first recorded missionary to reach China.

- Boniface was the first to organize Christian churches in what we now know as central and northern Europe (Netherlands, Switzerland, Germany, eastern France, and Celtic nations, such as Ireland).

- Anna Nitschmann was a Moravian Brethren missionary, poet, and hymnist who did itinerant missions work in Southeast Pennsylvania.

- William Carey was founder of the English Baptist Missionary Society. He worked as a missionary to India for most of his life, and his method of missionary activity became the pattern by which mission work is structured.

- Charlotte "Lottie" Digges Moon spent over forty years in missions, teaching and evangelizing in China. She was one of the first to embrace cultural adaptation, as she wore Chinese clothes and embraced Chinese culture.

- Anne Luther Bagby was the first woman from the Texas Baptists to become a foreign missionary, working in the nation of Brazil. For sixty-one-years, she pioneered in the mission field, inspiring six of her nine children to follow in her footsteps and also become missionaries.

- Amy Beatrice Wilson Carmichael was the founder of Welcome Evangelical Church in Belfast, Ireland, starting a Sunday class for women, working until they had five hundred people in attendance, weekly. She went on to spend more than half a century in mission work, and later more than fifty-five years as a missionary in India.

- Susanna Carson Rinjart, also known as "Doctor Susie," was a Canadian missionary and medical doctor in Tibet. She was the second woman from the west to visit, explore, and work in Tibet.

- Philip James "Jim" Elliot was a missionary of the Plymouth Brethren who worked among the Quichua Indians of Ecuador for his entire missionary life.

Chapter 11 Assignments

- Research the life of a missionary who inspires you. Present a one-to-two-page report on their life. Include the following: life, missionary activity, missions work, and what made their life and missionary work unique.

- Write a prayer for missionaries.

CHAPTER TWELVE:
TAKING ON THE WORK OF MISSIONS IN TODAY'S WORLD

What's your dream and to what corner of the missions world will it take you?
(Eleanor Roat[1])

THE proof of your true heart for missions lies in your willingness to see this entire program through, right to the end. Here we find ourselves at the last step of our introductory journey, which is to look at things we, as missionaries, must learn to handle our missions work in our modern world.

It's obvious in many ways that the world we live in is not the same as the world our spiritual ancestors worked in when they ventured out to work for the Gospel. We are much more aware; we are more aware of the world around us; we have a flood of media information and attention, showcasing cultures and current events in a slanted light; and we have the intense competition of things around us that demand our immediate attention and never seem to let up. Endeavoring into missions is not easy, and never has been, but as we live now, we need to examine outlooks and purposes that can help us to develop a proper sense of grace and ability in missions today.

Taking a more active role in supporting missions

LET'S NOT GET TIRED OF DOING GOOD, BECAUSE IN TIME WE'LL HAVE A HARVEST IF WE DON'T GIVE UP. (Galatians 6:9)

If we are interested in missions ourselves, we should also take an interest in seeing others at work in the mission field. Part of how we develop our connections for missions comes from our ability to support the work of missionaries worldwide, and we do that as we connect with other missionaries who are also doing the work of the Gospel in different places.

Missionary support is not all about money, although money is certainly a part of missions, and a necessary one, at that. There are lots of ways we can step up and show interest in missions activity that aren't all about money, however. I think it's a great idea to diversify the way that missions are supported, because there are times when missionaries need assistance beyond what money can buy. Some ways to support missionaries that aren't as simple as giving money include:

- **Pray for them**: Adding names of missionaries around the world to prayer lists, prayer calls, or prayer groups is a powerful way to remember those individuals in prayer. Too often, missionaries are nameless, faceless people that we don't ever think about as individuals until they die or take on another form of ministry that is more notable. Missionaries are people who face the same problems, stress factors, and temptations as other ministers, with them severely amped up. Missionaries are away from their comforts, their homes, all that is familiar to them, and that leaves them open to discouragement, depression, financial struggles, and feelings that don't always lead to good things. Praying for missionaries and reminding others to do the same gives the work of missions a powerful boost and purposed feel.

- **Tell others about them**: I'm not sure why we keep the best people, best leaders, and best work in Christianity to ourselves, but we certainly do. Word of mouth is important for missionaries to develop networks of support and interest so they can keep their missions work going. Yes, websites and social media are great for promoting general information, but they are often not enough to establish legitimacy and lasting support by themselves. Let others know about the mission, what work they are doing, and why you believe in that work – and those missionaries.

- **Send items/needed materials**: We like to think that money solves all problems, but when you're on the mission field, it can be difficult to turn money into needed items. Sometimes items aren't easily bought where a mission takes place. Sometimes the buying and selling of items is prohibitive or difficult. Missionaries should always keep a list of needed items, ranging from supplies to distribution items, to higher-end items, all of which are related to the continuation and expansion of the mission. Instead of sending money, consider sending items to help the work of missions.

- **Volunteer to assist on a mission trip**: If you are not in the place to run a missions trip yourself, consider volunteering to travel with another team or to visit the location where a mission is in full force and assist in that work and vision for a few days.

Putting your best foot forward for missions

SO, BROTHERS AND SISTERS, BECAUSE OF GOD'S MERCIES, I ENCOURAGE YOU TO PRESENT YOUR BODIES AS A LIVING SACRIFICE THAT IS HOLY AND PLEASING TO GOD. THIS IS YOUR APPROPRIATE PRIESTLY SERVICE. DON'T BE CONFORMED TO THE PATTERNS OF THIS WORLD, BUT BE TRANSFORMED BY THE RENEWING OF YOUR MINDS SO THAT YOU CAN FIGURE OUT WHAT GOD'S WILL IS—WHAT IS GOOD AND PLEASING AND MATURE. (Romans 12:1-2)

Many dislike discussion of ministry as a profession or a professional endeavor, because they feel it reduces ministry to an earthly level, void of spirituality. This is a misnomer, however, because ministry is a profession as well as a professional endeavor. It is something that a minister does as their primary purpose, it's professional work. It is something that has certain guidelines, protocol, disciplines, presentations, and conduct. Being in ministry represents something; it represents the service that one does throughout life, and missions is a part of that ministry work. That means as ministers who are preparing for missions or who are on a mission or even returning from a mission, we need to put our best foot forward to generate the proper response and image needed to convey dedication and success in ministerial work.

In older times, missionaries would spend the first year of a mission acclimating to the culture. They would engage in what we now call "instant immersion." This means they would subject themselves to be a part of that culture, no matter how much effort or work it took, and surround themselves with what they needed to learn in order to be successful. In modern times, this is not always practical, but all missionaries can and should receive training for their missions. Whether it's through a seminary program that is specifically designed for missionaries, a missions training program, or a missions initiative, missionaries should learn about their work and about where they are going to go, covering the essentials of culture, manners, language, economics, social customs, religion, geography, terrain, politics, and commerce for at least one year prior to a missions trip departure.

Whether we like it or not, missions work requires money. I am the first to admit that fundraising is not the most fun aspect of missions, but it is a necessary aspect, as we discussed earlier. The success or failure of obtaining funds for missions is not as simple as how we dress or carry ourselves, but it does help if we carry ourselves properly. We need to dress the part, attire ourselves appropriately, wearing appropriate professional clothing for fundraising, church, and speaking events. When we are in the countries where we will serve, we should attire ourselves within the bounds of the culture (not always in the sense of ethnic dress but following regulations for clothing as pertain to that nation), stand clean and neat, exemplify the best of what ministry has to offer, speaking properly and clearly.

We should also consider the realities of preparation and financial sponsorship. There are many individuals who operate businesses with Christian themes or who are Christians with their own businesses. These are people we want to meet, and we want to present ourselves in the best possible light, because they have the resources and ability to support missions in their work. Even though they probably never even considered the work of missionary support, this can all change with the right input, right letter, and right approach. If we are professional and courteous, we can trust that God will open doors for us to meet and mingle with the right people who can sponsor our every financial need.

Missionaries should also maintain a regular newsletter, newspaper, magazine, or mailing that lets sponsors, donors, and friends of the work see mission work in action. This can also be annexed on to an existing ministry publication, or even a few missionaries in different places can team up and create a joint publication. Publications should be attractive, informative, and give a visual component to the world of missions where only a few dare to venture.

Creating empowerment and independence during a mission

THE ONE WHO EMPOWERED PETER TO BECOME AN APOSTLE TO THE CIRCUMCISED EMPOWERED ME ALSO TO BE ONE TO THE GENTILES. (Galatians 2:8)

AFTER YOU HAVE SUFFERED FOR A LITTLE WHILE, THE GOD OF ALL GRACE, THE ONE WHO CALLED YOU INTO HIS ETERNAL GLORY IN CHRIST JESUS, WILL HIMSELF RESTORE, EMPOWER, STRENGTHEN, AND ESTABLISH YOU. (1 Peter 5:10)

We've already discussed the Gospel as the center of missions. Going somewhere just to do a social project is not the primary purpose of missions, but we have also examined that the social Gospel often overlaps with the heart of Gospel work. It's not always possible to do one without the other, and the complimentary nature of the two puts the Gospel in full frontal action for those who are serious about changing their lives and adopting the values of a Kingdom that offers so much more than the ones of this world.

As spiritual leaders, we cannot underestimate the value of creating empowerment and independence in those we instruct. Creating economic independence and cooperation with church members helps to create an economic impact for the church that is built or strengthened in mission activity. If people have no sustainable income, they will not have money to tithe or to build the church. Helping people to gain skills they can otherwise not obtain themselves helps build the church.

Economic sustainability is the ability to support economic production long-term, no matter what level of productivity may define that. This means that it is more important to give individuals tools for success and education for change than it is to go in and do things for people all the time. In missions, we should never do things for people that they can otherwise do or accomplish themselves. Depending on the nature of a mission and its location, methods for economic sustainability may vary considerably. Some examples of economic sustainability training may include:

- Entrepreneur programs
- Literacy initiatives
- GED classes
- Computer classes
- How to start your own business
- Small business training
- Job training seminars (not pyramid schemes or sales companies)
- Sewing classes
- Agriculture and farming
- Farming co-op structure
- Creation of crafts or goods
- Fishing
- Manufacturing

The goal of these programs is to equip individuals with skills so they can gain financial independence, tackle the difficulties that poverty often overtakes in one's life, and ultimately create an atmosphere where believers are able to sustain themselves, their families, and their churches, anywhere in the world.

Overcoming the shadows of missions past and present

BECAUSE OF THE GRACE THAT GOD GAVE ME, I CAN SAY TO EACH ONE OF YOU: DON'T THINK OF YOURSELF MORE HIGHLY THAN YOU OUGHT TO THINK. INSTEAD, BE REASONABLE SINCE GOD HAS MEASURED OUT A PORTION OF FAITH TO EACH ONE OF YOU. (Romans 12:3)

If we are going to honestly discuss missions, we must acknowledge the darker side of their history and often their present. Missions have not always been used to promote the Gospel, but often, to impose culture on imperialized or colonized nations. Even now, many use missions or mission activity to try and strong-arm nations, groups, and individuals into receiving and accepting certain aspects of culture or political values in the name of spirituality or religion. If we are going to be missionaries today, we need to know the issues that cause people to be wary of missionaries, uninterested in spiritual work, or who associate Christianity negatively.

- **Spiritual imperialism:** The use of religion to infiltrate for alternate reasons is not new. Spiritual imperialism, or the disguise of spiritual experiences or religious beliefs to try and influence a nation, people, or group with something else in mind, has been around for thousands of years. It is, however, alive and well in the world and camouflage in many different forms. The agenda behind spiritual imperialism is almost always political, with the end goal to change the thinking or ideals of a nation to transform them into something better for another group. Whether spiritual imperialism benefits crazy cult-like leaders interested in nothing more than control or it's about political ideals, ties, colonization and imperialism, spiritual imperialism deeply hurts the efforts of missionaries who are there to do Gospel work. It means we must pay that much more attention to the things we hand out, the propaganda that might seep into Christian items, even some Bibles (that promote nationalism or patriotism), and the manner in which we speak about things that relate to a secular nature. Politics have a way of damaging the best of intentions, and in missions, we must always remember the Kingdom we proclaim is not of this world.

- **Dominion theology:** Dominion theology is often lurking behind the scenes of spiritual imperialism in one form or another. The basics of dominion theology rest in Christian reconstructionism, which we discussed in an earlier chapter. It's the principle that Christians have authority and should create a kingdom based on the way the understand the Scriptures (usually through Mosaic Law) and that Christ will not return until this kingdom has been established.[2]

  The basic problem with dominion theology is the means of exerted control, which typically becomes a matter of spiritual imperialism. There's a fine line between asserting perceived authority and controlling everyone and everything around you. Those I have known who are heavily into dominion theology don't get along well with others and are disagreeable and dislikable, and most importantly, refuse to adapt or assimilate in any situation. These attitudes are contrary to the nature of Christ, and will make for bad missionary experience.

- **Alt-right politics:** It's difficult to describe the alt-right. I have deliberately left commentary on the alt-right for this last chapter rather than including it when we discussed fundamentalism earlier because it is an alternative movement, one that is not embraced by the majority, although it shouldn't be embraced by anyone. Regardless, it is embraced, and due to political electoral swings, it's obvious that it is becoming more of a dominating force within the United States. Because most who espouse these beliefs do consider themselves to be fundamentalist or evangelical, what they believe and how they operate will mix with missions materials and ideals. The alt-right, or "Alternative Right," is an extremely far "right" group of individuals who reject even mainstream conservatism as not being "conservative" enough. They are not formally organized but as a group, universally advocate racism, white supremacy, neo-Nazism, antisemitism, nativism, Islamophobia, antifeminism, homophobia, and white nationalism. This combination is slowly creeping into many mainline churches and spurring many to spread and espouse these beliefs in various forms, including the way the Bible is read and interpreted. If people believe these are Biblical teachings, their dissemination in a spiritual capacity can be catastrophic for missionaries. Those in other countries can believe missionaries espouse these belief systems and can be there to impose them on others.[3]

- **Racism:** Racism is the belief that one group is superior to another based on their race, while all other races are deemed as inferior. Missionaries have, throughout history, offered religion as a cover to infiltrate a group and try to conform the group to an inferior status or way of thinking, and this has led many to believe that all mission work is covert in nature, designed to get people to think a certain way spiritually so another group can come in and take over via control.

- **Sexism:** Sexism, or a belief that the sexes are unequal, is a basic problem worldwide, with or without Christianity. Most cultures in the world do not embrace equality between men and women and this leads to a host of societal problems that span everything from interpersonal marital relationships to economic issues. Sexism can also manifest against those who do not fall into categories of "gender norms" and are either violated, denied rights, or terrorized for their orientation. Because evangelicals and fundamentals are not getting their way in western politics, many are turning their focus to infiltrating spiritual communities, laws, and governances overseas. One of the ways they operate is, of course, through missionaries. This creates a terrifying prospect for people worldwide, as well as treating all missionaries with suspicion.

Nations that impede or prohibit missions activity

THIS GOSPEL OF THE KINGDOM WILL BE PROCLAIMED THROUGHOUT THE WORLD AS A TESTIMONY TO ALL THE NATIONS. THEN THE END WILL COME. (Matthew 24:14)

There are nations in the world that outright impede or prohibit missionary activity in their nations. This is usually because they associate missionary activity with spiritual imperialism, believing missionaries are coming to conform their nation with western ways and western ideals. Because this has often been true from a historical perspective (and is still very true in some missions today), missionary activity is seen as an invasion of culture, not just the threat of faith. This sad reality means Christians in many of these countries face horrific, unimaginable persecution because of their faith. More than 200 million Christians in over 60 nations face persecution every day, with about half of that number as children. Still, at least 150,000 Christians are martyred each year.[4]

Thanks to a bad mix of politics, negative former witnesses, and negative attitudes toward Christianity and Christian liberation. Christianity is illegal in many of these countries. In such nations:

- Missionaries are unwelcome. If a missionary enters the country under the guise of religious proselytism, they will either be refused entry, deported, or worse.

- Religious services are held underground, in homes, or in churches that are closely monitored by the government, who keeps track of the number of members. Conversion to Christianity is prohibited. If one is to be a Christian, they must be born into a Christian family, and even in these instances, many are still killed or punished by their governments.

- Converts to Christianity often cannot tell anyone, including relatives, who may have them killed or may kill them themselves.

- Events and services cannot be advertised.

- Bibles cannot be distributed or printed within the country.

These nations are[4, 5, 6]:

- China
- Indonesia
- North Korea
- Morocco
- Iran
- Afghanistan
- Saudi Arabia
- Uzbekistan
- Somalia
- Iraq
- Syria
- Maldives
- Sudan
- Libya
- Yemen
- Qatar

Nations that frown on missions activity

I'M NOT ASHAMED OF THE GOSPEL: IT IS GOD'S OWN POWER FOR SALVATION TO ALL WHO HAVE FAITH IN GOD, TO THE JEW FIRST AND ALSO TO THE GREEK. (Romans 1:16)

There are also nations that, while hostile to missionaries and Christian activity, don't outright prohibit it. On the surface, it might appear they are more tolerant to Christianity, especially considering nations that are downright hostile to it and forbid it. The truth is under the surface, however, and the realities of it are:

- Missionaries are generally unwelcome, at least in certain regions of the nation. If a missionary enters the country under the guise of religious proselytism, they will either be refused entry, deported, or worse.

- Churches may not be prohibited, but evangelism is suppressed or forbidden outside of church.

- As a rule, general evangelism is usually forbidden, in at least part of the nation, or all of it.

- The nation may be religiously divided, with one religion more dominant than the other, and certain laws impact and penalize Christians more than other groups.

- Not all Christian groups are always regarded in the same manner. Some may be considered state churches of sort, and free to practice their religion in public, while other Christian groups may be considered rebel groups and prohibited.

- Bibles may be permitted for churches, visitors to the nation, or for private devotion, but not for distribution among the general populace. They are often not printed within the nation itself but may sometimes be imported.

- Rebel groups may be hostile to missions activity and to Christian advances, especially if church leaders speak out against them, while government leaders are not. Due to rebel advances, however, the fact that rebel groups reject Christianity is more relevant in law-making and governance than the actual feelings the government may have about Christianity.

- Christians may be welcome to believe if they do not spread their faith, and/or they were born into their belief system.

- Conversion to Christianity is usually seen as a punishable offense.

- Christians may experience intense persecution or harassment, as they have limited legal protection.

These nations include[4, 5, 6]:

- Russia
- Nigeria
- Pakistan
- Cuba
- Columbia
- Belarus
- Commonwealth of Independent States
- Egypt
- Vietnam
- Eritrea
- Central African Republic
- Turkmenistan
- India
- Ethiopia
- Djibouti
- Burma

The most dangerous nations in the world for Christians[7]

IN THIS WAY, I HAVE A GOAL TO PREACH THE GOSPEL WHERE THEY HAVEN'T HEARD OF CHRIST YET, SO THAT I WON'T BE BUILDING ON SOMEONE ELSE'S FOUNDATION. (Romans 15:20)

All the nations we've mentioned are dangerous for missionaries, and most are dangerous for Christians, as well. When doing missions work, however, we don't always consider the conditions that those we convert may live under once we leave. These are the most dangerous nations for Christians worldwide:

- **Laos:** Christianity is associated with American ideals and considered a threat to the nation's communism.

- **Uzbekistan:** Churches losing government registrations, buildings lost, churches raided, fines for illegal religious activity, even prison terms for Christian activities.

- **Iraq:** Christians targeted, raided, bombed, and killed.

- **Yemen:** Sharia law is governance for entire nation; evangelism of any kind forbidden; citizens are prohibited from leaving Islam; terrorist movements.

- **Maldives:** Citizens of the nation must be Muslim; sharia law is governance for the entire nation; churches forbidden; importing Christian literature is forbidden.

- **Somalia:** No formalized government in place; insurgents seek out Christians.

- **Saudi Arabia:** No religious freedom; non-Muslim worship is forbidden; conversion to Christianity is punishable by death; only monitored foreign workers can practice other religions, in private.

- **Afghanistan:** Parliament called for the execution of Christians in 2010; believers keep low profile and do not meet publicly.

- **Iran:** Government instability; known to harass Christians.

- **North Korea:** Being a Christian in Communist North Korea is considered a crime; Christians must hide their faith at all times; Christian parents cannot teach their faith to their own children; owning a Bible can lead to execution or labor camp; Christians still arrested, sent to labor camps, and publicly executed.

International covering

BUT THE LORD STOOD BY ME AND GAVE ME STRENGTH, SO THAT THE ENTIRE MESSAGE WOULD BE PREACHED THROUGH ME AND SO ALL THE NATIONS COULD HEAR IT. I WAS ALSO RESCUED FROM THE LION'S MOUTH! (2 Timothy 4:17)

If you are in missions, you will probably reach a point where you must go home and life must resume its somewhat normal pace, at least for a while. If you are going to maintain contact and a certain sense of supervision over the church you've either started or helped to maintain, you need to have a plan for what you will do once you return.

Covering internationally is difficult for one reason: because you can't immediately jet off to that country and see the situation of the ministry. You may not be able to communicate via telephone on a regular basis due to high calling costs. You don't know what is true from what is not true, and much of what goes on goes on by trust. There can be communication difficulties. Covering internationally takes God's grace and extensive planning. It is different than covering others in the United States (which is where I am from and where I live when not on missions) In order to successfully cover those you can't jump in the car and see in a few hours, here are a few keys to bringing forth solid covering and instruction that can help people all over the world.

- **Have guidelines they must abide by:** It's essential that, when covering people, we have guidelines for them to follow. These guidelines should reflect Bible leadership, respect for leadership and investment made in that individual, and plain, old-fashioned common sense. It is especially important that those who are covered internationally have guidelines are required to follow - and that those requirements be upheld. Sometimes requirements may need adjusting to fit an international scenario, but those guidelines which are put into place must be upheld. Giving in on guidelines they just don't feel they can or want to meet shows that you, as their leader, can be manipulated and pushed around if they play the right buttons. This needs to be avoided - most certainly - especially given the next point.

258

- **Some individuals may have very fixed concepts about things that may need changing:** I'll never forget the day a man from Pakistan sent me a message on Facebook: "You come to MY country!" My response? "Oh no, I NOT come to YOUR country!" This is an example of a difference in cultural approach between nations. Other countries are not the United States - especially those in non-western nations. They have different social interactions, different concepts about men and women, different ideas about money, about ways money should be distributed, about giving, and about doctrinal concepts. They often have very romanticized notions about living in the United States, and if they've never been over here, they have a concept about the income levels we have and what we are able to do or not do. Coupled with things they may have been taught from other sources, they may be mixing any number of ideals together. Even though you may have dealt with and addressed these issues earlier in time, once you are away, it is possible some of those earlier ideals may come back. If you are to correct their incorrect understandings, it is essential that they understand your role in their life. They need to understand about the five-fold ministry and what you, as an apostle, prophet, etc., do in their life and ministry. They need to realize that you are an authority to them - and that they must speak with you in a certain manner, holding forth respect and courtesy, and do not have the right to undermine you or lie to you.

- **Don't send money overseas without a pinpoint contact person to filter finances through:** Even if you have been to their nation or their church, proceed with caution when sending money back if there is no administrator from your ministry to handle the finances. It is not the job of a covering to financially sponsor everyone they cover. When covering, you are giving time, teaching, some materials, and instruction to others. This is the covering's job; not to pay for everyone within that organization at a whim. A covering is not meant to meet every need an organization has, that's not a covering, it's a sponsor - and, while we are at it, a covering is under no obligation to meet personal financial needs, such as schooling or education. If you have gone on a mission to that nation, you have already spent a large sum of money to bring teaching and meet needs in this area, and a missionary is not obliged to extend themselves further.

- **Emphasize tithes, offering, and giving**: Everyone in the Kingdom is required to bring forth tithes and offerings into God's house. Many overseas believe that because they help widows or orphans, they don't have to tithe or give. Some believe they don't have to tithe or give offerings because they themselves feel they are too poor to give - and, therefore, feel somebody should be giving to them. Then there are those who still believe that tithing means giving to orphans and widows, because they have never had anyone properly explain tithes, gifts, and offerings to them. Everyone needs to understand about giving, and this should be something taught in missions as well as reiterated when a missionary returns. Teach them about giving, tithing, offerings, and the importance of giving - not just receiving.

- **Require them to communicate with you on a regular basis**: This is perhaps one of the most powerful ways international coverings falter: at first, you hear from the ministry you are covering all the time. It seems like they are always there, especially if you have recently left from a mission and now they miss your presence. Then, as time goes on...you hear from them less and less. Just as we require communication with American ministers, so too foreign ministers must be held to regular communication with their leader. Do not allow expenses to be an excuse to get out of the meetings. Schedule regular times to talk and discuss ministry matters. Whatsapp, Facebook, and Viber are all free and accessible to foreign ministries - so non-communication is never an option.

- **Require their presence at meeting times**: Group meetings by which everyone international (and even possibly national) are called upon to gather for a conference call or Whatsapp cal are essential. If time is a problem, have a "regional" or "time zone" meeting for each group, timed so they can all be online. These meetings should be teaching or instructionally based and should serve to get people together for instructional purposes - not social or recreational ones. Encourage the people on the conference line to pray for one another, meet, and share in joys and concerns.

- **Don't allow them to be covered by more than one ministry:** Once upon a time, a ministry came to me for covering, which I agreed to do on the spot, because I didn't handle things with a lot of discernment in those days. I learned a few days after the fact that, despite my acceptance of them, they went to a friend of mine for covering as well. Some ministries will go from person to person, ministry to ministry, gleaning what they want here and there, even if you have met someone in person. If someone is covered by your ministry, make it clear they may not be covered by another ministry, nor may they receive money from another ministry under the guise of covering or network extension.

- **Don't overlook the basics of Christian doctrine in instruction:** Missions are only for a period, unless someone makes the commitment to be a missionary in one region for life. This is rare, as even long-term missionaries move around after a few years. Just because you are gone doesn't mean you don't teach any longer. Don't overlook the basics of Christian doctrine, even if you have gone over some of them before, including the five-fold ministry, nature of God, Jesus, the Holy Spirit, baptism in the Spirit, spiritual gifts, baptism in water, communion, salvation, atonement, sanctification, holiness, order, church and Kingdom government, etc. Do your job as a leader and make sure they have a sure foundation to grow upon for ministry.

Changing the way missions are perceived

THE LORD ISN'T SLOW TO KEEP HIS PROMISE, AS SOME THINK OF SLOWNESS, BUT HE IS PATIENT TOWARD YOU, NOT WANTING ANYONE TO PERISH BUT ALL TO CHANGE THEIR HEARTS AND LIVES. (2 Peter 3:9)

The world almost moves at a dizzying pace. Anyone of us can go online and look up information about any topic and hear a variety of opinions on any one issue. This means that anyone, worldwide, with internet access has the same opportunity to look up whatever it is they want to learn about Christianity, as well. There's question in some minds if missions are even needed today, but I believe until Jesus returns, missions will be relevant. They may not look like what they looked like a long time ago, but they will look like what is needed for our world, right now.

Our world is in need of missions activity, maybe more than ever. People need the human contact they crave, the interest and attention to see God as a real entity, not some distant, uncaring spirit that's out there somewhere, but not interested here. Missions bridges that gap, makes God real, proves that God cares about us. He cares enough, so much, that He called and sent this individual to work with this group, these people, this one person who receives the light and Word of God in their lives. He cares so much, someone has been sent, across land and sea, to meet the needs of the church, the community, the spirituality, of these people, right where they are. There is no better message to be given, nor to receive. Nothing affirms life, speaks life, and embraces life better than the touch of a missionary who can change the way someone sees God and eternity.

This starts with us, as missionaries. It starts when we embrace the changes that we need to make, become the people God has called each of us to be, and to minister His Gospel exactly as He has called, and rightly as we are sent. It completes as we step out into this brave new world that in many ways is as it always has been and take on the challenge to center the Gospel at the heart of what we do and bring it to others. If God has called you to missions, now is the time to answer. The harvest is, indeed plentiful, but the laborers are few.

Chapter 12 Summary

- It's obvious in many ways that the world we live in is not the same as the world our spiritual ancestors worked in when they ventured out to work for the Gospel. We are much more aware; we are more aware of the world around us; we have a flood of media information and attention, showcasing cultures and current events in a slanted light; and we have the intense competition of things around us that demand our immediate attention and never seem to let up.

- If we are interested in missions ourselves, we should also take an interest in seeing others at work on the mission field.

- Missionary support is not all about money, although money is certainly a part of missions, and a necessary one, at that. There are lots of ways we can step up and show interest in missions activity that aren't all about money: pray for them, tell others about them, send items/needed materials, and volunteer to assist on a mission trip.

- Ministry is a profession as well as a professional endeavor. It is something that a minister does as their primary purpose, it's professional work. It is something that has certain guidelines, protocol, disciplines, presentations, and conduct. Being in ministry represents something; it represents the service that one does throughout life, and missions are a part of that ministry work.

- Whether it's through a seminary program that is specifically designed for missionaries, a missions training program, or a missions initiative, missionaries should learn about their work and about where they are going to go, covering the essentials of culture, manners, language, economics, social customs, religion, geography, terrain, politics, and commerce for at least one year prior to a missions trip departure.

- The success or failure of obtaining funds for missions is not as simple as how we dress or carry ourselves, but it does help if we carry ourselves properly.

- Economic sustainability is the ability to support economic production long-term, no matter what level of productivity may define that. This means that it is more important to give individuals tools for success and education for change than it is to go in and do things for people all the time. In missions, we should never do things for people that they can otherwise do or accomplish themselves.

- Missions have not always been used to promote the Gospel, but often, to impose culture on imperialized or colonized nations. Some things to beware are spiritual imperialism, dominion theology, alt-right politics, racism, and sexism.

- Nations that impede or prohibit missionary activity are China, Indonesia, North Korea, Morocco, Iran, Afghanistan, Saudi Arabia, Uzbekistan, Somalia, Iraq, Syria, Maldives, Sudan, Libya, Yemen, and Qatar.

- Nations that frown on missions activity are Russia, Nigeria, Pakistan, Cuba, Columbia, Belarus, Commonwealth of Independent States, Egypt, Vietnam, Eritrea, Central African Republic, Turkmenistan, India, Ethiopia, Djibouti, and Burma.

- The most dangerous nations in the world for Christians are Laos, Uzbekistan, Iraq, Yemen, Maldives, Somalia, Saudi Arabia, Afghanistan, Iran, and North Korea.

- When covering (leading) people from a distance, consider the following: guidelines they must abide by, changing fixed concepts, don't send money without a pinpoint contact person, emphasize tithes and giving, require them to communicate on a regular basis, require their attendance at meetings, don't allow them to be covered by more than one ministry, and don't overlook the basics of Christian doctrine in instruction.

- Our world is in need of missions activity, maybe more than ever. People need the human contact they crave, the interest and attention to see God as a real entity, not some distant, uncaring spirit that's out there somewhere, but not interested here. Missions bridges that gap, makes God real, proves that God cares about us.

Chapter 12 Assignments

1. Drawing on earlier assignments and information presented in the text, create a Missions Presentation Package. Include: Your mission vision, why you desire to go on mission, your

ministerial bio, photo, nations you desire to go to, all the information you have gathered on that nation throughout this course, your vision and purpose for the mission, contacts, long-term plan for mission work in that area (even if you are not remaining for that long a period of time) and a rough budget of what the mission will cost and how you intend to raise the money.

2. Write an essay (5-8 sentences) describing your heart for missions and how, as paralleling the beginning of this course, your vision has expanded, changed, improved, or clarified. What do you have to offer now that you did not have when you started?

The Telegu Christian Community (c. 1879)

OTHER BOOKS BY THE AUTHOR
RELATED TO THIS TOPIC

- *All That is Seen and Unseen: A Journey Through the Book of Revelation* (Righteous Pen Publications, 2015)

- *Ministry Officer Candidate School* (Righteous Pen Publications, 2025)

- *Stumbling to Nineveh: A Journey Through the Book of Jonah* (Righteous Pen Publications, 2015)

- *Surrounded by so Great a Cloud of Witnesses: Women of Faith Who Revolutionized Church History* (Photini Press, 2017)

- *Touching the Church in Eternity: A Journey Through the Book of Ephesians* (Righteous Pen Publications, 2016)

- *Understanding Demonology, Spiritual Warfare, Healing, And Deliverance: A Manual for the Christian Minister* (Apostolic University Press, 2017)

The Meltlakahtla Christian Mission Church, c. 1980

REFERENCES

Introduction
[1]"Quotes About Missions." http://www.goodreads.com/quotes/tag/missions. Accessed January 9, 2017.

Chapter 1
[1]"Quotes About Missions." http://www.goodreads.com/quotes/tag/missions. Accessed January 9, 2017.

Chapter 2
[1]Missions Slogans and Notable Quotes from Missionaries. https://home.snu.edu/%7EHCULBERT/slogans.htm. Accessed January 9, 2017.

Chapter 3
[1]Missions Slogans and Notable Quotes from Missionaries." https://home.snu.edu/%7EHCULBERT/slogans.htm. Accessed January 9, 2017.
[2]"Which Churches Today Send The Most Missionaries?" http://christianity.stackexchange.com/questions/25252/which-churches-today-send-the-most-missionaries. Accessed December 19, 2016.
[3]Ibid.
[4]Ibid.

Chapter 4
[1]Missions Slogans and Notable Quotes from Missionaries." https://home.snu.edu/%7EHCULBERT/slogans.htm. Accessed January 9, 2017.
[2]"Obadiah." https://en.wikipedia.org/wiki/Obadiah. Accessed December 26, 2016

Chapter 5
[1]Missions Slogans and Notable Quotes from Missionaries." https://home.snu.edu/%7EHCULBERT/slogans.htm. Accessed January 9, 2017.

Chapter 6
[1]Missions Slogans and Notable Quotes from Missionaries." https://home.snu.edu/%7EHCULBERT/slogans.htm. Accessed January 9, 2017.

Chapter 7

[1]"Missions Slogans and Notable Quotes from Missionaries."
https://home.snu.edu/%7EHCULBERT/slogans.htm. Accessed January 9, 2017.
[2] "Christian Fundamentalism."
https://en.wikipedia.org/wiki/Christian_fundamentalism. Accessed December 28,
2016.
[3]"Liberal Christianity." https://en.wikipedia.org/wiki/Liberal_Christianity.
Accessed December 28, 2016.
[4]"The Fundamentals." https://en.wikipedia.org/wiki/The_Fundamentals. Accessed
December 28, 2016.
[5]"Christian Reconstructionism."
https://en.wikipedia.org/wiki/Christian_Reconstructionism. Accessed December
29, 2016.
[6]Balmer, Randall. *Thy Kingdom Come: How The Religious Right Distorts The Faith
And Threatens America*. New York, New York: Basic Books, 2007.
[7]"Question: Who Were The Samaritans?"
https://www.gotquestions.org/Samaritans.html. Accessed December 30, 2016.
[8]"Why Did Jesus Call The Canaanite Woman a Dog?"
https://www.gotquestions.org/Canaanite-woman-dog.html. Accessed December
30, 2016
[9]"Syrophoenician."
http://classic.net.bible.org/dictionary.php?word=Syrophoenician. Accessed
December 30, 2016.

Chapter 8

[1]"Missions Slogans and Notable Quotes from Missionaries."
https://home.snu.edu/%7EHCULBERT/slogans.htm. Accessed January 9, 2017.
[2]Alkire, Sabina; Chatterjee, Mihika; Conconi, Adriana; Seth, Suman; and Vaz,
Anna. "Poverty In Rural And Urban Areas." http://www.ophi.org.uk/wp-
content/uploads/Poverty-in-Rural-and-Urban-Areas-Direct-Comparisons-using-the-
Global-MPI-2014.pdf. Accessed January 1, 2017
[3]Ibid.

Chapter 9

[1]"Missions Slogans and Notable Quotes from Missionaries."
https://home.snu.edu/%7EHCULBERT/slogans.htm. Accessed January 9, 2017.
[2]Oxenham, Jason. "15 Most Spoken Languages In the World, The."
https://www.rocketlanguages.com/blog/the-15-most-spoken-languages-in-the-
world/. Accessed January 3, 2017.
[3]"Economics." https://en.wikipedia.org/wiki/Economics. Accessed January 3, 2017.

Chapter 10

[1]"Missions Slogans and Notable Quotes from Missionaries."
https://home.snu.edu/%7EHCULBERT/slogans.htm. Accessed January 9, 2017.
[2]"Spirits Called By Name In The Bible."
http://bibleforums.org/showthread.php/230082-Spirits-called-by-name-in-the-Bible.
Accessed January 3, 2017.

Chapter 11

[1]"Missions Slogans and Notable Quotes from Missionaries."
https://home.snu.edu/%7EHCULBERT/slogans.htm. Accessed January 9, 2017.
[2]"Saint Peter." https://en.wikipedia.org/wiki/Saint_Peter. Accessed January 6, 2017.
[3]"Andrew The Apostle." https://en.wikipedia.org/wiki/Andrew_the_Apostle. Accessed January 6, 2017.
[4]"James son of Zebedee." https://en.wikipedia.org/wiki/James,_son_of_Zebedee. Accessed January 6, 2017
[5]"John the Apostle." https://en.wikipedia.org/wiki/John_the_Apostle. Accessed January 6, 2017.
[6]"Philip the Apostle." https://en.wikipedia.org/wiki/Philip_the_Apostle. Accessed January 6, 2017.
[7]"Bartholomew the Apostle."
https://en.wikipedia.org/wiki/Bartholomew_the_Apostle. Accessed January 6, 2017.
[8]"Matthew the Apostle." https://en.wikipedia.org/wiki/Matthew_the_Apostle. Accessed January 6, 2017.
[9]"James Son of Alphaeus." https://en.wikipedia.org/wiki/James,_son_of_Alphaeus. Accessed January 6, 2017.
[10]"Thomas the Apostle." https://en.wikipedia.org/wiki/Thomas_the_Apostle. Accessed January 6, 2017.
[11]"Simon the Zealot." https://en.wikipedia.org/wiki/Simon_the_Zealot. Accessed January 6, 2017.
[12]"Jude the Apostle." https://en.wikipedia.org/wiki/Jude_the_Apostle. Accessed January 6, 2017
[13]"Matthias." https://en.wikipedia.org/wiki/Saint_Matthias. Accessed January 6, 2017.
[14]Marino, Lee Ann B. "Thecla." *Surrounded By So Great A Cloud Of Witnesses: Christian Women Who Revolutionized History*, #126, Raleigh, North Carolina: Photini Press, 2017.
[15]"St. Pantaenus." http://www.catholic.org/saints/saint.php?saint_id=808. Accessed January 6, 2017.
[16]"Pantaenus." http://www.newadvent.org/cathen/11446b.htm. Accessed January 6, 2017.
[17]Marino, Lee Ann B. "Nina of Georgia." *Surrounded By So Great A Cloud Of Witnesses: A Devotional Study Of Women Who Revolutionized Church History*, Day 7. Raleigh, North Carolina: Righteous Pen Publications, 2013.
[18]"Saint Patrick." https://en.wikipedia.org/wiki/Saint_Patrick. Accessed January 6, 2017.
[19]"St. Patrick." http://www.catholic.org/saints/saint.php?saint_id=89. Accessed January 6, 2017.
[20]Marino, Lee Ann B. "Matrona, Abbess of Constantinople." *Surrounded By So Great A Cloud Of Witnesses: Christian Women Who Revolutionized History*, #75. Raleigh, North Carolina: Photini Press, 2017.
[21]Marino, Lee Ann B. "The Apostles of Ireland."
http://www.slideshare.net/powerfortoday. Accessed January 6, 2017.
[22]"Alopen." https://en.wikipedia.org/wiki/Alopen. Accessed January 5, 2017.

[23]"Saint Boniface." https://en.wikipedia.org/wiki/Saint_Boniface. Accessed January 6, 2017.

[24]"Anna Nitschmann." https://en.wikipedia.org/wiki/Anna_Nitschmann. Accessed January 6, 2017.

[25]"William Carey." https://www.britannica.com/biography/William-Carey. Accessed January 6, 2017.

[26]Marino, Lee Ann B. "Charlotte "Lottie" Digges Moon." *Surrounded By So Great A Cloud Of Witnesses: Christian Women Who Revolutionized History*, #23. Raleigh, North Carolina: Photini Press, 2017.

[27]"Anne Luther Bagby." http://www.wow.com/wiki/Anne_Luther_Bagby. Accessed January 6, 2017.

[28]Marino, Lee Ann B. "Amy Beatrice Wilson Carmichael." *Surrounded By So Great A Cloud Of Witnesses: Christian Women Who Revolutionized History*, #16. Raleigh, North Carolina: Photini Press, 2017.

[29]"Susanna Carson Rijnhart." https://en.wikipedia.org/wiki/Susanna_Carson_Rijnhart. Accessed January 5, 2017.

[30]"Petrus and Susie Rijnhart." http://www.bdcconline.net/en/stories/r/rijnhart-petrus-and-susie.php. Accessed January 5, 2017.

[31]"Jim Elliot." http://www.wheaton.edu/isae/hall-of-biography/jim-elliot. Accessed January 6, 2017.

Chapter 12

[1]Missions Slogans and Notable Quotes from Missionaries." https://home.snu.edu/%7EHCULBERT/slogans.htm. Accessed January 9, 2017.

[2] "Dominion Theology." https://www.gotquestions.org/dominion-theology.html. Accessed January 7, 2017.

[3]"Alt-right." https://en.wikipedia.org/wiki/Alt-right. Accessed January 7, 2017.

[4]"Countries Where Christianity Is Illegal." http://www.sharondalecc.org/fire/countries_where_christianity_is_illegal.pdf. Accessed January 7, 2017.

[5]Map of persecuted Christians. https://www.christianfreedom.org/persecuted-christians-map/. January 7, 2017

[6]"Where in the world is the worst place to be a Christian." https://www.theguardian.com/world/ng-interactive/2015/jul/27/where-in-the-world-is-it-worst-place-to-be-a-christian Accessed January 7, 2017.

[7]"Top 10 most dangerous countries for Christians." http://listverse.com/2011/11/24/top-10-most-dangerous-countries-for-christians/. Accessed January 7, 2017.

ABOUT THE AUTHOR:
DR. LEE ANN B. MARINO, PH.D., D.MIN., D.D.

These that have turned the world upside down have come hither also.
[Acts 17:6, KJV]

Dr. Lee Ann B. Marino, Ph.D., D.Min., D.D. (she/her) is "everyone's favorite theologian" leading Gen X, Millennials, and Gen Z with expertise in leadership training, queer and feminist theology, general religion, and apostolic theology. She has served in ministry since 1998 and was ordained as a pastor in 2002 and an apostle in 2010. She founded what is now Sanctuary Apostolic Fellowship Empowerment (SAFE) Ministries in 2004. Under her ministry heading Dr. Marino is founder and Overseer of Sanctuary International Fellowship Tabernacle (SIFT) (the original home of National Coming Out Sunday) and The Sanctuary Network, and Chancellor of Apostolic Covenant Theological Seminary (ACTS).

Affectionately nicknamed "the Spitfire," Dr. Marino has spent over two decades as an "apostle, preacher, and teacher" (2 Timothy 1:11), exercising her personal mandate to become "all things to all people" (1 Corinthians 9:22). Her embrace of spiritual issues (both technical and intimate) has found its home among both seekers and believers, those who desire spiritual answers to today's issues.

Dr. Marino has preached throughout the United States, Puerto Rico, and Europe in hundreds of religious services and experiences throughout the years. A history maker in her own right, she has spent over two decades in advocacy, education, and work for and within minority spiritual communities (including African American, Hispanic, and LGBTQ+). She has also served as the first woman on all-male synods, councils, and panels, as well as the first preacher or speaker welcomed of a different race, sexual orientation, or identity among diverse communities. Today, Dr. Marino's work extends to over 150 countries as she hosts the popular *Kingdom Now* podcast, which is in the top 20 percentile of all podcasts worldwide. She is also the author of over 35 books and the popular Patheos column, *Leadership on Fire*. To date, she has had five bestselling titles within their subject matter: *Understanding Demonology, Spiritual Warfare, Healing, and Deliverance: A Manual for the Christian Minister*; *Ministry School Boot Camp: Training for Helps Ministries, Appointments, and Beyond*; *Discovering Intimacy: A Journey Through the Song of Solomon*; *Fruit of the Vine: Study and Commentary on the Fruit of the Spirit*; and *Ministering to LGBTQ+ (and Those Who Love Them): A Primer for Queer Theology* (and its accompanying workbook).

As a public icon and social media influencer, Dr. Marino advocates healthy body image (curvy/full-figured), representation as a demisexual/aromantic, and albinism awareness as a model. Known to those she works with, she is a spiritual mom, teacher, leader, professor, confidant, and friend. She continues to transform, receiving new teaching, revelation, and insight in this thing we call "ministry." Through years of spiritual growth and maturity, Dr. Marino stands as herself, here to present what God has given to her for any who have an ear to hear.

For more information, visit her website at kingdompowernow.org.